D1626088

DATE DUE			

TL2951

TRENDS IN PSYCHOTHERAPY RESEARCH

TRENDS IN PSYCHOTHERAPY RESEARCH

M.E. ABELIAN
EDITOR

Nova Science Publishers, Inc.
New York

NOTICE TO THE READER

The Publisher has taken reasonable care in the preparation of this book, but makes no expressed or implied warranty of any kind and assumes no responsibility for any errors or omissions. No liability is assumed for incidental or consequential damages in connection with or arising out of information contained in this book. The Publisher shall not be liable for any special, consequential, or exemplary damages resulting, in whole or in part, from the readers' use of, or reliance upon, this material.

This publication is designed to provide accurate and authoritative information with regard to the subject matter covered herein. It is sold with the clear understanding that the Publisher is not engaged in rendering legal or any other professional services. If legal or any other expert assistance is required, the services of a competent person should be sought. FROM A DECLARATION OF PARTICIPANTS JOINTLY ADOPTED BY A COMMITTEE OF THE AMERICAN BAR ASSOCIATION AND A COMMITTEE OF PUBLISHERS.

LIBRARY OF CONGRESS CATALOGING-IN-PUBLICATION DATA
Available upon request

ISBN 1-59454-373-9

Published by Nova Science Publishers, Inc. ✛New York

CONTENTS

PREFACE

Psychotherapy is the treatment of mental and emotional disorders using psychological methods. Psychotherapy, thus, does not include physiological interventions, such as drug therapy or electroconvulsive therapy , although it may be used in combination with such methods. Behavior therapy aims to help the patient eliminate undesirable habits or irrational fears through conditioning. Techniques include systematic desensitization, particularly for the treatment of clients with irrational anxieties or fears, and aversive conditioning, which uses negative stimuli to end bad habits. Humanistic therapy tends to be more optimistic, basing its treatment on the theory that individuals have a natural inclination to strive toward self-fulfillment. Therapists such as Carl Rogers and Abraham Maslow used a highly interactive client-therapist relationship, compelling clients to realize exactly what they are saying or how they are behaving, in order to foster a sense of self-awareness. Cognitive therapies try to show the client that certain, usually negative, thoughts are irrational, with the goal of restructuring such thoughts into positive, constructive ideas. Such methods include rational-emotive therapy, where the therapist argues with the client about his negative ideas; and cognitive restructuring therapy, in which the therapist works with the client to set attainable goals. Other forms of therapy stress helping patients to examine their own ideas about themselves

The emerging paradigm of integrative health and medicine has provoked new perspectives on health as well as complementary treatment modalities. It has been suggested that cancer is in need of a broader theoretical framework that includes psychosocial factors in order to provide a more comprehensive model of disease. A unique perspective termed here as *developmental health contextualism* will be proposed in chapter 1. Specifically, the first purpose will be to explore a developmental biopsychosocial approach to disease by integrating attachment theory with the Type C Behavior Pattern (TCBP) for cancer. Traditionally, attachment is a theory of socio-emotional development with stress reactivity and affect regulation patterns. Some questions are....could attachment with its known influence on social and emotional patterns and stress and coping, play a clinically relevant role in the medical context of the chronically ill? Could attachment processes have therapeutic value for health-care interactions and psychosocial therapies for individuals with cancer? Lastly, the issue of therapeutic value leads to the second purpose of this chapter. That is, a psychosocial intervention for cancer patients that combines mindfulness meditation with attachment theory will be presented as a complement to traditional treatment.

As reported in chapter 2, the skin and the nervous system develop side by side in the ectoderm of the fetus and remain intimately interconnected throughout life. Cutaneous innervation represents the largest sense organ of the body and is also vital to skin protection and health. There is a significant psychosomatic or behavioral component to many skin disorders. This interaction permits nondrug psychotherapeutic interventions that have positive impacts on many cutaneous diseases. Cognitive-behavioral techniques that address dysfunctional cognitions (thought patterns) or behaviors (actions) can be useful for skin disorders with a significant psychosomatic or behavioral component, such as the picking component of acne excoriee, scratching in atopic dermatitis, habits such as lip licking or biting, hyperhidrosis, lichen simplex chronicus, neurotic excoriations, onychotillomania, trichotillomania, and psychosomatic triggering or exacerbation of urticaria. Cognitive-behavioral methods can also desensitize individuals with needle phobia. Biofeedback has some limited usefulness in a few selected skin disorders. Galvanic skin resistance (GSR) feedback can be utilized for teaching control of hyperhidrosis. Skin temperature feedback allows individuals to learn how to warm the fingers for Raynaud's syndrome and scleroderma. Neurofeedback of electroencephalographic (EEG) spectral frequency is in its infancy but may prove useful for certain habit disorders that affect the skin, hair, or nails by picking, scratching, or other manipulation. Hypnosis has been found useful to treat a number of skin disorders including acne excoriée, alopecia areata, atopic dermatitis, congenital ichthyosiform erythroderma, dyshidrotic dermatitis, erythromelalgia, furuncles, glossodynia, herpes simplex, hyperhidrosis, ichthyosis vulgaris, lichen planus, neurodermatitis, nummular dermatitis, postherpetic neuralgia, pruritus, psoriasis, rosacea, trichotillomania, urticaria, verruca vulgaris, and vitiligo. Hypnosis can also help individuals feel more comfortable about having their skin diseases. Hypnotic relaxation utilizing self-guided imagery reduces anxiety and discomfort during dermatologic procedures. For resistant skin disorders, hypnoanalysis using ideomotor signaling and the affect bridge technique can often identify original incidents and promote healing. Subtle energy intuitive techniques are an almost lost art that have so far been relatively difficult to explore on a scientific basis. They are still utilized by various indigenous practitioners and shamans, and are sometimes capable of clearing or improving otherwise refractory skin disorders. A psychiatrist has described their modern use. This area has potential for significant future development.

In chapter 3, chronic tinnitus has a very high prevalence in Europe and other industrialized countries. Latest studies found 4% of the German population with chronic tinnitus, almost 2 % suffering severely in their daily life. Because there is no curative therapeutic approach available, neither pharmacological nor surgical, the main focus lies on treatments enhancing the habituation of tinnitus. Habituation occurs in almost 50 % of the patients as a normal process, leading to a complete compensation. This is based on the ability of the auditory perception to habituate random noise and focus on important acoustic information. However, habituation is impossible, if tinnitus is connected to hyperacusis, to fear of severe otologic disabilities such as impending deafness or to fear of brain damage, tumors or other diseases. With thorough audiological diagnosis these complications or basic causes of tinnitus can be found or excluded - counseling of the patients then can explain the symptom and thus facilitate the habituation process, often with the help of apparative therapy such as hearing aids or noise generators. If tinnitus is held responsible for psychic disturbances such as lack of concentration, sleep disorders or manifest depressions, neither of these can be cured with psychotherapy alone, leaving aside the symptom tinnitus. On the other hand, tinnitus habituation is impossible without treating the psychosomatic imbalance. Therefore an integrative psychosomatic and otologic model is needed. This therapeutic approach combines hearing therapy based on proper knowledge about the individual's auditory abilities and psychotherapy, mostly cognitive and/or behavioral therapies. Retraining (TRT) alone is only sufficient for patients without psychosomatic symptoms and imbalance, whereas integrative psychosomatic models provide tinnitus sufferers with self-competence and facilitate the habituation of tinnitus. Selected cases are presented to explain these models.

Chapter 4 informs about a patient's death by suicide constitutes a common but rarely examined occupational hazard in psychiatry and nursing. Clinicians need to determine patients' risk for suicide to manage suicidal patients, prevent suicide, estimate stability for discharge and cope with the aftermath if their preventive efforts fail. Evaluating and differentiating suicide attempters from completers are a serious clinical challenge; miscalculation of risk and inadequate vigilance can have lethal consequences. When preventive efforts fail, clinicians feel poorly prepared to cope with the aftermath of suicide even though bereavement is a universal human response. Losing a patient to suicide may trigger ongoing distress and/or promote the clinician's professional growth. The clinician may experience various feelings including sadness, guilt, and doubt about suicide prevention skills and may also threaten the clinician's health and work performance until tasks of grief and mourning are accomplished. This retrospective study compared suicide attempters (SA) and completers (SC) and examined the clinician's response to the suicide of a patient. Suicide messages and distressing symptoms were examined among a matched cohort of suicide completers (SC) (n=25) and suicide attempters (SA) (n=25) at a Veterans Administration Medical Center. Although the clinicians documented and reported patients' clear, direct, and frequent messages about suicide, patients were still able to complete their suicide. Themes within psychiatric patients' suicide messages and the number of documented suicide messages helped differentiate SA s from SCs. SCs were more likely to have a fear of being killed, hopelessness, and perceived symptom distress. SA s (28.6%) typically made a contract with staff not to commit suicide in the hospital while no SCs did so. Over 50% of the suicide messages were clear and directly referred to suicide. Indirect or unclear messages about suicide are more likely to be overlooked or discounted. In a secondary analysis of suicide messages using Leenaars' categories (1992), completers' and attempters differed in their messages about unbearable psychological pain and dissatisfaction with interpersonal relationships. The SCs who completed suicide after hospital discharge, did so within 6 weeks of discharge; during this time patients face high risk and require careful follow-up. To examine the aftermath of suicide, primary clinicians were interviewed about their interactions with the patient and their response to the SC patient's suicide. They experienced their own grief as well as their lack of omnipotence over suicide, and the fear of their colleagues' responses. Understanding bereavement and factors influencing bereavement after suicide may help therapists process their own grief more effectively.

It is well established in the child abuse literature that children born to adolescent mothers are at a heightened risk for the perpetration of child abuse. However, little is known about the extent to which this relationship persists among those who became mothers as adolescents but are now within adulthood. Such knowledge is important since adolescence is a relatively short period in the lifecycle, but is one that sets the stage for a lifetime of parenting, including abusive parenting. Applying Erikson's theory, it is argued that impaired identity resulting from adolescent parenthood will increase the risk of child abuse. The purpose chapter 5 is to investigate the manner in which variables that serve as proxies for identity formation, namely education, employment, and self-esteem, operate in the production of child abuse for formerly adolescent mothers (FAMs). Using a representative sample of 4,387 Canadian mothers, both descriptive and logistic regression analyses are conducted. The results demonstrate that children of FAMs are, indeed, more likely to be abused than children of non-FAMs. With few exceptions, the identity variables operate as hypothesized. However, the multivariate analyses show that identity formation alone is an insufficient explanation for the higher likelihood of child abuse for children of FAMs. Not only do the results suggest that Erikson's theory is inadequate as an explanation of the heightened risk of child abuse of children born to FAMs', but the analyses also imply that a more holistic approach is needed to fully comprehend is phenomenon. The paper concludes with a proposed holistic framework for understanding FAMs higher likelihood of child abuse.

In chapter 6, every year thousands of youth participate in residential substance abuse treatment. The purpose of this study was to analyze the process of substance abuse treatment at the Generations Program and determine if the process of treatment was consistent with the constructs of the Positive Youth Development Model. A qualitative case study design was used for this study. A multi-method data collection approach was used for this case study including, field observations, interviews, and document analysis. Data analysis was an ongoing process. Analysis began with construction of computer files of each interview and observation. Each file was reviewed and memos were written ranging from marginal notes to several paragraphs. These memos were used to generate additional interview questions. Data were compiled and reviewed; a case study record was constructed. A constant-comparative process was used to analyze all data. Analysis of the treatment process revealed the primary goal of treatment was to assist youth develop a belief in their ability to remain alcohol and drug free. This goal was achieved through the use peer support network, the development of self-control, and acquisition of treatment knowledge. Consistency was found between the process of substance abuse treatment and the Positive Youth Development Model. The content and process of substance abuse treatment at Generations Youth Program includes a number of components and strategies that provide the clients an opportunity to meet their basic human needs. Clients have the opportunity to develop a variety of competencies that are essential to healthy development. The Youth Development Model provides a unique framework for the delivery of primary, secondary, and tertiary prevention services to substance abusing adolescents. Specifically, this framework focuses on developing fully functioning adolescents prepared not only for sobriety, but also for complete living.

There is a well-recognised association between substance use and psychotic disorders, sometimes described as 'dual diagnosis'. Approximately one half of individuals in the community with a psychotic disorder have a substance use disorder, and the same proportion of those who abuse substances have a psychiatric disorder. Most interventions have concentrated on opiates, psychostimulants, hallucinogens and marijuana and there has been much less emphasis on the treatment of co-morbid nicotine use. Tobacco use is especially high in chronic schizophrenia and people with this diagnosis are more likely to be nicotine dependent than smokers in the general population or those with other psychiatric disorders. Smoking may contribute to the 60 percent increase in deaths from respiratory disorders, and a 30 percent increased chance of heart disease. Patients with psychotic disorder may also spend up to 40% of their income on tobacco. Chapter 7 looks at possible psychological and pharmacological treatments such as nicotine replacement and bupropion. It particularly focuses on the effectiveness of a manualised group intervention based on motivational interviewing and cognitive behavioural therapy, which also includes advice on nicotine replacement. Using a waitlist-treatment crossover design, we recruited 38 subjects of whom nineteen completed the waitlist and intervention phases. There were no significant differences between subjects and dropouts. During the waitlist period there were no significant changes in tobacco use. At the end of the intervention, almost a quarter had stopped smoking, (z=-2.24, p=0.02). Other outcome measures included smoking cessation, motivation to stop, the Fagerstrom Test for Nicotine Dependence (FTND), urinary cotinine and psychiatric symptoms on the General Health Questionnaire. Subjects showed significant improvements on state of change, FTND score and urinary cotinine levels. These improvements were maintained at three-month follow-up (n=10), with no adverse effect on psychiatric morbidity. Although this intervention shows promise, larger randomised controlled trials are indicated to determine the relative contributions of nicotine replacement, bupropion and group interventions to smoking cessation in this population. The authors also need to consider intervention early on in the course of schizophrenia and other psychotic disorders. In a subsequent survey of patients attending an early psychosis service (n=60), half were smokers, of whom 60% wished to stop. These smoking rates were roughly mid-way between the general population and a long-term psychiatric population and they may be more susceptible to intervention than patients with chronic psychotic illness. This should include primary prevention aimed at ensuring that non-smokers do not start smoking, and a secondary prevention programme aimed at existing smokers

As reported in chapter 8, in 1986 Pennebaker and Beall published their renowned study on the long-term beneficial health effects of disclosing traumatic events in 4 brief sequential writing sessions. Their results have been confirmed in various studies, but conflicting results have also been reported. The intent of the study was to replicate the experiments from Pennebaker and Beall (1986), Pennebaker et al. (1988), and Greenberg and Stone (1992) using a German student sample. Additionally, essay variables that point to the emotional processing of events (e.g., depth of self-exploration, number of negative/positive emotions, intensity of emotional expression) were examined as potential mechanisms of action. Trait measures of personality which could moderate the personal consequences of disclosure (alexithymia, self-concealment, worrying, social support) were also assessed. In a second study the experimental condition (disclosure) was varied by implementing "coping" vs. "helping" instructions as variations of the original condition. Under the coping condition participants were asked to elaborate on what they used to do, continue to do, or could do in the future to better cope with the event. Under the helping condition participants were asked to imagine themselves in the role of a adviser and elaborate on what they would recommend to persons also dealing with the trauma in order to better cope with the event. The expected beneficial effects of disclosure on long-term health (e.g., physician visits, physical symptoms, affectivity) could not be corroborated in either the first or the second study. None of the examined essay variables of emotional processing and only a single personality variable was able to explain significant variance in the health-related outcome variables influence. Nevertheless, substantial reductions in posttraumatic stress symptoms (e.g., intrusions, avoidance, arousal), were found in both experiments. These improvements were significantly related to essay variables of emotional expression and self-exploration and were particularly pronounced under the activation of a prosocial motivation (helping condition). Repeated, albeit brief, expressive writing about personally upsetting or traumatic events resulted in an immediate increase in negative mood but did not lead to long-term positive health consequences in a German student sample. It did, however, promote better processing of stressful or traumatic events, as evidenced by reductions in posttraumatic stress symptoms. The instruction to formulate recommendations for persons dealing with the same trauma seems more helpful than standard disclosure or focusing on one's own past, present, and future coping endeavours. Overall, expressive writing seems to be a successful method of improving trauma processing. Determining the appropriate setting (e.g., self-help vs. therapeutic context) for disclore can be seen as an objective of future research.

In: Trends in Psychotherapy Research
Editor: M. E. Abelian, pp. 1-32

ISBN 1-59454-373-9
© 2006 Nova Science Publishers, Inc.

Chapter 1

DEVELOPMENTAL HEALTH CONTEXTUALISM: FROM ATTACHMENT TO MINDFULNESS-BASED THERAPY IN CANCER

*A. M. Tacón**

Texas Tech University, Department of Health, Exercise and Sport Sciences; Joint Appoint, Human Development and Family Studies, Texas Tech University, Lubbock, Texas

ABSTRACT

The emerging paradigm of integrative health and medicine has provoked new perspectives on health as well as complementary treatment modalities. It has been suggested that cancer is in need of a broader theoretical framework that includes psychosocial factors in order to provide a more comprehensive model of disease. A unique perspective termed here as *developmental health contextualism* will be proposed in this chapter. Specifically, the first purpose will be to explore a developmental biopsychosocial approach to disease by integrating attachment theory with the Type C Behavior Pattern (TCBP) for cancer. Traditionally, attachment is a theory of socio-emotional development with stress reactivity and affect regulation patterns. Some questions are....could attachment with its known influence on social and emotional patterns and stress and coping, play a clinically relevant role in the medical context of the chronically ill? Could attachment processes have therapeutic value for health-care interactions and psychosocial therapies for individuals with cancer? Lastly, the issue of therapeutic value leads to the second purpose of this chapter. That is, a psychosocial intervention for cancer patients that combines mindfulness meditation with attachment theory will be presented as a complement to traditional treatment.

* Dr. A.M. Tacón, Assistant Professor of Health; Department of Health, Exercise and Sport Sciences; Box 43011; Texas Tech University; Lubbock, Texas 79409-3011; Phone 806-742-1685 x409; fax 806-742-3423; E-mail: anna.tacon@TTU.EDU

Can models of health and development be integrated in order to provide a more holistic, multidimensional approach to stress, illness and disease vulnerability, and psychosocial treatment? Are there certain contexts of developmental systems and biopsychosocial experience that create pathways---a biopsychosocial pruning---of health trajectories? One purpose here is to explore these possibilities and stimulate theoretical and empirical interest in the area of a developmental biopsychosocial approach to health (e.g., Maunder & Hunter, 2001) or what is termed here as developmental health contextualism; this will be done by application of attachment theory to the disease of cancer . The second purpose is to explore the potential utility of attachment-related mindfulness group therapy program for cancer patients.

A broader theoretical framework that includes psychosocial components in the cancer process has been suggested because the traditional biomedical model does not account for all factors in this disease (Greer, 1999). Attachment, a biobehavioral theory of socio-emotional development provides an explanation for lifelong social, affective, and stress response patterns that are acquired during childhood. The issue is whether patterns associated with attachment development, such as affect regulation and stress response, contribute to an individual's response to life events and illness vulnerability. Attachment may play some complementary ---not causal---role in physical illness, disease, and health behavior (Feeney,2000; Kotler, Buzwell, Romeo & Bowland, 1994; Tacón, Caldera & Bell, 2001). Attachment theory will be introduced followed by a conceptual application to cancer. Next, attachment-related issues in psychosocial therapy for cancer patients will be reviewed. Lastly, a psychosocial intervention in the form of a group mindfulness therapy specific to cancer patients will be presented.

THE DEVELOPMENTAL CONTEXT AND ATTACHMENT THEORY

A developmental contextual or developmental systems perspective involves the idea of integrated multi-contextual levels or systems of organization (i.e., biology, physiology, psychology, society), that are dynamically interactional in nature (Ford & Lerner, 1992). Specifically, various developmental systems are embedded within each other and human life exists in this holistic context or ecology of system embeddedness and reciprocal relatedness. For example, developmental contextualism would suggest that factors from organized levels of one's biological systems interact with factors from other contextual levels (e.g., interpersonal, ecological, etc.) within which the biological systems are embedded. It is this embeddedness of context that attachment serves as a lynchpin; for, early experiences of threat and stress response, emotional and coping patterns, physiological and immune system development, as well as brain development, all occur with the biopsychosocial and biobehavioral domain of attachment. In that developmental milieu, parents serve as the original external regulators of a child's encounters with distress---the psychological and physiological response to stress. Hopefully, the parents will have the ability to soothe the child and decrease the levels of arousal and induce homeostatic balance between the sympathetic and parasympathetic nervous systems. It is within the context of attachment that cancer will now be explored.

ATTACHMENT THEORY

Background

Attachment is a theory of socio-emotional development that emphasizes the salience of human relations within an evolutionary-ethological context of adaptation and species survival. John Bowlby (1973,1988) proposed an attachment system that evolved to regulate the sense of security and protection through activation of the independent biological system of attachment. During perceived threat, this system increases the chances of survival by motivating closeness to preferred others. Attachment is conceptualized as a behavioral control system rooted in neuro-physiological processes within the central nervous system. The system maintains proximity to an "attachment figure", usually a parent, who serves as a "secure base" for the child (Ainsworth, 1989; Bowlby, 1988). A major tenet is that sensitive and responsive care to the child's signals provides the context within which the child learns to organize and regulate distress in regard to "felt security"---in a word, cope. Attachment figures appear to be the original regulators of the child's affective and physiological reactivity to stress, as well as a model for using social support when needed. Seminal studies of early rearing experiences of mother and infant monkeys and rats, specifically work by Harlow (Harlow & Zimmerman, 1958) and Hofer (1973,1976,1984, 1995), support Bowlby's evolutionary-ethological approach and the existence of this relational, regulating biobehavioral system.

A concept of attachment theory is internal working models. These are mental representations organized from childhood that provide explanations for continuity: these structures guide perception and expectations, affect and behaviors, physiological responses, and cognitions (Bowlby, 1973). The premise that early experiences lead to different attachment styles, and thus differing internal models, has been supported by research. The traditional classification is one secure and two insecure patterns---avoidant and ambivalent (Ainsworth, Blehar, Waters & Wall, 1978). Attachment research also indicating different affect patterns has led attachment to be considered a theory of affect regulation (Kobak & Sceery, 1988). Research indicates that children of sensitive or responsive caregivers develop a secure style, and as adults have positive images of self and others, are comfortable with intimacy, are not restricted in affect, and have high self-esteem (Ainsworth et al., 1978; Collins & Read, 1990). Children of inconsistent caregivers tend to develop an ambivalent style; characteristics of these adults include intense affect and emotional neediness, fear of abandonment, and low self-esteem (Collins & Read, 1990; Hazan & Shaver, 1987).

Lastly, children whose caregivers are emotionally cold and rejecting develop the avoidant style, who as adults exhibit compulsive self-reliance, high distrust with fear of intimacy, and hyper-regulation of affect (Collins & Read, 1990; Hazan & Shaver, 1987). A striking characteristic of this style is the inhibited display of negative emotions—the "masking" of negative affect—especially of anger (Bowlby, 1973; Hazan & Shaver,1987). Also, avoidant individuals tend to restrict acknowledgement of distress by appearing unperturbed, yet displaying contradictory physiological arousal during exploration of threatening issues (Dozier & Kobak, 1991; Main, Kaplan & Cassidy, 1985; Main & Weston, 1982). This fact has implications for well-being; research indicates that the non-expression of negative emotions is linked to health (Gross, 1989, 1999).

Attachment and the Development of Stress Regulation

The attachment system and processes are important in that they impact future social relations, affect patterns, and the development of stress-regulatory systems. Basically, attachment influences how children respond to stress by moderating affective, physiological and neuroendocrine responses; the attachment system is activated during times of fear, threat, or illness, hence, the sympathetic nervous system's fight-or-flight response. Distress-alleviation in the sense of safety and protection is a core function of attachment which has been viewed directly in terms of affect and physiological arousal regulation (Brennan & Shaver, 1995; Kobak & Sceery, 1988; Reite & Boccia, 1994). Thus, one's style of attachment becomes a system of organized affect, behaviors, cognitions where felt security involves modulating emotional and physiological reactivity so that the individual will be able to cope appropriately with the environment (Porges, Doussard-Roosevelt & Maiti, 1994; Thompson, 1994).

During stress the hypothalamus releases corticotrophin-releasing hormone, which stimulates the pituitary gland to secrete adrenocorticotropic hormone, which in turn stimulates the adrenal cortex to release corticosteroids such as cortisol. Persistent activation of the HPA axis, for example chronic elevated cortisol levels, may be associated with harmful effects on development of the brain as well as cognitive, emotional, and physical functioning in humans (Gunnar 1998; Liu et al., 1997). Caregiving and separation has been linked to rat infant stress responses and consequent effects on the development of stress-regulatory systems that include permanent changes in stress reactivity (Francis, Diorio & Liu, 1999; Liu, Diorio, Day, Francis, Mar & Meaney, 2000). Gunnar's lab has shown attachment security to moderate stress reactivity in toddlers; for example, securely attached children are less likely to exhibit elevated cortisol responses to innoculations than insecure counterparts (Gunnar, Brodersen, Nachimias, Buss & Rigatuso, 1996; Nachimias, Gunnar, Mangelsdorf, Parritz & Buss, 1996). Other studies, however, have not found an exaggerated HPA reactivity to stress in those classified as insecurely attached (Hertsgaard, Gunnar, Erickson & Nachimias, 1995).

Flinn and England (1997) found that poor family interactions as well as unavailable or inconsistent parental attention was associated with abnormal cortisol response profiles, diminished immunity and frequent illness among children and adolescents. Lueckin investigated the relation between attachment experiences in childhood and cortisol responses in adulthood (1998,2000). Results showed that those who had lost a parent or reported poor family relations showed higher cortisol levels following a stress task relative to the control group. These findings are consistent with animal research suggesting that attachment disruption in the early environment may impact stress responses later in life (Coe, 1999). In sum, while attachment processes appear to be implicated in physiological and neuroendocrine stress responses in both animal and human studies, findings remain inconsistent.

Attachment and Developmental PNI?

The effect of security on stress response and neuroendocrine reactivity advances the question of early psychosocial influences on the immune system and vulnerability to illness, or Ader's "developmental" psychoneuroimmunology (1983). Several studies support for the notion that early interactions involve a developmental psychobiological attunement between mother and infant, however, most of these are from animal research. Laboratory studies of rodents and monkeys indicate that early rearing conditions can affect immune responses (e.g., Laudenslager, Reite & Harbeck, 1982). An example is Coe's work which has investigated the effects of psychosocial factors on immune function via a lifespan approach to psycho-neuroimmunology (PNI).

Coe's findings of early effects on immunity in rhesus monkeys suggests critical periods for PNI, and that changes in immune development may be age dependent (Coe, 1993; Lubach, Coe & Ershler, 1995). Some effects may involve more permanent changes upon the trajectory of immunity---especially when events occur at younger ages. Thus, his research emphasizes the importance of the social context and other psychological influences on the development of the immune system. In human studies, relevant here is Gunnar's work on neurobiological activity in young children and the perspective that security is a coping resource (e.g., Gunnar et al., 1996). A study investigated the role of security in moderating stress responses of the hypothalamic-pituitary-adrenocortical (HPA) system in inhibited children. Results supported the prediction that security moderated stress reactivity; insecurely attached, inhibited children had the highest elevations of cortisol post-session in contrast to secure children (Nachimias et al., 1996).

Attachment, Illness Vulnerability and Behavior

In terms of illness, there is a paucity of research into attachment and physical health. However, from several existing studies, associations have been found between children diagnosed with epilepsy, asthma and congenital heart disease and insecure attachment (Goldberg, Simmons, Newman, Campbell & Fowler, 1991; Marvin & Pianta, 1996; Mrazek, Casey & Anderson, 1987). In adults, the research suggests that insecure attachment in general, and avoidant attachment, in particular, may be a risk factor for physical health (Kotler et al., 1994). Adult insecurity has been found to be associated with higher reports of psychosomatic and physical illness (Hazan & Shaver, 1990) symptom reporting (Feeney & Ryan, 1994), decrease in immune function (Kiecolt-Glaser, Fisher, Ogrocki, Stout, Speicher & Glaser, 1987) and emotion focused coping related to illness reports (Feeney & Ryan, 1994). Avoidant attachment, specifically, has been found to be inversely related to health care visit behavior and emotional inhibition with contradictory physiological arousal (Dozier & Kobak, 1991; Feeney & Ryan, 1994). Additionally, women with cancer scored significantly higher on avoidant attachment and emotional control than women in the control group (Tacón et al., 2001). Of course, further study needs to differentiate between avoidance as a pre-morbid pattern or a coping response to cancer.

In sum, be it animals or humans, findings reflect the process and power of the attachment system to promote enduring bonds that serve the survival of the species. A developmental contextual approach to health is advocated via developmental psychobiology in the form of reciprocal biobehavioral attunement between caregiver and child. The quality of early interactions may play some role in sculpting the template for physiological and affective regulatory patterns, immune function, and responses to stress—especially if no life-altering event or change in environment presents itself (Coe, 1999; Gunnar et al., 1996). As Hofer proposes, it is likely that interactions which involve biological regulation by the mother become organized into cognitive and emotional states that would constitute Bowlby's concept of internal working models (1995). This approach fits with Maunder and Hunter's (2001) view that attachment has the potential for a biopsychosocial model of development and health, and aid in explaining individual vulnerability to stress and disease.

PSYCHOSOCIAL FACTORS AND CANCER

Type C Behavior Pattern

The Type C Behavior Pattern (TCBP) was developed by Temoshok and Heller in working with melanoma patients (Temoshok & Heller, 1981), and includes such factors as coping, emotional expressiveness, and helpless/hopeless orientations. They were the first to define and operationalize the notion of a Type C repressive coping style by proposing a constellation of cognitive, behavioral, and emotional factors that related to cancer progression. Temoshok hypothesized the Type C individual as being: cooperative, overly patient, unassertive and appeasing, non-expressive of emotions, especially anger, inattentive to or unaware of one's needs and signals, and compliant with authority (1987). This particular pattern was conceived as being the polar opposite of Rosenman & Friedman's Type A pattern for heart disease (Rosenman et al., 1964). Empirical support has been found for this position. For example, self-reported anxiety and physiological activity were assessed for repressive coping reactions in melanoma patients, heart patients, and controls. The melanoma patients exhibited significantly more repressed coping reactions than the other groups, and cardiovascular patients exhibited the least repressive reactions (Temoshok & Kneier, 1984).

The basic proposition being put forth is that a connection may exist between attachment theory and the Type C pattern. Two areas of research suggest connections: parent-child relations and emotional patterning involving the non-expression of emotion.

The Family Context: Parent-Child Relations

The view that troubled relations in childhood is distally related to cancer is not new. LeShan espoused this position in the 1950s based on interviews of patients (LeShan, 1966; LeShan & Worthington, 1956). Unfortunately, his work and others at the time had methodological problems: inappropriate or no use of control groups, subjective methods, and retrospective reports (Eysenck, 1996). Recently, better designed retrospective and prospective studies, using both within and between-group designs have yielded findings similar to LeShan (Grassi & Molinari, 1986; Shaffer, Duszynski & Thomas, 1982).

One association in the literature is that of loss or separations in childhood. That is, some researchers have reported that adults with cancer were more likely to have experienced significantly higher incidences of parental deprivation via parental death, than controls (Baltrusch, Gehde, Titze & Heine, 1992; Tacón, 2003). In contrast, other researchers have reported no group differences for parental loss between lung cancer and benign lung disease groups (Grassi & Lodi, 1989). Unfortunately, these studies focus on the experience of loss alone, while not reporting or addressing the need to assess the cause of parental death, especially if it was from cancer. In one case, while not reporting specific causes for parental deaths, results showed that the majority of cancer patients reported a family history of cancer (Tacón, 2003). This admittedly, is a hole in the research, and supports a uni-dimensional genetic view. Again, the goal here is to explore contributing psychosocial factors in cancer, not dominant causality factors, for the purpose of stimulating the collaboration of a more holistic, multidimensional and interdisciplinary model that integrates both endogenous and exogenous factors.

Second is the issue of closeness to parents, or the degree to which emotional needs were met. Cross-sectional and longitudinal studies have shown cancer patients report significantly less closeness to parents, which also predicted later cancer (Grassi & Molinari, 1986; Shaffer et al., 1982). However, perhaps the largest source implicating parent-child relations is the prospective Precursors Study begun at Johns Hopkins in 1948 (Thomas, 1988). Data analysis on family relations from 1337 white male medical students during 40 years of follow-up showed that scores on closeness to parents significantly differentiated the disorder groups; that is, those who developed cancer during the follow-up years had premorbidly reported the lowest scores on closeness to their parents in childhood. As Thomas noted, findings that people who would develop cancer held less close relations, especially with their parents in early years, suggest the hypothesis that the quality of human relationships, specifically with parents, may be an important component in the development of cancer (Thomas, p.55).

Emotional Patterns

The non-expression of emotion, particularly anger, is described by Temohsok as the pathogenic core of Type C coping. In 1987, Temoshok proposed a model of explanation as to how the Type C pattern may have developed. A brief summary follows.

Because of an inherited predisposition and/or family interaction patterns, a child learns early to cope with stressors and challenges in a way that involves acquiring an orientation where needs and feelings of self become nullified or negated to those of others in the environment, most likely, those upon which the child is dependent. An example is given where a child consciously suppresses a physical need so as not to "bother" a parent (p.558). This shows the possible developmental pathway where initial conscious, suppressive behaviors and expression go unconsciously underground; consistent entrainment of these strategies becomes an enduring, maladaptive pattern of repressive coping and self-unawareness.

As noted by Temoshok, consistent findings in the literature indicate "that repressive behaviors or tendencies, coping strategies in which anxiety-provoking events, emotions, or ideas are denied, suppressed, repressed, minimized, rationalized away, or otherwise avoided, are often associated with higher incidences of cancer and with poorer prognosis" (Temoshok & Kneier, p.145). The issue at point regarding attachment, cancer, and emotions is that of a particular emotional regulation pattern or style in cancer patients that distinguishes them from other disease groups, i.e., cardiovascular patients, or the well-known conceptual differences between Type A and Type C prone individuals (Rosenman et al., 1964; Temoshok, 1987). That is the lynchpin of focus here. Evidence indicating an over-arching proclivity of emotional patterning that involves the inhibition of emotional expression in cancer individuals is relevant to this thesis regarding attachment theory.

Several studies indicate that individuals with cancer are more likely to control or suppress their emotions than those with benign disease or healthy controls (Jansen & Muenz, 1984;

Pettingale, Watson & Greer, 1985). Perhaps the most distinctive work in this area is that of Steven Greer and colleagues. They developed an emotional control scale, from which individuals with cancer have been found to exhibit higher emotional control of negative emotions than comparison groups (Greer & Morris, 1975; Watson & Greer, 1983; Watson, Pettingale & Greer, 1984). Alternately, an early study by Greer and Morris regarding breast biopsy patients found an abnormal release of anger in breast cancer patients, with most displaying extreme suppression. However, not all cancer patients were consistent in this pattern; some displayed high-expression and not suppression (Greer & Morris, 1978). Despite this lack of consistency, the data indicate that emotional regulation, including external emotional expressiveness, is a major factor of consideration in cancer patients. Additionally, this non-expressiveness of emotion has been found across cancer type and gender, for example, in cancer of the lung in men (Kissen, 1963) and in women with breast cancer (Tacón et al., 2001).

A discrepancy between emotional expression and physiological arousal has been also found. Individuals with different types of malignancy (melanoma, breast cancer) as compared to other diagnosis groups or controls, have shown significant and contradictory physiological arousal while expressing low self-distress and exhibiting a calm façade during induced stress (Temoshok & Kneier, 1984; Watson et al., 1984). Also, findings regarding variables associated with thicker, more invasive tumors in melanoma patients were congruent with more of a Type C than a Type A style during interviews using semantic differential scales which distinguished the Type A and C characteristics (Temoshok, 1985). Along the same lines, skin conductance activity during adult attachment interviews showed that individuals who used avoidant or deactivating attachment strategies during the discussion of threatening issues showed a discrepancy between external facade and internal arousal (Dozier & Kobak, 1991). This suggests that those with this affective style deal with stress at the cost of increased physiology, which likely impacts immuno-competence. Lastly, in terms of the development of the Type C when dependence and socialization are prominent, Ader and Solomon suggest that socialization is linked to neuro-endocrine development, which may be an important determinant of adult immuno-competence (Ader, 1983; Solomon, 1987). Such views support the position that the development of socio-emotional processes may be important to the Type C pattern.

CONCEPTUAL INTEGRATION

This section will begin with a discussion as to connections among attachment theory, health, and cancer.

Global Links: Attachment and Health

Although research in attachment has focused on the precursors and outcomes of social and emotional development across the lifespan, there are several reasons to deduce a general relation between attachment and health which include the following issues: 1) social variables, 2) negative affect, regulation and behavior, 3) brain development and stress neuroimmunology, and 4) neural substrates of affective style.

Social Variables

Research has demonstrated associations between health and social variables, with social support probably being the most investigated variable in this area. An extensive review of 81 studies concerning the relation between social support and physiological processes showed that social support was reliably related to beneficial health effects on cardio-vascular, endocrine, and immune systems (Uchino, Cacioppo & Kiecolt-Glaser, 1996). Likewise, links also have been found between physiological-immunological data and relationship quality; decreased immune function has been associated with loneliness, divorce and bereavement (Irwin, Daniels, Risch, Craig & Bloom, 1988; Kennedy, Kiecolt-Glaser & Glaser, 1999; Kiecolt-Glaser et al., 1987). Also, Kulik and Mahler found that coronary bypass patients who perceived their marital relationship as good prior to surgery and who received high support from their attachment figure postoperatively---as measured by the number of hospital visits---used less pain medication and recovered more quickly than their counterparts (1989).

While the exact mechanisms by which relationships specifically affect health are unknown, attachment theory may help to explain such mechanisms because it provides a framework within which to understand the development of relationships. Attachment is also the initial process that establishes if and by what behavioral strategies individuals will seek support when distressed. Accordingly, it would be both logical and intuitive to suggest that the supportiveness from an attachment figure would impact one's sense of security and well-being during stressful circumstances, be it a child or an adult. Consequently, attachment is an important psychosocial variable in health; secure attachments are part of and foster healthy development, and provide a sense of security and support with which to deal with and recover from life's challenges.

As discussed previously, Temoshok described how the Type C might develop, during which the child learns to subvert needs and feelings in order to please, appease or otherwise not burden others in the early environment (1987). Of course, the selected coping strategy needs to be effective in reducing anxiety and re-establishing multiple levels of homeostasis for adaptational merit. As the seminal work of Han Selye (1956) demonstrated, organisms can only endure so much stress arousal until exhaustion or breakdown occurs. Some degree of returning to a sense of safety, comfort and security can be manifested via the processes that achieve psychological, biological, and environmental homeostasis (Temoshok, 1987). As Temoshok referred to environmental homeostasis, so too, did Bowlby (1973). In fact, it is a major concept that helps to explain the dynamics of the attachment behavioral control system. Bowlby viewed it similar to a thermostat or regulatory mechanism such as temperature or blood pressure.

Specifically, there are environmental "rings" of security within which the child operates during exploration or proximity-seeking in relation to a secure base. Thus, environmental homeostasis involves the social milieu and the child's literal landscape position to a secure base during distress. Avoidantly attached children distance themselves from their caregivers during stressful laboratory analogs and do not seek aid during events that would normally evoke activation of the attachment system and proximity-seeking. They are described as having "given up" the expectation of aid being forthcoming which derives from previous rejecting and unfulfilling experiences with attachment figures (Bowlby, 1973, 1988). These children prematurely move into a modus operandi of strong self-reliance and hyper-regulation of affect that includes the non-expression of emotions (especially anger) or the need of support, as well an avoidant attitude toward the discussion of emotionally laden issues. This apparently helps to maintain the avoidantly attached individual's sense of integrity by re-establishing multiple levels of homeostasis within a social, relational context.

Negative Affect, Regulation, and Behavior

Second, it has been established that sustained negative emotions and affect regulation impact physiology and health quality (Gross, 1999), and are factors associated in disease processes such as cancer and cardiovascular disease. This is a lynchpin with attachment because it is a theory of affect regulation that is impacted by the quality of the secure base function provided by an attachment figure in childhood. These experiences establish the blueprint for coping with negative events and affect in later life. Also, attachment is conceptually related to health or self-care behaviors. Bowlby postulated that the attachment system is activated during stressful times of threat, fatigue, and sickness, which typically initiates proximity seeking behaviors to a stronger, wise, or protective figure (1973). In childhood, this would be a parent, however in adulthood, this proximity-seeking or approach-oriented behavior could be directed to a spouse, friend, therapist/support group, or a physician.

According to theory, responses will differ by attachment classification, which may possibly play a role in health outcomes. For example, while following health variables of undergraduate students, Feeney and Ryan (1994) found that visits to health care professionals were inversely related to avoidant attachment, even when the level of symptoms were controlled. This finding is consistent with theory in that during times of need avoidant persons do not behaviorally seek aid or support. Rather, they tend to use hyper-avoidant and distancing strategies that could have implications for compliance. The issue of delay in seeking medical attention is especially salient for malignancies, and models specific to delay in cancer diagnosis have been generated (Andersen, Cacioppo & Roberts, 1995).

Brain Development and Stress Neuroimmunology

Recent research has shown that early experiences are crucial for the development of neural structure and function because the brain is use-dependent, thus children require stimulating and nurturing experiences for appropriate brain maturation. This is especially important for the emotional region of the brain, the limbic system, which is associated with the development of empathy and inhibition of violent behavior. The development of attachment plays a key role in shaping the structure and function of the brain as well as the neurobiology of stress and trauma responses, including cortisol activation (Perry, 1998; Shore, 1994).

The development of the stress response is impacted by early attachment experiences and whether the attachment figure provides the secure base function during distress and threat. Also, as mentioned previously, child attachment security to a parent was found to moderate stress reactivity and predict child cortisol responses to the event (Nachiamas et al., 1996). Research has concluded that the quality of daycare received early in life appears to be important in the development and regulation of stress-related neurobiological processes (Dettling, Parker, Lane, Sebanc & Gunnar, 2000). Thus, there is evidence to support the notion that early secure base experiences play a role in shaping later neurobiological responses to stress.

Neural Substrates of Emotion: Affective Style

For several decades, Davidson's lab has investigated the neural substrates of emotion and affective patterns, which has resulted in the definition of "affective style." Specifically, "affective style" refers to consistent individual differences in emotional reactivity and regulation; broadly, it refers to processes that include individual emotional response to challenge, mood, and emotion-relevant cognitive processes (Davidson, 2000). Affect regulation is considered a key component of affective style. This research has involved examining physiological activity of the prefrontal cortex (PFC), amygdala, and the central neural circuitry of emotion. Replicated findings demonstrate that baseline asymmetric activation in certain brain regions reflect trait-like, dispositional affective styles that are reliable and stable over time. For example, in studies of 10-month old infants, affective reactivity was recorded during a lab situation similar to the attachment lab Strange Situation where infant EEG reactivity was obtained during maternal separation and reunion episodes (Davidson & Fox, 1989). From this study and others, large individual differences in baseline electrophysiological measures of PFC activation in both infants and adults indicate that left-frontal activation is related to positive affect while right-frontal activation is associated with negative affect.

Other studies by Davidson and colleagues have found that measures of affective style predicted repressive defensiveness (Davidson & Tomarken, 1989), baseline immune function (Kang, Davidson, Coe & Ershler, 1991), and reactivity of the immune system to emotional challenge (Davidson, Coe, Dolski & Donzella, 1999). Recall that Bowlby conceptualized the attachment system as rooted in neurophysiological processes. Interdisciplinary research among the fields of socio-emotional development and neurophysiology could help to clarify whether Davidson's affective styles are possibly the neural substrates of attachment affect patterns. Findings that affective style is related to baseline immune function and reactivity may implicate possible links between attachment, stress response and coping, and immune function.

Specific Links: Attachment and Cancer

Interpersonal Links

Attachment includes affective, behavioral, cognitive and interpersonal components and is the conceptual foundation for later relational quality. As noted previously, associations have been found between inadequate or disrupted relationship quality and cancer diagnosis, which can be framed in an attachment perspective. First, the longitudinal findings from the Precursor's study (Thomas,1988), showing that individuals who developed cancer held the lowest scores on closeness to parents in childhood, could be interpreted as attachment quality in the early relationship.

Second, research conducted regarding "early family relationships" and the family "affective climate" in the childhood of cancer patients, can be cast within an attachment framework. That is, the family "affective climate", according to Grassi and Molinari

(1986)includes unresolved conflict within the family as indicated by coldness, estrangement, and disaffection in the relationship between parents and their offspring. This is consistent with early socio-emotional experience and primary attachments. Also, the psychosocial findings and descriptions of cancer patients' history by researchers for over 40 years---early parental loss, major loss, unresolved emotional tension with parents, emotionally distant, less loving parents, and emotional needs not met in childhood (e.g., Grassi & Molinari 1986; LeShan, 1966) ---can be integrated into and reconceptualized according to attachment. The reciprocal world of socio-emotional relations where a sense of security, affection and worth, as well as the expression and signaling of needs and feelings, are essential components of attachment theory and process.

Affective and Behavioral Links

The non-expression of emotions, is an important component of the Type C configuration. Such a distinct style can be integrated into an attachment framework precisely because attachment is a theory of affect regulation (Kobak & Sceery, 1988). Also, there are parallels with Temoshok's view that the Type C may develop as the child acquires the tendency to put others before self, a self-sabotage, so to speak, of needs and feelings. The psychosocial dynamics that are embedded within a given context can be connected with attachment relationships and the maintenance of some form of attachment for a dependent child. For, whether one is securely attached, or insecurely attached because one has experienced and expects rejection or inconsistent care and protection by a caregiver--- it is still the state of being attached to another. Indeed, attachment and the inability or non-expression of negative emotions linked to cancer "may have its roots in the lack of a *secure base* in childhood" (Baltrusch & Waltz, 1987).

SUMMARY

In this first section, a developmental contextualistic approach to health was presented by applying and integrating attachment theory with psychosocial factors in cancer. Attachment involves the establishment and relative endurance of acquired behavioral styles with corresponding affect regulation patterns. Essential to the development of a particular style is early experience during distress and the degree to which an attachment figure serves as a secure base and externally regulates a child's stress response and coping. Added to this is the neurophysiological research from Davidson's lab and neuro-physiological designation of reliable trait-like affective styles. Possible links exist between these areas in terms of attachment's emotional regulation patterns and Davidson's "reliable" affective styles. While the influence of psychosocial and behavioral factors in health and immunocompetence has received attention in both infrahuman and human research, the role of developmental contextual factors and processes has not. It may be that chronic maladaptive coping which includes contradictory emotional regulation tendencies(internal-to-external incongruence) that originates within a relational context, may have implications for physiological and immunological functioning, and hence, health outcomes. For, health trajectories are contextually dependent on developmental processes that are embedded within given genotypic potentials and biological constraints, environmental and lifestyle factors.

The likely development of Type C coping during childhood may link with developing neural substrates of affective style and brain activity as reported from Davidson's lab (e.g., Davidson, 2000). As previously discussed, attachment not only impacts brain development, but also stress reactivity in the form of security moderating cortisol activation as shown by Gunnar's work (Nachiamias et al., 1996). Attachment also has consequences for emotional regulation and expressive patterns of communication; and, these factors are salient to coping and support-seeking during crisis. This is especially relevant during major health conditions such as cancer where physician-patient interactions and psychosocial interventions are an essential part of coping with such a frightening disease. We now turn to attachment-related factors in psychosocial therapies for chronically ill patients.

PSYCHOSOCIAL THERAPIES – WHAT'S ATTACHMENT GOT TO DO WITH IT?

Over the last 20 years, the field of psycho-oncology has progressed in understanding and providing psychological strategies and social support to treat the needs of people coping with cancer. Overall, by the late 1980s and early 1990s evidence indicated that certain negative psychological states of mind could enhance the neoplastic process, while social connections and social support might slow down its progression (Spiegel & Fawzy, 2002). In particular, types of group therapy have been found to be helpful in providing psychological support to people suffering with cancer. Specifically, a variety of group interventions with cancer patients have improved anxiety and mood, coping strategies, psychological adjustment, and social support (Bloom, D'Onofrio & Banks, 1999; Tacón, Caldera & Ronaghan, in press; Telch & Telch, 1986; Worden & Weisman, 1984). One salient area of stress research is an individual's ability to maintain positive states of mind during challenge, and three psychosocial domains associated with positive states of mind are coping, social support and attachment style (Horowitz et al.,1988). All three of these factors are therefore important to psychosocial therapy, and as well, are all associated with attachment theory. Consequently, attachment concepts and processes, in general, can be considered a dynamic in the therapeutic process.

First, Bowlby's position that early experiences with caregivers are internalized as working models which then develop into a unique attachment style with concomitant affect regulation and coping patterns are related to stress responses. He basically theorized that the different attachment styles defined different strategies of stress management; moreover, such attachment style differences have been found in the way people cope with internal and external sources of distress (Bowlby, 1973; Mikulincer & Florian, 1998). For example, secure individuals have been shown to both perceive and seek higher levels of emotional and instrumental support than avoidant or ambivalently attached persons, whereas insecurely attached individuals tend to perpetuate distress and increase vulnerability by suppressing negative emotions with attachment deactivation and avoiding seeking support when it is needed (Mikulincer & Florian,1995). Buffering distress amidst threatening chaos and adjusting to health stressors are highly important for chronically ill populations; hence, attachment is relevant to psychosocial therapies for these individuals.

Next, attachment has important implications for therapy in the specific domain of the therapist-client relationship (a form of support). Bowlby suggested that the therapist's role was to serve as a secure base for the client while disconfirming the client's problematic working models of relationships, which would include views of self (Bowlby, 1988). This view of clinicians as caregivers thus sees the therapist acting as an attachment figure who is consistently available, responsive and provides a base of safety from which the client can explore issues, feelings and self-disclose within a therapeutic alliance that is benevolent and secure (e.g., Dozier, Cue & Barnett, 1994). This is akin to Winnicott's "holding environment" for the client (Winnicott, 1971). Unlike a caregiver, however, the therapist has the role of facilitating the client's updating and changing of internal working models as well as enhancing coping and affect regulation strategies that are appropriate and reality-based for the present---not the past.

Lastly, organizational attachment-style differences have been found in affective responses to stress and psycho-physiological arousal (Dozier & Kobak, 1991; Mikulincer & Florian, 1995, 1998; Simpson, 1990). Remember also that attachment has been viewed as a theory of affect regulation since the 1980s. How might this relate to chronic illness, treatment regimen and recovery? Individuals classified as securely attached---which involves positive mental representations of self and others and a healthy range of feelings--experience an optimistic and hopeful attitude, are characterized by a strong sense of self-efficacy, and are more likely to acknowledge distress and seek support from others (Bartholomew & Horowitz, 1991; Collins & Read, 1990;Mikulincer, Florian & Weller, 1993). Clearly, the ability to acknowledge rather than deny one's health condition combined with a strong sense of self-efficacy and a hopeful [versus a hopeless or fatalistic] attitude would enhance one's coping with a chronic disease. Perhaps the most well-known psychosocial group intervention specific to cancer patients that can be interpreted as including attachment factors in therapy has been that of David Spiegel at Stanford University.

In the late 1980s, Spiegel and colleagues began a psychotherapy intervention called Supportive-Expressive group therapy for women with metastatic breast cancer based on the hypothesis and research findings of longstanding links between affective and behavioral inhibition in cancer populations (Spiegel, Bloom, Kraemer, & Gottheil, 1989). As previously presented, the core characteristic of the Type C coping style is that of emotional suppression-repression of negative affect (e.g., Temoshok, 1987); or in attachment terms, the developmentally acquired socio-emotional style of hyper-regulation of negative affect. The emphasis in supportive-expressive therapy is to encourage and increase overall emotional self-efficacy via facilitating emotional expression---rather than the continued lifestyle pattern of suppression/repression---in a supportive context that leads to improved coping skills with cancer. What was ground-breaking about this group intervention? In the decade-long follow-up study of these 86 women it was found that patients who participated in the expressive psychotherapy group lived twice as long (mean of 36.6 months) as control subjects who did not participate (mean of 18.9 months) (Spiegel et al., 1989). Spiegel and colleagues were surprised by the unexpected findings and are in the process of replicating findings.

Spiegel has emphasized that the intervention was designed to encourage emotional expression, as well as the sharing and processing of emotions within this life threatening experience of cancer. It is this specified focus of the therapy that deals with styles of emotional expression and coping during threat that is considered to be the lynchpin with attachment. Attachment theory offers a framework for the study and process of interrelationships between stress, social support and health and activation of the attachment system precisely during periods of threat, danger and illness. Additionally, the threat of cancer is certainly a context in which the attachment system would become activated and hence, should be considered to have clinical relevancefor psychosocial intervention. Afterall, the quality of social support and intimate relationships is generally considered to moderate harmful effects of stressful events on both physical and mental health, and attachment provides this theoretical foundation (Gerlsma & Luteijn, 2000).

The position here is that attachment concepts and processes have clinicalimplications for psychotherapy, and that attachment factors play a salient role in psychosocial aspects of individuals dealing with chronic illness and terminal disease. In of itself, the original premise of attachment is that social and emotional processes play a major, adaptational role in survival of the individual, and hence, in the survival of the species as a whole. Furthermore, the neurophysiologically-based, biobehavioral attachment system is activated precisely during times of threat, stress, fear and illness.......all of which are components of being diagnosed with the chronic and potentially fatal disease of cancer. As such, the stance here is that attachment issues should be considered a standard psychosocial factor in clinical treatment when working with chronically ill patients, especially those with cancer.

It could be said that Spiegel's intervention emphasizes two therapeutic foci on the individual level that are separate from group social support: emotional patterns of expression and emotional and cognitive awareness. First, Spiegel's *supportive-expressive* group focuses on increasing emotional expression in a safe and socially supportive context. This includes being able to recognize one's feelings as well as modify the attachment-related affect pattern of behavioral suppression of emotions, especially of negative emotions. Second, this program emphasizes awareness on emotional and cognitive levels. While awareness does not automatically lead to peaceful acceptance of one's situation, it does, at least, place the individual in accord with reality.This is necessary in order to problem-solve and cope which requires less energy on the part of the patient than maintaining a façade of denial.

Spiegel's group-work includes topics such as improved doctor-patient relationship dynamics, detoxification of death and dying issues, and facilitation of active coping via techniques such as relaxation and imagery (Classen, Diamond, & Spiegel, 1999). Each of these topics can be consecutively interpreted from an attachment perspective. For example, regarding doctor-patient dynamics, this involves relationships and communication within a socially supportive context where the physician is viewed as a professional form of an attachment figure in a frightening, attachment-system arousing situation of dealing with a serious life-threatening disease. Dying is the most direct threat to self, and more importantly, death can be considered the ultimate separation from loved ones---the final severing of attachment bonds.

Lastly, due to the generally consistency of one's cognitive models----unless a major experience updates or revises one's internal representations---a given attachment style with associated affect patterns and coping strategies is believed to remain relatively stable and enduring throughout adulthood. Following from this, attachment could be an important psychosocial factor related to stress reactivity and coping which would include one's use of stress reduction and/or relaxation techniques to combat stress, anxiety and fatigue during chronic illness. For, attachment theory's comprehensive framework makes it a truly holistic perspective: it has biological and neurophysiological, cognitive and behavioral, as well as social and emotional components. This brings us to the final purpose of presenting a mindfulness psychosocial intervention that is embedded within an attachment framework designed for cancer patients.

MINDFULNESS MEDITATION- A COMPLEMENTARY PSYCHOSOCIAL THERAPY IN CANCER

Over the past decades, the number of cancer patients seeking complementary therapies has increased steadily, with thousands of patients seeking unconventional therapies independent of standard health care (Cassileth, 1999). Research in the field of psycho-neuroimmunology has demonstrated support for the view of mind-body holism and the biopsychosocial model in health and medicine (Kiecolt-Glaser, McGuire, Robles & Glaser, 2002). The idea that the mind or psychosocial factors may play a role in the neoplastic disease process has been notably advanced by prominent researchers such as Greer (1983) and Speigel (1991). One mind-body technique is meditation. Research investigating the effects of meditation as well as its use in intervention programs has existed for several decades and spans different health populations (Alexander, Robinson, Orme-Johnson & Schneider, 1994; Murphy & Donovan, 1997). While programs using meditation have been developed for specific health populations, such as heart disease (Ornish, 1990) and addictions patients (O'Connell & Alexander, 1994), a comparable, standardized program for cancer patients has yet to be established. The purpose here is to review the literature and propose a program for use in cancer.

PSYCHOSOCIAL CONSIDERATIONS IN CANCER

Psychological and psychosocial variables that have been associated with cancer patients will be reviewed. Specifically, psychological consequences of the disease as well as psychosocial factors found to be salient in cancer populations will be discussed.

Psychological Sequelae and Indications

The diagnosis of cancer, especially breast cancer which is the most common type of cancer among American women, elicits greater distress than any other diagnosis, regardless of the prognosis (NCI, 1997). The literature historically documents various negative psychological consequences for patients that include depression, anxiety and anger; depression and anxiety are the most prevalent (Shapiro, Lopez & Schwartz, 2001). Such psychological concomitants of the disease reduce the overall well-being and effectiveness of individuals to actively participate in their own healing process. Thus, the ability to confront their life-changing challenge and work with their stress---rather than be incapacitated by it--- is severely limited. Stress reduction and relaxation programs are indicated as a cancer therapy due to the above findings regarding depression and anxiety. However, other psychosocial variables also have special relevance for cancer patients. While cancer is different for each individual, research suggests that certain psychosocial factors play a role in disease onset, progression and psychological adjustment. What follows is a review of several salient factors: stress, sense of control, repressive coping, social support and spirituality.

Psychosocial Factors and Cancer

Stress is the one variable that has been found likely to be associated with every kind of psychological insult. Stress has been associated with increases in depression, anxiety and worry, and other forms of mental distress; physiologically, stress, depression and anxiety have been found to impact immune function (e.g., Delongis, Folkman & Lazarus, 1988). In regards to cancer, a higher frequency of stressful life events in cancer patients has been found in comparison to controls (Baltrusch, Stangel & Waltz, 1991; Tacón, 2003). Additionally, stressful critical life events have been found to be significantly higher in adolescents who developed cancer; one study showed that the mean score of critical life events (loss, separations, change of residence, etc.) in a group of adolescent cancer patients was more than double the mean found for the healthy control group (Eiser, 1990; Johnson, 1986) Lastly, research by Andersen and colleagues found that stress levels significantly modulated immune parameters of NK cell activity in a sample of 116 post-op cancer patients (Anderson, Anderson & DeProsse, 1989).

Research suggests that one's perception of control during stressful encounters in the environment is salient to psychological and physical health. Relevant here is Seligman's concept of learned helplessness. For example, tumor growth has been found to be accelerated in rats exposed to inescapable shock in comparison to rats who were allowed escape from the stressor (Peterson, Maier, & Seligman, 1993; Visintainer, Volpicelli, & Seligman, 1982). Having breast cancer has been found also to elicit feelings of helplessness and loss of control (Andersen, Kiecolt-Glaser & Glaser, 1994). Furthermore, a recent study by Greer and colleagues indicated that responding to cancer diagnosis with feelings of helplessness or hopelessness increases the risk of recurrence and death (Watson, Haviland, Greer, Davidson & Bliss, 1999). The above is consistent with studies that found that feelings of loss of control in response to cancer was a significant predictor of first recurrence and death; that is, an attitude of helplessness toward cancer is related to poor prognosis and recovery (Antoni & Goodkin, 1988; Pettingale, Morris, Greer & Haybitle, 1985). Feelings of loss of control or helplessness are associated with anxiety and depression, as well as decreased longevity of survival (Derogatis et al., 1983; Watson et al., 1991). Alternately, a sense of control during the threat of cancer was found to be significantly related to adjustment at six-months (Ell, Nishimoto, Movay, Mantell & Hamovitch, 1989).

A specific style of coping that involves a pattern of repression and denial is a major component of the Type C Behavior Pattern (TCBP) as conceptualized by Temoshok (1987). The Type C is operationally defined as a constellation of cognitive (decreased awareness of needs, feelings and sensations), verbal expression (non-expression of emotion, especially anger, with a pleasant façade), and behavioral-coping patterns (denying or minimizing problems, appeasing and unassertive behaviors) (e.g., Temoshok & Dreher, 1992). In a prospective study of women with breast cancer, Jensen found that those with repressive coping and low emotional expression of negative feelings were associated with poorer outcomes and decreased longevity (1987). Also, as previously presented, emotional expression is the focus of Spiegel's psychosocial *supportive-expressive* therapy program (e.g., Spiegel et al., 1989)

The benefits of social support during stress and illness are documented as evidence of this relational variable's positive impact on health and well-being (Uchino et al., 1996). Again, the work by Spiegel serves as a primary example. As discussed previously, women with breast cancer who participated in group with traditional treatment plus group therapy sessions lived significantly longer than those with only traditional treatment (see Spiegel, 1991). It has been suggested that this intervention increased participants' sense of social support which was related later to longevity. This is consistent with other findings relating social support to higher survival rates in cancer patients at four-years of follow-up (Waxler-Morrison, Hislop, Mears & Kan, 1991).

Finally, spirituality is a variable that possibly plays a role in the cancer experience. For example, spirituality may be a protective factor in the buffer model of stress where it shields against stressful events. Research has demonstrated the positive effects of this variable in physical and psychological health, well-being and its efficiency as a predictor of health outcomes (Levin, 1994). A recent review of spiritually-based interventions indicates that some programs demonstrate effectiveness or clinical validity (Harris, Thoresen, McCullough & Larson, 1999). However, more rigorous studies with improved designs and methodology are needed to clarify the role of spirituality in health.

The above psychosocial variables are considered important to the quality of life for cancer patients and therefore merit attention in cancer intervention therapies. The import of these factors indicate that a complementary therapy which decreases stressful effects and repressive coping, while enhancing a sense or locus of control, social support, emotional expression and spirituality, would be an efficient research-based protocol and provide benefits to cancer patients. Here an attachment foundation is useful for such a framework is associated with each of these factors.

Specifically, Bowlby's proposition that different attachment styles are associated with different patterns of emotional regulation, stress reactivity and coping strategies has been previously documented in this chapter (e.g., Bowlby, 1973; Mikulincer & Florian, 1998). This indicates attachment's role in stress and related repressive coping and emotional expression. Likewise, one's sense or locus of control is related to one's view of self, which is influenced by early attachment interactions with caregivers and the development of internal working models of self and others. One must have a positive, internal representation of self to be able to view self as having an agency or locus of control. Next, attachment style, as a socio-emotional process built from previous experience with attachment figures, plays an influential role as to interpersonal trust and proximity-seeking behaviors of an individual for social support during distress. Lastly, in terms of spirituality, research has documented attachment styles being associated withreligious and spiritual issues; for example, secure attachment was positively correlated with and found to be a predictor of spiritual maturity (TenElshof & Furrow, 2000). Likewise, research has investigated God as a substitute attachment figure (Kirkpatrick, 1998). Thus, attachment working models appear to go beyond positive or negative views of self and others, and to yield a universal, spiritual or religious representation as well.

In sum, a psychosocial therapy program that addresses the above factors as well as reduces mental distress/anxiety during chronic illness and treatment may be a clinically effective protocol of treatment. Meditation will be now presented followed by a discussion of its application to psychosocial variables associated with cancer.

MEDITATION

Meditation is basically the self-regulation of attention and awareness. Although a predominantly cognitive and sometimes emotional activity, meditation immerses the individual into the fullness of psycho-physiological experience. It enhances concentration and awareness as one intentionally focuses on inner or outer experience. Simply put, it is a disciplined way of paying attention to the present moment with uncritical, non-judging acceptance. This alert, yet calm attentiveness is practiced in two basic forms: exclusive/restrictive meditation (e.g., transcendental meditation) or inclusive/insight meditation (e.g., mindfulness) (Harris et al., 1999). The focus here will be on the latter.

Mindfulness is an example of inclusive meditation that involves including rather than excluding stimuli from the field of consciousness. This practice starts from a one-pointed focus of attention, however the field of awareness gradually expands to include a range of stimuli and objects present within the context of experience. Inclusive or mindfulness meditation is exemplified in the vipassana and soto zen traditions which cultivate an intentionally non-reactive, non-judging moment-to-moment awareness of reality as it is. This provides also a means of self-monitoring and regulating one's own arousal and potential distress with detached awareness. Learning to be mindful in the present moment can make mindfulness a practical and realistic strategy for people with busy, hectic lives and multiple responsibilities. The most prominent mindfulness program today is the mindfulness-based stress reduction/relaxation program (MBSR) of Kabat-Zinn at the University of Massachusetts Medical Center (Kabat-Zinn, 1990).

Mindfulness-Based Meditation Interventions

Interventions with mindfulness meditation truly became an area for research in the 1980s, based on Kabat-Zinn's stress reduction and relaxation program at the University of Massachusetts Medical Center. Since the program's inception, mindfulness stress reduction programs have rapidly increased: currently over 100 MBSR programs exist in health settings across the United States (Astin, 1997). Mindfulness-based meditation program of Kabat-Zinn is single-focused in that the modality taught via various techniques is mindfulness, in contrast to multi-faceted interventions where the meditative practice is just one of several components such as diet, exercise, group sessions, etc. (e.g., Ornish, 1990). A program with a singular modality of stress reduction & relaxation may be more feasible for a variety of patients---at least initially to give them tools to work with---in different circumstances.

Research has shown that mindful stress reduction decreases general physical and psychological symptoms including demonstrated decreases in chronic pain (Kabat-Zinn, Lipworth & Burney, 1985), anxiety (Miller, Fletcher & Kabat-Zinn, 1995), fibromyalgia (Kaplan, Goldenberg & Galvin-Nadeau, 1993), and mental symptoms with an increased sense of control (Astin, 1997). The use of meditation with cancer patients is sparse. As noted by

Kabat-Zinn in 1998, the use of meditation in cancer had not yet been tested scientifically in clinical trials (Kabat-Zinn, Massion, Hebert & Rosenbaum, 1998). In 2000, the first major clinical trial with cancer patients was conducted (Speca, Carlson, Goodey & Angen, 2000). Ninety-patients with different types of cancer participated in a randomized, wait-list control design to evaluate the effectiveness of a mindfulness-based program on mood disturbance and stress symptoms. Results indicated beneficial outcomes for the MBSR training: pre and post measures showed that the intervention group had significantly lower scores on mood disturbance and fewer stress symptoms than the control group after completing the training. The application of a mindfulness-based program for cancer patients will be now considered.

MBSR APPLICATION

The mindfulness stress reduction and relaxation program will be examined as it relates to variables that research has shown are associated with cancer. This will be then followed by a description of a mindfulness-based stress reduction and relaxation program geared for cancer patients.

Mindfulness and Psychosocial Variables

Mindfulness and Stress
As discussed earlier, stress has been associated with increases in depression, anxiety and worry as well as other forms of mental distress; and, physiologically, stress, depression and anxiety impact immune function (Delongis et al., 1988). Also, a higher frequency of stressful life events in cancer patients has been found in comparison to controls (e.g., Johnson,1986). The practice of mindfulness encourages the discipline of being present and mindful of the present moment to the exclusion of thinking about the past or ruminating and worrying about the future--- which at this present moment---does not even exist yet. Through attention, mindfulness directs individuals to attend to and deal with the current reality so as to reduce overwhelming stress regarding issues not presently in the field of experience. Mindfulness meditation has been shown to significantly and effectively reduce anxiety and stress-related symptoms of participants in several studies (Miller et al., 1995; Speca et al., 2000).

Mindfulness and Control
As mentioned previously, the diagnosis of breast cancer elicits feelings of helplessness and loss of control. Feelings of loss of control or helplessness are associated with anxiety and depression, as well as decreased longevity of survival (Watson et al., 1991). Alternately, a sense of control during the threat of cancer was significantly related to adjustment at six-months (Ell et al., 1989). A major aspect of mindfulness meditation precisely involves an increase in a sense of control: one must learn to first be aware of one's thoughts and actions in order to then be able to better regulate such thoughts and behaviors. Following participation in an MBSR 8-week stress reduction and relaxation program, participants in the experimental group indicated a significant increase in overall sense of control compared to the nonintervention group (Astin, 1997).

Mindfulness and Repression-Denial

As previously discussed, a style of coping where negative emotions and experiences are typically repressed and denied is strongly linked to the TCBP (Temoshok, 1987). The principle of mindfulness is directly opposed to that of denial; mindfulness emphasizes being aware of and paying attention to one's experience in the present moment with uncritical acceptance of reality as it is. It is possible that this complementary strategy may be useful in gradually enhancing conscious awareness and acceptance of events, and also foster a healthier mode of coping and dealing with the difficulties of life. It is emphasized that this is only a suggestion that is based on principle and relation; no study has investigated this and no data are currently available for empirical support.

Mindfulness, Social Support and Spirituality

The benefits of social support during stress and illness are documented throughout the literature (Uchino et al., 1996). The structure of the mindfulness reduction and relaxation program, similar to other therapies, is that of a group format. In this setting, individuals who all share a common suffering or challenge can offer true empathic support which others not facing such a crisis could do. Lastly, research has demonstrated positive effects of spirituality in physical and psychological health, as well as its ability to predict health outcomes (Levin, 1994). Most meditative techniques that have been transformed into western therapies stem from eastern religious-spiritual philosophies, i.e., Hinduism and Buddhism. Thus, mindfulness-based stress reduction programs have this historically spiritual origin within it.

In sum, based on the relations above as well as the rigorous research studies that support the effectiveness of the MBSR with various populations, it is concluded that Kabat-Zinn's mindfulness program could be an appropriate application for use with cancer patients. Additionally, this intervention is conceptualized from an attachment theory perspective. Thus, a group format is necessary in order to provide socio-emotional support with a facilitator who understands theory in order to recognize and utilize attachment concepts and processes as they arise. An attachment perspective, for example, would be relevant during discussions of loss of salient emotional bonds in the patients' lives as well as discussing the patient's role of being an attachment figure for loved ones who will be left behind to grieve if/when the patient dies. A mindfulness therapy intervention that is grounded in an attachment framework will now be presented which combines two primary therapeutic goals from mindfulness practice and attachment: cognitive/emotional awareness and emotional expression.

MBSR PROGRAM FOR CANCER PATIENTS

Before the program begins, participants will need to have received approval from their physicians and bring that approval form to an intake interview with a member of the MBSR staff. At that time, health information will be obtained to understand their current condition, i.e., health status, stage of disease, treatment regimen, etc. An adult attachment interview (AAI) will be conducted to assess the current state of mind with regards to attachment and determine unresolved status regarding loss and trauma.

The AAI is a semi-structured interview (George, Kaplan & Main, 1985) with questions that start out about the individual's childhood relationships with parents, what happened during times of illness, injury or emotional upset, experiences considered a setback to development, the overall impact of childhood experiences on adult personality, and the status of current relations with parents, if living. Additionally, a salient section of questions probe into early and adult loss/death issues as well as traumatic experiences. The AAI is unique in that it is not only what is said during the narrative that is important, but *how* it is said, for the AAI focuses on linguistic components of coherence during the narrative. Specifically, the concept of coherence is based on Grice's maxims that a coherent narrative is of high quality if it meets the standards of believability, relevance and detail, manner and clarity (George et al., 1985). The individual is classified as "secure", "dismissing" (avoidant), or "preoccupied" (ambivalent) on ratings from multiple scales. In addition, individuals are assigned a secondary classification of "unresolved" based on low coherence or disorientation during the portion of the interview related to loss and trauma. It is the position here that knowing a participant's AAI classification would be helpful for several reasons.

First, it would help the clinician understand interaction processes (between an individual and the therapist as well as among group members) manifested during group when the content and context of topics is related to loss, relationships, grieving, and specific fear-laden issues in the therapy room. For example, knowing that a participant has been classified as "dismissing" or avoidant of attachment-related issues would help to analyze the individual's behavior as well as target potential goals specific to that patient. Second, knowing an individual's attachment history in regards to being unresolved due to death or traumatic experiences within this group context of cancer would be valuable therapeutic information when working through discussions related to one's possible fear of mortality due to disease. Third, an AAI classification focuses on one's narrative and the coherence or disorientation of language. This focus would be consistent with the therapeutic goal of enhancing emotional expression since emotional inhibition is considered by some to be a core characteristic of the Type C behavior pattern (e.g., Geise-Davis & Spiegel, 2001).

Structure

Individuals participating in a Kabat-Zinn mindfulness-based stress reduction program meet for two-hours one night per week for 8 weeks. Participants attend these weekly meetings and are exposed to didactic, inductive, and experiential modes of learning regarding mindfulness strategies for stress reduction and relaxation.

Components

During the 8-week group meetings participants receive training in three basic mindfulness meditative practices that serve as the heart of the program.

(1) The body scan, a gradual sweeping of attention through the entire body from feet to head, focusing non-critically on any sensations or feelings in bodily regions with periodic suggestions of breath awareness and relaxation. This is done in supine position.

(2) Sitting meditation, which involves mindful attention of the breath and other perceptions. This is intended to create a heightened state of observational yet non-judging awareness of cognitions, stream of thoughts, and distractions that constantly attempt to engage the mind. It is practiced in a dignified sitting position on a chair or mat. (3) Hatha yoga, simple stretches and postures (asanas) that strengthen, relax, and increase flexibility of the musculoskeletal system and body. It fosters the development mindfulness during movement; yoga is sometimes known as "meditation in motion".

Participants are given audiotapes to facilitate daily homework practice of the meditative techniques learned during the weekly sessions.

Content

This adapted program for cancer patients is modeled closely after Kabat-Zinn's original program along with the fundamental principles and basic practices. However, the training will be adjusted to reflect concerns and issues of cancer patients.

Weeks 1 & 2

At the first meeting, introductions and reasons for participation are shared as well as special concerns or problems they wish to individually work on and address during the next weeks. An overview of the intervention and its philosophy are presented as well as group rules (confidentiality, regular attendance, home practice, etc.,) are discussed. Participation in a basic experiential exercise of mindfulness is performed followed by discussion of the experience and the use of mindfulness principles to daily life. Also, using the experiential exercise as a frame of reference, participants will be asked to share their expectations, beliefs and how their typical way of forecasting compared with their outcome cognitions and feelings after experience. This leads into a discussion as to our "attachment" to certain expectations, beliefs, that is, our patterned cognitive perception that may impact our experience of the event itself, and equally important, self-awareness of such patterned views of interpreting the world. This is consistent with Martin's proposal that mindfulness is a core cognitive psychotherapy process which is present within all psychotherapy orientations (Martin, 1997).

Basically, Martin's position is that mindfulness can be defined as psychological freedom where a client's self-observing awareness allows detachment from one's pattern of thinking or feeling which appears to then "help facilitate an optimal circumstance for psychotherapeutic change (p. 292). This is similar to Deikman's concepts of the observing self and deautomatization in psychotherapy; that is, self-awareness leads to an undoing of the automatic processes that control perception and cognition (1982). Other similar concepts include nonattachment (Safran & Segal, 1990), detachment (Bohart, 1983), and mindfulness as a creative cognitive process (Langer, 1989). Whatever the term, a window of psychological freedom from entrenched perception is needed in psychotherapy in order to facilitate different interpretations of self and problems, as well as therapeutic change in behaviors and responses. According to Martin's thesis of mindfulness as a core psychotherapy process, this state of psychological freedom occurs when attention is quiet and receptive, without attachment to any particular point of view. Martin's position is incorporated into this current psychosocial intervention being presented for cancer patients. Throughout this program, awareness in the present moment is continually emphasized since that is the state of being mindful. The practice of such disciplined awareness---whether it may lead to "cognitive reframing" or "updating of internal working models" is a strong opponent to defensive denial or cognitive distortion of reality, regardless of the terminology.

During the second week, a visualization exercise is used to indicate the connection between mind, imagery, and body response; that is, the conditioned response of salivation due to the visualization of food. Awareness of the breath and sitting meditation are introduced, as well as the body scan technique. Beginning early in the program, ongoing discussions will address how to apply techniques to medical procedures, treatments, and conditions (e.g., lymphadema). Role-plays with available props will be done of patients as they receive chemo while also practicing the body scan, seated or lying down meditation, guided imagery or visualization, etc. Dramatizations will be applied to waiting for or undergoing radiation treatments, and attempting to maintain self-awareness as to how our cognitive and emotional expectations may impact our behavioral and physiological reactions when placed in such situations. Application to interpersonal interactions will be also worked through as needed during the eight weeks, be it discussing painful issues with loved ones or enhancing communication with a physician, including if needed, confrontation.

Weeks 3 & 4

Group discussions as to the progress with the homework and clarifying any questions is done. Sitting meditation (the breath as an anchor) and Hatha yoga are the focus as participants are gently guided through different postures (asanas). In the fourth week, the topic of stress and the physiological stress response is presented with a discussion of tuning in to the body's language. Participants are encouraged to identify early bodily/behavioral signals or areas that indicate stress or discomfort. Once one begins paying attention to the body as a trusted advisor, early detection of stress can aid in strategies to reduce tension.

Weeks 5 & 6

Continued discussions as needed regarding the home practice or application to treatments or interpersonal issues. The issue of helplessness (external locus) versus a sense of control (internal locus) will be explored in regards to patterns of thoughts, feelings, and irrational beliefs. The value of support, be it from social others or spiritual-religious domains, as well as communicating and expressing one's feelings to loved ones and health professionals, are discussed as tools of empowerment. Walking meditation is practiced during these sessions. Participants walk silently at a slow pace and gradually pick up speed while focusing attention on the bodily sensations of walking. Extended sitting meditation and yoga continues in remaining sessions.

Weeks 7 & 8

The last two weeks involve extended practice periods of sitting meditation/breath awareness alternating with yoga and the body scan, which provide a review of the stress reduction training. Group discussions are conducted as to how to apply these complementary techniques to their regimen of treatment and challenges. At the end of the eighth session, closing comments are made along with goodbyes.

SUMMARY AND CONCLUSION

A developmental contextualistic approach to health and disease as well as a therapy program for cancer patients that combined mindfulness meditation with attachment theory was presented in this chapter. The goal in the latter section was to explore an intervention that is more holistic and that addresses multiple aspects of human beings within a medical context. This attempt was motivated by my stress reduction work with cancer patients as they shared their journeys with cancer and what they felt was missing in their treatment.

Basically, the consensus was that the physical was the focus of which they highly commended their physicians and medical team. However, attention to the psychological, emotional and spiritual aspects of themselves as human beings struggling with a life-threatening disease was severely lacking. They expressed regret that no well-rounded program was in place as part of a standard mind-body treatment protocol that addresses coping with cancer on mental, emotional and spiritual levels. This would have eased the multiple "how do I get through" *present moments* of anxiety, of fear, or of pain: not just each chemo or radiation treatment, but the waiting before each treatment.....the agonizing minutes sitting in the waiting room of my doctor's office... the waiting for the next doctor's appointment... And also, needing some program where coping tools were provided to the family members, so that the whole family---a family with cancer---was addressed. Afterall, the entire structure and dynamics of the family unit are perturbed when homeostasis is threatened by a loved one having cancer, be it a child or adult.

In conclusion, attachment is a psychosocial factor and process that exists whenever a human being is present, especially during times of distress and danger. Thus, attachment is embedded within the medical context everyday and should be acknowledged as having potential for a more integrative, humanistic and holistic model of health and medicine. This approach is biopsychosocial. Engel put forth the seminal argument in his contribution suggesting a biopsychosocial model in his landmark 1977 article in *Science*. In this chapter, attachment and mindfulness were viewed as being psychosocially relevant in treating chronically ill patients in general, and in particular, were explored as playing therapeutic roles in psychotherapy for cancer patients as a complement to traditional medicine.

REFERENCES

Ader, R. (1983). Developmental psychoneuroimmunology. *Developmental Psychbiology,* 16, 251-267.

Ainsworth, M. (1989). Attachments beyond infancy. *American Psychologist,* 44, 709-716.

Ainsworth, M., Blehar, M., Waters, E. & Wall, S. (1978). Patterns of attachment A psychological study of the strange situation. *Hillsdale, NJ: Erlbaum.*

Alexander, C., Robinson, P., Orme-Johnson, D., & Schneider, R. (1994).The effects of transcendental meditation compared to other methods of relaxation and meditation in reducing risk factors, morbidity, and mortality. *Homeostasis Health and Disease,* 35, 243-263.

Andersen, B., Cacioppo, J., & Roberts, D. (1995). Delay in seeking a cancer diagnosis: Delay stages and psychophysiological comparison processes. *British Journal of Social Psychology,* 34, 33-52.

Andersen, B., Kiecolt-Glaser, J., & Glaser, R. (1994). A biobehavioral model of cancer stress and disease course. *American Psychologist,* 49, 389-404.

Anderson, B., Anderson, B., & deProsse, C. (1989). Controlled prospective longitudinal study of women with cancer: Psychological outcomes. *Journal of Consulting and Clinical Psychology,*57, 692-697.

Antoni, M., & Goodkin, K. (1988). Host moderator variables in the promotion of cervical neoplasia. Personality facets. *Journal of Psychosomatic Research,*32, 327-338.

Astin, J. (1997). Stress reduction through mindfulness meditation. *Psychology and Psychosomatics,* 66, 97-106.

Baltrusch, H., Gehde, E., Titze, I., & Heinze, H. (1992). Early socialization and development of cancer in later life: Biopsychosocial psychoneuroimmunologic aspects. *In N. Fabris, B. Jankovic,* (Eds.), Ontogenetic and phylogenetic mechanisms of neuroimmunomodulation: From molecular biology to psychosocial sciences, (pp. 99-108). New York: New York Academy of Sciences.

Baltrusch, H., Stangel, W., & Waltz, M. (1991). Stress, cancer and immunity: New developments in biopsychosocial and psychoneuroimmunologic research. *Acta Neurologica,* 13, 315-327.

Baltrusch, H., Waltz, M. (1987). Stress and cancer: A sociobiological approach to aging, neuroimmunomodulation and the host-tumor relationship. *In J. Humphrey* (Ed.), Human stress: current selected research (vol 2, pp. 241-257). New York, NY: AMS Press.

Bartholomew K., & Horowitz, L. (1991). Attachmetn styles among young adults: A test of a four-category model. *Journal of Personality and Social Psychology,* 61, 226-244.

Bloom, J., D'Onofrio, C., & Banks, P. (1999). A psychoeducational group intervention for young women with breast cancer: Design and process valuation. *Cancer Research, Therapy, and Control,* 8, 93-102.

Bohart, A. (1983). Detachment: A variable common to many psychotherapies? Paper presented at the 63rd Annual Convention of the Western Psychological Association, San Francisco, CA.

Bowlby, J. (1973). Attachment and loss. vol. 2. New York, NY: *Basic Books.*

Bowlby, J. (1988). A secure base. New York, NY: *Basic Books.*

Brennan, K., & Shaver, P. (1995). Dimensions of adult attachment, affect regulation and romantic relationship functioning. *Personality and Social Psychology Bulletin,* 21, 267-283.

Cassileth, B. (1999). Complementary therapies. *Cancer Nursing,* 22, 85-90.

Classen, C., diamond, S., & Spiegel, D. (1999). In L. VandeCreek & T. Jackson, (Eds.), Innovations in clinical practice: A source book, (vol. 17., pp. 119-134). Sarasota, FL: Professional Resource Press.

Coe, C. (1993). Psychosocial factors and immunity in nonhuman primates: A review. Psychosomatic Medicine, 55, 298-308.

Coe, C. Psychosocial factors and psychoneuroimmunology within a lifespan perspective.(1999). In D. Keating & C. Hertzman, (Eds.), Developmental health and the wealth of nations: social, biological and educational dynamics (pp.201-219). New York: Guilford Press.

Collins, N. & Read, S. (1990). Adult attachment, working models, and relationship quality in dating couples. *Journal of Personality and Social Psychology,* 58, 644-663.

Davidson, R. (2000). Affective style, psychopathology and resilience: brain mechanisms and plasticity. *American Psychologist,*55, 1196-1214.

Davidson, R., & Fox, B. (1989). Frontal brain asymmetry predicts infants' response to maternal separation. *Journal of Abnormal Psychology,*98, 127-131.

Davidson, R., & Tomarken, A. (1989). Laterality and emotion: An electrophysiological approach. In F. Boller & J. Grafman, (Eds), *Handbook of neurophysology.* (vol. 3. pp. 419-441). NY: Elsevier.

Davidson, R., Coe, C., Dolski, C., & Donzella, B. (1999). Individual differences in prefrontal activation asymmetry predict natural killer cell activity at rest and in response to challenge. *Brain and Behavioral Immunity,*13, 93-108.

Deikman, A. (1982). The observing self. Boston: *Beacon Press.*

Delongis, A., Folkman, S., & Lazarus, R. (1988). The impact of daily stress on health and mood: Psychological and social resources as mediators. *Journal of Personality and Social Psychology,* 58, 486-495.

Derogatis, L., Morrow G., & Fetting, J. (1983). The prevalence of psychiatric disorders among cancer patients. *Journal of the American Medical Association,* 249, 751-757.

Dettling,A., Parker, S., Lane, S., Sebanc, A., & Gunnar, M. (2000). Quality of care and temperament determine changes in cortisol concentrations over the day for young children in daycare. *Psychoneuroendocrinology,*25, 819-836.

Dozier, M. & Kobak, R. (1991). Psychophysiology in attachment interviews: Converging evidence for deactivating strategies. *Child Development,* 63, 473-1480.

Dozier, M., Cue, K., & Barnett, L. (1994). Clinicians as caregivers: Role of attachment organization in treatment. *Journal of Consulting and Clinical Psychology,* 62, 793-800.

Eiser, C. (1990). Chronic childhood disease. New York: *Springer Verlag.*

Ell, K., Nishimoto, R., Movay, T., Mantell, J., & Hamovitch, M. (1989). A longitudinal analysis of psychological adaptation among survivors of cancer. *Cancer,* 63, 406-413.

Engel, G. (1977). The need for a new medical model: A challenge for biomedicine. *Science,* 196, 129-136.

Eysenck, H. Personality and cancer. (1996). In C. Cooper, (Ed.), Handbook of stress, medicine, and health, (pp. 63-79). *Boca Raton, FL: CRC publishing.*

Feeney, J. (2000). Implications of attachment style for patterns of health and illness. *Child: Care, Health, and Development,* 26, 277-288.

Feeney, J., & Ryan, S. (1994). Attachment style and affect regulation: Relationships with health behavior and family experiences with illness in a student sample. *Health Psychology,* 13, 334-345.

Flinn, M. & England, B. (1997). Social economics of childhood gluticosteroid stress responses and health. *American Journal of Physical Anthropology,* 102, 33-53.

Ford, D., Lerner, R. (1992). Developmental systems theory. *Newberry Park, CA: Sage.*

Francis, D., Diorio, J., Liu, D., & Meaney M. (1999). Nongenomic transmission across generations of maternal behavior and stress responses in the rat. *Science,* 286, 1155-1158.

Geise-Davis, J., & Spiegel, D. (2001). Suppression repression-defensiveness, restraint and distress in metastatic breast cancer: Separable or inseparable constructs? *Journal of Personality,* 69, 417-449.

George, C., Kaplan, N, & Main, M. (1985). The Adult Attachment Interview. Unpublished manuscript, University of California, Berkeley.

Gerlsma, C., & Luteijn, F. (2000). Attachment style in the context of clinical and health psychology. *British Journal of Medical Psychology,* 73, 15-34.

Goldberg, S., Simmons, R., Newman, J., Campbell, K.,& Fowler, R. (1991). Congenital heart disease, parental stress, and infant-mother relationships. *Journal of Pediatrics,* 119, 661-666.

Grassi, L., & Lodi, M. (1989). Early family relationships and parental losses among lung cancer patients. *New Trends in Experimental and Clinical Psychology,* 5, 245-256.

Grassi, L., Molinari, S. (1986). Family affective climate during the childhood of adult cancer patients. *Journal of Psychosocial Oncology,*4, 53-62.

Greer, S. (1983). Cancer and the mind. *British Journal of Psychiatry,* 143, 535-543.

Greer, S. (1999). Mind-body research in psycho-oncology. *Advances in Mind Body Medicine,* 15, 236-244.

Greer, S., & Morris, T. (1975). Psychological attributes of women who develop breast cancer: A controlled study. *Journal of Psychosomatic Research,* 19, 147-153.

Greer, S., & Morris, T. (1978). The study of psychological factors in breast cancer: Problems of method. *Social Science and Medicine,* 12, 129-134,

Gross, J. (1989). Emotional expression in cancer onset and progression. *Social Science and Medicine,* 28, 1239-1248.

Gross, J. (1999). Antecedent and response-focused emotion regulation: Divergent consequences for experience, expression and physiology. *Journal of Personality and Social Psychology,*74, 224-237.

Gunnar, M. (1998).Quality of early care and buffering of neuroendocrine stress reactions: Potential effects on the developing human brain. *Preventive Medicine,* 27, 208-211.

Gunnar, M., Brodersen, L., Nachmias, M., Buss, K. & Rigatuso, J. (1996). Stress reactivity and attachment security. *Developmental Psychobiology,* 26, 191-204.

Harlow, H., & Zimmerman, R. (1958). The development of affective responsiveness in infant monkeys. *Processes in American Philosophic Society,*102, 501-509.

Harris, A., Thoresen, C., McCullough, M., & Larson, D. (1999). Spiritually and religiously oriented health interventions. *Journal of Health Psychology,*4, 413-433.

Hazan, C., & Shaver, P. (1987). Romantic love conceptualized as an attachment process. *Journal of Personality and Social Psychology,* 52, 511-524.

Hazan, C., & Shaver, P. (1990). Love and work: An attachment-theoretical perspective. *Journal of Personality and Social Psychoogy,*59, 270-280.

Hertsgaard, L., Gunnar, M., Erickson, M. & Nachimias, M. (1995). Adrenocortical responses to the strange situation in infants with disorganized/disoriented attachment relationships. *Child Development,* 66, 1100-1106.

Hofer, M. (1973). The effects of brief maternal separations on behavior and heart rate of two-week old rat pups. *Physiological Behavior,* 10, 423-427.

Hofer, M. (1976). The organization of sleep and wakefulness after maternal separation in young rats. *Developmental Psychobiology,* 9,189-205.

Hofer, M. (1984). Relationships as regulators: A psychobiological perspective on bereavement. *Psychosomic Medicine,* 46, 183-197.

Hofer, M. Hidden regulators in attachment and loss. (1995) In S. Goldberg, R. Muir, & J. Kerr (Eds), Attachment theory: Social developmental and clinical Perspectives, pp. 357-376. *Hillsdale, NJ: The Analytic Press.*

Horowitz, M, Adler, N., & Kegeles, S. (1988). A scale for measuring the occurrence of positive states of mind: A preliminary report. *Psychosomatic Medicine,* 50, 477-483.

Irwin, M., Daniels, M., Risch, S., Craig, S., & Bloom, E. (1988). Plasma cortisol and natural killer cell activity during bereavement. *Biological Psychology,* 24, 173-178.

Jansen, M., & Muenz, L. (1984). A retrospective study of personality variables associated with fibrocystic disease and breast cancer. Journal of Psychosomatic Research, 28, 35-42.

Jensen, M. (1997). Psychobiological factors predicting the course of breast cancer. *Journal of Personality,* 55, 317-342.

Johnson, J. (1986). Life events as stressors in childhood and adolescence. *Beverly Hills: Sage.*

Kabat-Zinn, J. (1990). Full catastrophe living: Using the wisdom of your body and mind to face stress, pain, and illness. New York: *Dell Publishing.*

Kabat-Zinn, J., Lipworth, L., & Burney, R. (1985). The clinical use of mindfulness meditation for the self-regulation of chronic pain. *Journal of Behavioral Medicine, 8,* 163-190.

Kabat-Zinn, J., Massion, A., Hebert, J., & Rosenbaum, E. (1998). Meditation. In J. Holland, (Ed.), Psycho-oncology (pp. 613-622). Oxford, England: *Oxford University Press.*

Kang, D., Davidson, R., Coe, C., & Ershler, W. (1991). Frontal brain asymmetry and immune function. *Behavioral Neuroscience, 105,* 860-869.

Kaplan, K., Goldenberg, D., & Galvin-Nadeau, M. (1993). The impact of a meditation-based stress reduction program on fibromyalgia. *General Hospital Psychiatry, 15,* 284-289.

Kennedy, S., Kiecolt-Glaser, J., & Glaser, R. Immunological consequences of acute and chronic stressors: Mediating role of interpersonal relationships. *Journal of Medical Psychology,* 61, 77-85.

Kiecolt-Glaser, J, McGuire, L, Robles, T, & Glaser, R. (2002). Psychoneuroimmunology and psychosomatic medicine: Back to the future. *Psychosomatic Medicine,* 64, 15-28.

Kiecolt-Glaser, J., Fisher, L., Ogrocki, P., Stout, J., Speicher, C., & Glaser, R. (1987). Marital quality, marital disruption and immune function. *Psychosomatic Medicine,* 49, 13-34.

Kirkpatrick, L. (1998). God as a substitute attachment figure: A longitudinal study of adult attachment style and religious change in college students. *Personality and Social Psychology Bulletin,* 24, 961-973.

Kissen, D. (1963). Personality characteristics in males conducive to lung cancer. *British Journal of Medical Psychology,* 36, 27-34.

Kobak, R., & Sceery, A. (1988). Attachment in late adolescence: working models, affect regulation, and representation of self and others. *Child Development,* 59, 135-146.

Kotler, T., Buzwell, S., Romeo, Y. Bowland, J. (1994). Avoidant attachment as a risk factor for health. *British Journal of Medical Psychology,* 67, 237-245.

Kulik, J., & Mahler, H. Social support and recovery from surgery. *Health Psychology,* 8 221-238.

Langer, E. (1989). Mindfulness. New York: *Addison-Wesley.*

Laudenslager, M., Reite, M., & Harbeck, R. (1982). Suppressed immune response in infant monkeys associated with maternal separation. *Behavior and Neurological Biology,* 36, 40-48.

LeShan, L. (1966). An emotional life history pattern associated with neoplastic disease. *Annals of the New York Academy of Science,* 125, 780-793.

LeShan, L., & Worthington, R. (1956). Personality as a factor in the pathogenesis of cancer: A review of the literature. *British Journal of Medical Psychology,* 29, 49-56.

Leucken, L. (1998). Childhood attachment and loss experiences affect adult cardiovascular and cortisol function. *Psychosomatic Medicine,* 60, 765-772.

Leucken, L. (2000). Parental caring and loss during childhood and adult cortisol responses to stress. *Psychological Health,* 15, 841-851.

Levin, J. (1994). Religion and health: Is there any association and it is valid? Social Science and Medicine, 38, 1475-1482.

Liu, D., Diorio, J., Day, J., Francis, D., Mar, A., & Meaney, M. (2000). Maternal care, hippocampal synaptogenesis and cognitive development in rats. *Nature and Neuroscience,* 3, 799-806.

Liu, D., Diorio, J., Tannenbaum, B., Caldji, C., Francis, D., Freedman, A., Sharma, S., Pearson, D., Plotsky, P., & Meaney, M. (1997). Maternal care, hippocampal glucocorticoid receptors and hypothalamic-pituitary-adrenal responses to stress. *Science,* 277, 1659-1662.

Lubach, G., Coe, C, & Ershler, W. (1995). Effects of early rearing on immune responses in infant rhesus monkeys. *Brain and Behavioral Immunity,* 9 31-46.

Main, M., & Weston, D. (1982). Avoidance of the attachment figure in infancy. In C. Parkes & J. Stevenson-Hinde, (Eds.), The place of attachment in human behavior. London, England: *Tavistock.*

Main, M., Kaplan, N., & Cassidy, J. (1985). Security in infancy, childhood and adulthood: A move to the level of representation. In I. Bretherton, I.& E. Waters, (Eds.), Growing points of attachment theory and research. (50:209, pp. 66-104). *Monographs of the Society for Research in Child Development.*

Martin, J. (1997). Mindfulness: A proposed common factor. *Journal of Psychotherapy Integration,* 7, 291-312.

Marvin, R., & Pianta, R. (1996). Mother's reaction to their child's diagnosis: relations with security of attachment. *Journal of Clinical Child Psychology,* 25, 436-445.

Maunder, R., & Hunter, J. (2001). Attachment and psychosomatic medicine: Developmental contributions to stress and disease. *Psychosomatic Medicine,* 63, 556-567

Mikulincer, M., & Florian, V. (1995). Appraisal of coping with a real life stressful situation: The contribution of attachment styles. *Personality and Social Psychology Bulletin,* 21, 406-414.

Mikulincer, M., & Florian, V. (1998). The relationship between adult attachment styles and emotional and cognitive reactions to stressful events. In J. Simpson & W. Rholes, (Eds.), Attachment theory and close relationships (pp. 143-165). New York: *Guilford.*

Mikulincer, M., Florian, V., & Weller, A. (1993). Attachment styles, coping strategies, and posttraumatic psychological distress: The impact of the Gulf War in Israel. *Journal of Personality and Social Psychology,* 64, 817-826.

Miller, J., Fletcher, K., & Kabat-Zinn, J. (1995). Three-year follow-up and clinical implications of a mindfulness meditation-based stress reduction intervention in the treatment of anxiety disorders. *General Hospital Psychiatry,* 17, 192-200.

Mrazek, D., Casey, B., & Anderson, I. (1987). Insecure attachment in severely asthmatic preschool children: is it a risk factor? *Journal of American Academy of Child and Adolescent Psychology,*26, 516- 520.

Murphy, M, Donovan, S. (1997). The Physical and Psychological Effects of Meditation. Sausalito, California: Institute of Noetic Sciences.

Nachimias, M., Gunnar, M., Mangelsdorf, S., Parritz, R. & Buss, K. (1996). Behavioral inhibition and stress reactivity: the moderating role of attachment security. *Child Development,* 67, 508-522.

National Cancer Institute. (1997). Cancer facts. Washington, DC.

O'Connell, D., & Alexander, C. (1994). Recovery from addictions using transcendental meditation. *Alcohol Treatment Quarterly,* 11, 1-10.

Ornish, D. (1990). Dr. Dean Ornish's Program for Reversing Heart Disease. NY: *Random House*

Perry, B., & Pollard, R. (1998). Homeostasis, stress, trauma, and adaptation. Child and Adolescent Psychiatric Clinics of North America,7, 33-51.

Peterson, C., Maier, S, & Seligman, M. (1993). Learned Helplessness. New York: Oxford.

Pettingale, K., Morris, T., Greer, S., & Haybittle, J. (1985). Mental attitudes to cancer: An additional prognostic factor. *Lancet, I,* 750.

Pettingale, K., Watson, M., & Greer, S. (1985). The validity of emotional control as a trait in breast cancer patients. *Journal of Psychosocial Oncology, 2,* 21-30.

Porges, S., Doussard-Roosevelt, J. & Maiti, A. (1994). Vagal tone and the physiological regulation of emotion. In N. Fox, (Ed.), The development of emotion regulation: Biological and behavioral considerations (59:240, pp. 167-186).*Monographs of the Society for Research in Child Development.*

Reite, M. & Boccia, M. (1994). Physiological aspects of adult attachment. In M. Sperling & W. Berman, (Eds.), Attachment in adults: Clinical and developmental perspectives,(pp. 98-127). New York: Guilford.

Rosenman, R., Friedman, M., Straus, R., Wurm, M., Kositchek, R., Hahn, W., & Werthessen, N. (1964). A predictive study of coronary heart disease. *Journal of American Medical Association,*189, 15-26.

Schore, A. (1994). Affect regulation and the origin of the self. *Trenton, NJ: Erlbaum.*

Selye, H. (1956). The stress of life. New York: McGraw-Hill.

Shaffer, J., Duszynski, K., & Thomas, C. (1982). Family attitudes in youth as possible precursor of cancer among physicians. *Journal of Behavioral Medicine, 5,* 143-163.

Simpson, J. (1990). Influence of attachment styles on romantic relationships. *Journal of Personality and Social Psychology,*59, 971-980.

Solomon, G. (1987). Psychoneuroimmmunology: Interactions between central nervous system and immune system. *Journal of Neuroscience Research,*18, 1-9.

Speca, M., Carlson, L., Goodey, E., & Angen, M. (2000). A randomized, wait-list controlled clinical trial: The effect of a mindfulness meditation-based stress reduction program on mood and symptoms of stress in cancer outpatients. *Psychosomatic Medicine,*62, 613-622.

Spiegel, D. (1991). A psychosocial intervention and survival time of patients with metastatic breast cancer. *Advances, 7,* 10-19.

Spiegel, D., & Fawzy, I. (2002). Psychosocial interventions and prognosis in cancer. In H. Koenig & H. Cohen, (Eds.), Links between religion and health: Psychoneuro-immunology and the faith factor. (pp. 84-100). London: *Oxford University Press.*

Spiegel, D., Bloom, J., Kraemer, H., & Goottheil, E. (1989). Effect of psychosocial treatment on survival of patients with metastatic breast cancer. *Lancet, 2,* 888-891.

Tacón, A. (2003). Attachment experiences in women with breast cancer. *Family and Community Health, 26,* 147-156.

Tacón, A., Caldera, Y. Bell, N. (2001). Attachment, emotional control and breast cancer. *Families, Systems, and Health, 19,* 319-326.

Tacón, A., Caldera, Y., & Ronaghan, C. (in press). Mindfulness-based stress reduction in women with breast cancer. *Families, Systems and Health.*

Telch, C. & Telch, M. (1986). Group coping skills instruction and supportive group therapy for cancer patients: a comparison of strategies. *Journal of Consulting and Clinical Psychology,* 54, 802-808.

Temoshok, L. (1985). Biopsychosocial studies on cutaneous malignant melanoma: Psychosocial factors associated with prognostic indicators, progression, psychophysiology, and tumor-host response. *Social Science and Medicine,* 20, 833-840.

Temoshok, L. (1987). Personality, coping style, emotion, and cancer: Towards an integrative model. *Cancer Surveys,*6, 545-567.

Temoshok, L., & Dreher, H. (1992). The Type C Connection: The Behavioral Links to Cancer and Health. New York: *Random House.*

Temoshok, L., & Kneier, A. (1984). Repressive coping reactions in patients with malignant melanoma as compared to cardiovascular disease patients. *Journal of Psychosomatic Research,* 28, 145-155.

Temoshok,L., & Heller, B. Stress and "Type C" versus epidemiological risk factors in melanoma. Paper presented at the 89th Annual Convention of the American Psychological Association, Los Angeles, August, 1981.

TenElshof, J. & Furrow, J. (2000). The role of secure attachment in predicting spiritual maturity of students at a conservative seminary. *Journal of Psychology and Theology,* 28, 99-108.

Thomas, C. (1988). Cancer and the youthful mind: A forty year perspective. *Advances in Mind Body Medicine,* 5, 42-58.

Thompson, R. (1994). Emotion regulation: A theme in search of definition. In N. Fox, (Ed.), The development of emotion regulation: Biological and behavioral considerations (59:240, pp. 25-52). *Monographs of the Society for Research in Child Development.*

Uchino, B., Cacioppo, J., & Kiecolt-Glaser, J. (1996). The relationship between social support and physiological processes: A review with emphasis on underlying mechanisms and implications for health. *Psychological Bulletin,*119, 488-531.

Visintainer, M., Volpicelli, J., & Seligman M. (1982). Tumor rejection in rats after inescapable or escapable shock. Science, 216, 437-439.

Watson, M., & Greer, S. (1983). Development of a questionnaire measure of emotional control. *Journal of Psychosomatic Research,* 27, 299-305.

Watson, M., Greer, S., & Rowden, L. (1991). Relationships between emotional control, adjustment to cancer and depression and anxiety in breast cancer patients. *Psychological Medicine,*21, 51-57.

Watson, M., Haviland, J., Greer, S., Davidson, J., & Bliss JM. (1999). Influence of psychological response on survival in breast cancer: A population-based cohort study. *Lancet,* 354, 1331-1336.

Watson, M., Pettingale, K., & Greer, S. (1984). Emotional control and autonomic arousal in breast cancer patients. *Journal of Psychosomatic Research,* 28, 467-474.

Waxler-Morrison, N., Hislop, T., Mears, B. & Kan, L. (1991). Effects of social relationships on survival for women with breast cancer: A prospective study. *Social Science and Medicine,*33, 177-183.

Winnicott, D. (1971). Playing and reality. New York: *Basic Books.*

Worden, J & Weisman, A. (1984). Preventive psychosocial intervention with newly diagnosed cancer patients. *General Hospital Psychiatry,* 6, 243-249.

In: Trends in Psychotherapy Research
Editor: M. E. Abelian, pp. 33-51

ISBN 1-59454-373-9
© 2006 Nova Science Publishers, Inc.

Chapter 2

NONDRUG PSYCHOTHERAPEUTIC OPTIONS FOR SKIN DISORDERS

Philip D. Shenefelt

James A. Haley VA Hospital
12901 Bruce B. Downs Blvd., Tampa, Florida 33612

ABSTRACT

The skin and the nervous system develop side by side in the ectoderm of the fetus and remain intimately interconnected throughout life. Cutaneous innervation represents the largest sense organ of the body and is also vital to skin protection and health. There is a significant psychosomatic or behavioral component to many skin disorders. This interaction permits nondrug psychotherapeutic interventions that have positive impacts on many cutaneous diseases.

Cognitive-behavioral techniques that address dysfunctional cognitions (thought patterns) or behaviors (actions) can be useful for skin disorders with a significant psychosomatic or behavioral component, such as the picking component of acne excoriee, scratching in atopic dermatitis, habits such as lip licking or biting, hyperhidrosis, lichen simplex chronicus, neurotic excoriations, onychotillomania, trichotillomania, and psychosomatic triggering or exacerbation of urticaria. Cognitive-behavioral methods can also desensitize individuals with needle phobia.

Biofeedback has some limited usefulness in a few selected skin disorders. Galvanic skin resistance (GSR) feedback can be utilized for teaching control of hyperhidrosis. Skin temperature feedback allows individuals to learn how to warm the fingers for Raynaud's syndrome and scleroderma. Neurofeedback of electroencephalographic (EEG) spectral frequency is in its infancy but may prove useful for certain habit disorders that affect the skin, hair, or nails by picking, scratching, or other manipulation.

Hypnosis has been found useful to treat a number of skin disorders including acne excoriée, alopecia areata, atopic dermatitis, congenital ichthyosiform erythroderma, dyshidrotic dermatitis, erythromelalgia, furuncles, glossodynia, herpes simplex, hyperhidrosis, ichthyosis vulgaris, lichen planus, neurodermatitis, nummular dermatitis, postherpetic neuralgia, pruritus, psoriasis, rosacea, trichotillomania, urticaria, verruca vulgaris, and vitiligo. Hypnosis can also help individuals feel more comfortable about having their skin diseases. Hypnotic relaxation utilizing self-guided imagery reduces anxiety and discomfort during dermatologic procedures. For resistant skin disorders, hypnoanalysis using ideomotor signaling and the affect bridge technique can often identify original incidents and promote healing.

Subtle energy intuitive techniques are an almost lost art that have so far been relatively difficult to explore on a scientific basis. They are still utilized by various indigenous practitioners and shamans, and are sometimes capable of clearing or improving otherwise refractory skin disorders. A psychiatrist has described their modern use. This area has potential for significant future development.

NEUROCUTANEOUS INTERACTIONS

Connections between the skin and the nervous system arise in the developing fetus and play important roles throughout life. As the fetus develops during the third week after fertilization, the human embryo forms by a process called gastrulation three primary germ layers called ectoderm, mesoderm, and endoderm. The ectoderm further subdivides into epidermis and neuroectoderm. The skin forms from epidermis derived from the ectoderm and dermis derived in part from ectoderm but more from mesoderm. The melanocytes that pigment the skin migrate from the neural crest that is part of the neuroectoderm. The nervous system forms from neuroectoderm that generates the neural tube. The neural tube develops into the brain, spinal cord, and peripheral nerves. Cutaneous peripheral nerves parallel blood vessels in their development. They consist of somatic sensory and sympathetic autonomic nerve fibers.

The skin innervation consists of myelinated branches of musculocutaneous nerves that arise from cranial and spinal nerves. The cutaneous branches form a deep plexus and ascend to a superficial subpapillary plexus. Nerve fibers extend from both plexes to innervate various structures of the skin. Free nerve endings extend into the epidermis from the papillary dermis and around the hair follicles as well as into the deeper tissues. These transmit touch, pain, itch, heat, and cold sensations. Specialized receptors called Meissner's corpuscles are mechanical receptors in the skin of the digits. Pacinian corpuscles in the deep dermis of the weight-bearing areas are vibrational mechanical receptors. Free nerve endings are also associated with Merkel cells as complex receptors. The skin serves as a massive sensory organ intimately connected with the nervous system. In addition, neuropeptides released by the sensory nerve fibers activate neuropeptide receptors on skin cells to induce inflammatory activities. Cholinergic sympathetic fibers innervate the eccrine sweat glands and control sweating. Thermal sweating occurs globally in the skin, while emotional sweating is accentuated on the forehead, palms, soles, and axillae. Sweating can be measured by galvanic skin resistance (GSR). Adrenergic and cholinergic fibers innervate the arrector pili muscles, causing hairs to stand up. This occurs both with exposure to cold and with a strong sudden emotional fear reaction. Adrenergic fibers innervate the cutaneous blood vessels. Alpha adrenergic receptors mediate vasoconstriction, while beta adrenergic receptors mediate vasodilitation, controlling cutaneous blood flow. Emotional embarrassment can cause facial blushing, while fear can cause facial pallor. Skin temperature is related to cutaneous blood flow [1].

The central nervous system (CNS) also mediates hormone release through the hypothalamus with its actions on the pituitary and other endocrine glands. Skin and hair are influenced by thyroid and sex hormones. Melanocytes are stimulated by melanocyte-stimulating hormone to produce more melanin. Stress hormones influence the immune system, affecting inflammatory processes in the skin. Many inflammatory skin diseases such as acne, alopecia areata, aphthous stomatitis, atopic dermatitis, herpes simplex recurrences, lichen planus, rosacea, psoriasis, seborrheic dermatitis, telogen effluvium, vitiligo, and others are exacerbated by excessive stress [2].

Habits (CNS conditioned responses) determine skin exposure to environmental hazards such as ultraviolet light, chemicals, physical injury, and temperature extremes. Manipulation of normal or diseased skin can result in excoriations (damage from scratching), lichenification (thickening in response to rubbing), factitial (intentional) trauma, aggravation of existing skin conditions, and subsequent dyspigmentation or scarring.

Conversely, the appearance of the skin and hair can have a significant impact on self image (in the CNS) and social interactions. Skin diseases also can affect self image, social interactions, and behavior. Chronic skin disorders such as acne, alopecia areata, atopic dermatitis, or psoriasis can induce or aggravate depression in susceptible individuals [3]. The large sums expended on skin care and hair care products, cosmetics, hair coloring, straightening, or curling, and nail care and coloring indicate the importance that individuals and social values place on appearance.

COGNITIVE-BEHAVIORAL METHODS

Cognitive-behavioral methods deal with dysfunctional thought patterns (cognitive) or actions (behavioral) that damage the skin or interfere with dermatologic therapy. Responsive diseases include acne excoriée, atopic dermatitis, factitious cheilitis, hyperhidrosis, lichen simplex chronicus, needle phobia, neurodermatitis, onychotillomania, prurigo nodularis, trichotillomania, and urticaria. The addition of hypnosis to cognitive-behavioral therapy can facilitate aversive therapy and enhance desensitization and other cognitive-behavioral methods.

The first step is to identify specific problems by listening to the patient's verbalization of thoughts and feelings such as fear of needles or by directly observing behaviors such as scratching. The second step is for the dermatologist or therapist and patient to determine the goals of cognitive-behavioral therapy, such as a reduction in anxiety about needles or cessation of scratching. The third step is for the dermatologist or therapist to develop a hypothesis about the underlying beliefs or environmental events that precede (stimulate) or that maintain (reinforce) or minimize (extinguish) these thought patterns and behaviors. The fourth step is for the dermatologist or therapist to test the hypothesis of cause and effect by altering the underlying cognitions, the behavior, the environment, or all three, and to observe and document the effects on the patient's dysfunctional thoughts, feelings, and actions. The fifth step is for the dermatologist or therapist to revise the hypothesis if the desired results are not obtained, or to continue the treatment if the desired results are obtained until the goals of therapy are reached (modified from Levenson [4]).

The above method draws in part on the cognitive therapies of identifying dysfunctional negative self-talk and substituting positive self-talk or reframing the thought picture by offering a new perspective. It also draws in part on alterations of behavior based on the classic conditioning described by Pavlov with dogs and by John B. Watson with people, and on the operant conditioning described by B. F. Skinner. For a more detailed description of systematic desensitization, aversion therapy, operant techniques, and assertive training as applied to skin disorders, see Bär and Kuypers [5].

The picking behavior in acne excoriée responded in a young adult woman to cognitive-behavioral therapy coupled with biofeedback, minocycline, and sertraline [6]. Such a multimodal approach is often beneficial in resistant cases.

In atopic dermatitis, scratching can become a conditioned response [7, 8], often associated with and exacerbated by feelings of anxiety or hostility. When an itch stimulus was paired with the neutral stimulus of a sound tone (classical conditioning) and the amount of scratching and GSR changes were measured, atopic patients had a significantly higher scratching and GSR response than did a control group. Atopic patients also scored significantly higher in anxiety levels and in levels of suppressed hostility. Most atopic patients report some relief of anxiety or hostility through scratching (operant conditioning). Substituting other activities for scratching, such as sports, music, artwork, meditating, or yoga can with repetition change the conditioning.

Adverse habits such as lip licking or biting produce factitious cheilitis [9]. Topical anti-inflammatory agents combined with cognitive-behavioral counseling were generally effective in producing improvement or resolution.

Severe palmar hyperhidrosis in a 19 year old woman responded with improvement in the hyperhidrosis and in her approach to social situations following assertiveness training and systemic desensitization [5]. After twelve months she continued to show no return to her prior anxiety about social situations, and she was able to accept the milder hyperhidrosis that she still experienced.

Lichen simplex chronicus (LSC) can arise from repetitive focal rubbing and scratching. Bär and Kuypers [5] treated a 6 year old girl with a 3 year history of vulvar LSC by having the mother ignore all scratching but reward nonscratching behavior with a token. The girl exchanged the tokens each night for rewards. After 5 weeks the scratching lessened, and by 13 weeks the condition resolved. They also treated a 33 year old male with LSC by aversive therapy with resolution of the scratching behavior after 19 days.

For needle phobia interfering with needed treatment, systemic desensitization using participant modeling has been effective [10]. The dermatologist or therapist first gives information about needles and interacts with them in a way that shows that the patient's fear is unrealistic or excessive. After modeling handling a needle, the dermatologist or therapist has the patient join in this performance, starting with situations that provoke relatively little anxiety and culminating in the performance of the feared activity. The patient is then instructed in self-directed practice to complete the desensitization. Since about 10 percent of the population has needle phobia [11], desensitization may be very helpful in these individuals to permit performance of needed dermatologic procedures.

Neurodermatitis produced by neurotic excoriations occurs in its typical distribution on shoulders, neck, extremities, and face, sparing the butterfly pattern on the back where the hands cannot reach. Ratliff and Stein reported improvement of neurodermatitis in a 22 year old male using aversion therapy techniques [12]. Rosenbaum and Ayllon used habit reversal treatment for neurodermatitis [13]. They taught awareness of scratching, reviewed the inconveniences produced by the habit, developed a competing response practice of isometric exercise by fist clenching that was incompatible with scratching, and did symbolic rehearsal. At one month and six month followup, all three patents had improved and healed.

Onychotillomania is damage to the nails produced by rubbing, picking, or tearing at the proximal and lateral nailfold. This differs from onychophagia, the habit of biting the free ends of the nails [14]. Onychotillomania can lead to onychodystrophy [15]. Teaching picking awareness, a competing response practice of isometric exercise gripping the hands together and pulling, and rehearsal under observation can help to reverse this habit.

Trichotillomania is caused by repetitive hair twisting and pulling resulting in hair loss. Habit reversal training involves self-monitoring of the frequency and duration of hair-pulling, habit control motivation by reviewing the inconveniences produced by the behavior, awareness training including situational precursors or triggers, competing response training that substitutes a different motor action to prevent or interrupt hair pulling, relaxation training to reduce stress levels, and generalization training to identify and manage high-risk situations [16]. Of three patients using this process, one discontinued hair pulling and the other two noticeably decreased their hair pulling.

Urticaria psychosomatically triggered or exacerbated was reduced in a young professional woman using cognitive-behavioral therapy with specific self-talk and relaxation techniques [6]. Biofeedback was also used along with multiple-agent antihistamines in a multimodal approach to reduce the urticaria.

Hypnosis may be employed in cognitive-behavioral therapy in patients with medium to high hypnotic ability to produce desensitization, facilitate relaxation, or produce imagined aversive experiences [17]. It is much easier and safer to have the patient experience the aversive stimulus in the imagination than in real life. For patients with low hypnotic ability, biofeedback may be more appropriate.

BIOFEEDBACK

Biofeedback can improve skin problems that have an autonomic nervous system component. Examples include biofeedback of galvanic skin resistance (GSR) for hyperhidrosis and biofeedback of skin temperature for Raynaud's syndrome. Hypnosis may enhance the effects obtained by biofeedback.

The most commonly used biofeedback techniques measure and provide auditory or visual feedback of galvanic skin resistance (GSR), skin temperature, electromyography (EMG), or electroencephalography (EEG) [18]. The polygraph is a combined instrument that can measure these simultaneously along with heart rate and respiratory rate. Individual instruments may also be employed. Larger, more complex units typically are used in the clinic, while a small handheld unit may be used by the patient at home.

Skin problems that have an autonomic nervous system component can be improved by biofeedback with or without hypnosis. Examples include biofeedback of GSR for hyperhidrosis and biofeedback of skin temperature for Raynaud's syndrome. Using biofeedback, individuals may learn consciously how to alter the autonomic response, and with enough repetition (typically 20 to 40 sessions) may establish new habit patterns. Hypnosis or autogenic training may enhance the effects obtained by biofeedback.

A case of hyperhidrosis in a young man described in Panconese [19] as translated by Sarti [18] with a very low initial GSR at the beginning of treatment improved slowly over 20 sessions combining GSR biofeedback with autogenic relaxation training. Autogenic training is considered to be a variant of hypnosis. Followup at three and six months after treatment, during which the patient continued to practice the autogenic training exercises, showed persistent reduction in palmar sweating to near normal levels.

Patients with Raynaud's as a feature of systemic sclerosis have been able to increase finger skin temperature by an average of about 4 degrees Centigrade using either hypnosis or autogenic training [20]. Two of six patients using autogenic training in addition to biofeedback reported that they could shorten the duration of Raynaud attacks by autogenic training. In another study, measurement of finger blood flow with venous occlusion plethysmography, finger temperature, and GSR in patients with Raynaud's disease showed significant elevations in finger blood flow, finger temperature, and GSR conductance level in those given finger temperature biofeedback compared with those who received autogenic training but no biofeedback [21]. A recent large study of Raynaud's patients compared learned hand warming results using different biofeedback methods and found that attention to emotional and cognitive aspects of biofeedback training was important [22].

There was a significant correlation between degree of hypnotic ability and ability to lower finger temperature using biofeedback in 30 subjects given the Stanford Hypnotic Susceptibility Scale, Form C (SHSS-C) in a study by Piedmont [23]. Hypnotized subjects were instructed to lower the temperature of a finger while receiving biofeedback. Those who scored high on the SHSS-C were able to maintain a lower mean temperature than those who scored low. In another study, biofeedback combined with hypnosis permitted voluntary control of skin temperature in some individuals with moderate to high hypnotic ability as measured by the SHSS-C [24]. This can be used to increase local peripheral circulation in such conditions as Raynaud's disease.

Biofeedback of muscle tension via EMG can enhance teaching of relaxation. Relaxation can have a positive effect on inflammatory and emotionally triggered skin conditions such as acne, atopic dermatitis, lichen planus, neurodermatitis, psoriasis, and urticaria. The mechanism is through influencing immunoreactivity [25]. Patients who have low hypnotic ability may be especially suitable for this type of relaxation training utilizing EMG biofeedback.

Brainwave spectral biofeedback via filtered EEG can with multiple repetitions (20 to 40 sessions) alter pain discomfort [26], which may prove useful for chronic posterherpetic neuralgia. It also has the potential to correct impulse control disorders and obsessive compulsive disorders. In the skin these can manifest as acne excoriée or neurodermatitis [27]. Whether quantitative EEG with neurofeedback with prove useful in neurogenic chronic pruritus and habit disorders such as acne excoriée, neurodermatitis, trichotillomania, and onychotillomania remains to be explored.

HYPNOSIS

Hypnosis is a tool with many useful dermatologic applications. It involves guiding the patient into a trance state for a specific purpose such as relaxation, pain or pruritus reduction, or habit modification. Hypnosis may improve or clear numerous skin disorders. Examples include acne excoriée, alopecia areata, atopic dermatitis, congenital ichthyosiform erythroderma, dyshidrotic dermatitis, erythromelalgia, furuncles, glossodynia, herpes simplex, hyperhidrosis, ichthyosis vulgaris, lichen planus, neurodermatitis, nummular dermatitis, post-herpetic neuralgia, pruritus, psoriasis, rosacea, trichotillomania, urticaria, verruca vulgaris, and vitiligo [28]. Hypnosis can also reduce anxiety and pain associated with dermatologic procedures. See Table 1.

Table 1. Skin disorders reported responsive to hypnosis

Randomized Control Trials (representing strong evidence of effectiveness)
    Hypnotic relaxation during procedures
    Verruca vulgaris
    Psoriasis
Nonrandomized Control Trials
    Atopic dermatitis
Case Series
    Urticaria
Single or Few Case Reports (representing weak evidence of effectiveness)
    Acne excoriee
    Alopecia areata
    Congenital ichthyosiform erythroderma
    Dyshidrotic dermatitis
    Erythromelalgia
    Furuncles
    Glossodynia
    Herpes simplex
    Hyperhidrosis
    Ichthyosis vulgaris
    Lichen planus
    Neurodermatitis
    Nummular dermatitis
    Post-herpetic neuralgia
    Pruritus
    Rosacea
    Trichotillomania
    Vitiligo

We all experience spontaneous mild trances daily while absorbed in watching television or a movie, reading a book or magazine, or other focused activity. After appropriate training, we may intensify this trance state and use this heightened focus to induce mind-body interactions that help to alleviate suffering or to promote healing. We may induce the trance state using guided imagery, relaxation, deep breathing, meditation techniques, self-hypnosis, or hypnosis induction techniques.

Hypnosis is the intentional induction, deepening, maintenance, and termination of the trance state for a specific purpose. Trance has been used since antiquity to assist the healing process. The purpose of medical hypnotherapy is to reduce suffering, to promote healing, or to help the person alter a destructive behavior. Some people are more highly hypnotizable, others less so, but most can obtain some benefit from hypnosis. Low hypnotizability is to a large extent hard-wired into individuals' brains and tends to be consistent over time as measured by the Hypnotic Induction Profile [29]. One biological factor that has been associated with degree of hypnotizability is the catechol-o-methyl-transferase gene. At position 148 in this enzyme, gene coding for the amino acid valine on both alleles (homozygous) is associated with a four times more rapid degradation of dopamine and lower hypnotizability compared with gene coding for methionine on both alleles (homozygous) with slower degradation of dopamine and medium hypnotizability. Heterozygous coding for valine and methionine is associated with medium to high hypnotizability [30].

Hypnosis can hasten the resolution of some skin diseases, including verruca vulgaris (warts). Hypnosis may also help to reduce skin pain, pruritus, or psychosomatic aspects of skin diseases. Suggestion without formal trance induction may be sufficient in some cases. Bloch [31] and Sulzberger [32] used suggestion to treat verrucae successfully.

The precise definition of hypnosis is still somewhat controversial. Marmer [33] defined hypnosis as a psychophysiological tetrad of altered consciousness consisting of narrowed awareness, restricted and focused attentiveness, selective wakefulness, and heightened suggestibility. Further discussions of the definitions of hypnosis are available in Crasilneck and Hall [34] or Watkins [35]. There are many myths about hypnosis that distort, overrate, or underrate the true capabilities of hypnosis. Recent evidence from EEG studies and positron emission tomography (PET) studies comparing brain activity in the same individual when alert and when in trance lend support to the theory that hypnosis is a describable altered state of consciousness rather than simply a social compliance with expectations. Quantitative EEG findings by Freeman et al [36] in a study of hypnosis versus distraction effects on cold pressor pain showed significantly greater high theta (5.5-7.5 Hz) activity for high hypnotizables (based on Stanford Hypnotic Susceptibility Scale, Form C, or SHSS:C scores) compared with low hypnotizables at parietal and occipital sites during hypnosis and also during waking relaxation. PET subtraction studies by Faymonville et al [37] demonstrated specific areas of the cerebral cortex with higher bloodflow during hypnosis and others with lower bloodflow, presumably related to cerebral activity. In their study, pain reduction mediated by hypnosis localized to the mid anterior cingulate cortex.

The mechanisms by which hypnosis produces improvement in symptoms and in skin lesions are not fully understood. Hypnosis can help regulate bloodflow and other autonomic functions not usually under conscious control. The relaxation response that accompanies hypnosis alters the neurohormonal systems that in turn regulate many body functions. [25]

For skin disorders, hypnosis may be used to help control harmful habits such as scratching. It can also be used to provide immediate and long term analgesia, reduce symptoms such as pruritus, improve recovery from surgery, and facilitate the mind-body connection to promote healing.

Skin diseases responsive to hypnosis are described in the relatively old book by Scott [38] and in the chapter on the use of hypnosis in dermatological problems in Crasilneck and Hall [34]. Koblenzer [39] also mentions some of the uses of hypnosis in common dermatologic problems. Grossbart and Sherman [40] include hypnosis as recommended therapy for a number of skin conditions in an excellent source book for patients. Skin disorders that have responded to hypnotherapy are discussed below.

MEDICAL HYPNOTHERAPY

Hypnosis can be used to reduce psychological or behavioral impediments to healing. Hypnosis facilitates supportive therapies (ego-strengthening), direct suggestion, symptom substitution, and hypnoanalysis [38,41,42,43]. Mentioning hypnosis to patients will allow the practitioner to gauge the patient's receptiveness to this treatment modality. The time needed to screen patients, educate them about realistic expectations for results from hypnosis, and actually perform the hypnotherapy are similar to or less than those for screening, preparing, and educating patients about cutaneous surgery and then actually performing the surgery. Practitioners who prefer to refer patients to hypnotherapists or who desire further information about training in hypnotherapy may obtain referrals or training information from the American Society of Clinical Hypnosis or similar professional organizations.

Some advantages of medical hypnotherapy for skin diseases include nontoxicity, cost-effectiveness, ability to obtain a response where other treatment modalities have failed, and ability of patients to self-treat and gain a sense of control when taught self-hypnosis reinforced by using audiotapes. Disadvantages include the practitioner training required, the low hypnotizability of some patients, the negative social attitudes still prevalent about hypnosis, and the lower reimbursement rates for cognitive therapies such as hypnosis when compared with procedural therapies such as cutaneous surgery. Patient selection is an important aspect of successful medical hypnotherapy. With proper selection of disease process, patient, and provider, hypnosis can decrease suffering and morbidity from skin disorders with minimal side effects.

Induction of the hypnotic state in adults is achieved by methods that focus attention, soothe, and/or produce monotony or confusion [34,35]. The hypnotic state may be induced in children by having the child make-believe that he or she is watching television, a movie, or a play or by using some other distractive process that employs the imagination [44].

Supportive (ego-strengthening) therapies include positive suggestions and posthypnotic suggestions for self-worth and effectiveness. Reinforcement can be achieved by recording an audiocassette tape that the patient can use subsequently for repeated self-hypnosis. The strengthened ego is better able to deal with psychological elements that inhibit healing.

Direct Suggestion During Hypnosis may be Used to Decrease Skin

Discomfort from pain, pruritus, burning sensations, anxiety, and insomnia. Posthypnotic suggestion and repeated use of an audiocassette tape by the patient for self-hypnosis helps to reinforce the effectiveness of direct suggestion. In highly hypnotizable individuals, direct suggestion may produce sufficiently deep anesthesia to permit cutaneous surgery. Direct suggestion can also reduce compulsive acts of skin scratching or picking, nail biting or manipulating, and hair pulling or twisting [38]. Autonomic responses in hyperhidrosis, blushing, and some forms of urticaria can also be controlled by direct suggestion. Verrucae can be induced to resolve using direct suggestion (see below).

Symptom substitution replaces a negative habit pattern with a more constructive one [38]. For example, another physical activity, such as grasping something and holding it so tightly for a half minute that it almost hurts, can be substituted for scratching. Other activities that can be substituted for scratching include athletics, artwork, verbal expression of feelings, or meditation.

Hypnoanalysis may help patients with skin disorders unresponsive to other simpler approaches. Using hypnoanalysis, results may also occur much more quickly than with standard psychoanalysis [38]. See Table 2.

Table 2. Hypnotic trance sequence during medical hypnotherapy

Trance induction

Rapid
Eyeroll
Slow
Progressive relaxation or other method
Trance deepening

Trance work (one or more)
Ego strengthening
Direct suggestion
Indirect suggestion
Hypnoanalysis
Relaxation for procedures
Trance termination

MEDICAL HYPNOTHERAPY FOR
TREATING SPECIFIC SKIN DISORDERS

Until recently, reports of the effectiveness of hypnosis on specific dermatologic conditions were mostly based on one or a few uncontrolled cases. Since the validity of such findings await further confirmation, "may" is used below to qualify recommendations that are based on weak evidence. The trend toward more controlled trials has produced more reliable information [45], although randomized controlled trial results are still not available for most skin disorders. The list of responsive skin conditions below is not all-inclusive.

Posthypnotic suggestion was successful in reducing or stopping the picking associated with acne excoriée in two reported cases [46]. One patient was instructed to remember the word "scar" whenever she wanted to pick her face and to refrain from picking by saying "scar" instead. I have had similar success in one case [27]. Hypnosis may be an appropriate treatment for the picking habit aspect of acne excoriée in conjunction with standard treatments for the acne itself.

In a small clinical trial of medical hypnotherapy with five patients having extensive alopecia areata alopecia areata, only one patient showed significant increase in hair growth. Although three patients had only slight increase in hair growth and one had no change, hypnosis did improve psychological parameters in these five patients [47]. Hypnosis may be appropriate as a complementary supportive treatment for the psychological impact of having alopecia areata, while not having much effect on the condition itself.

A number of case reports describe improvement of atopic dermatitis in both children and adults as a result of hypnotherapy [48]. In a nonrandomized controlled clinical trial. Stewart and Thomas [49] treated 18 adults with extensive atopic dermatitis who had been resistant to conventional treatment with hypnotherapy that included relaxation, stress management, direct suggestion for non-scratching behavior, direct suggestion for skin comfort and coolness, ego strengthening, posthypnotic suggestions, and instruction in self-hypnosis. The results were statistically significant (p < 0.01) for reduction in itch, scratching, sleep disturbance, and tension. Patient use of topical corticosteroid decreased by 40% at 4 weeks, 50% at 8 weeks, and 60% at 16 weeks. For atopic dermatitis, hypnosis can be a very useful complementary therapy that can decrease the needed amount of other treatments.

Remarkable clearing of congenital ichthyosiform erythroderma of Brocq in a 16 year old boy was reported following direct suggestion for clearing under hypnosis [50]. Similar though less spectacular results were confirmed with two sisters aged eight and six [51], with a 20 year old woman [52], and with 34 year old father and his four year old son [53]. Based on these case reports, hypnosis may be potentially very useful as a complementary therapy in addition to emollients.

Reduction in severity of dyshidrotic dermatitis has been reported with using hypnosis as a complementary treatment [54].

There is one case report of successful treatment of erythromelalgia in an 18 year old woman using hypnosis alone followed by self-hypnosis [55]. Permanent resolution occurred.

A 33 year old man with a negative self image and recurrent multiple Staphylococcus aureus containing furuncles since age 17 was unresponsive to multiple treatment modalities. Hypnosis and self-hypnosis with imagined sensations of warmth, cold, tingling, and heaviness brought about dramatic improvement over 5 weeks with full resolution of the recurrent furuncles [56]. The patient also improved substantially from a mental standpoint. Conventional antibiotic therapy is the first line of treatment for furuncles, but in unusually resistant cases with significant psychosomatic overlay, complementary use of hypnosis may help to end the chronic susceptibility to recurrent infection.

Oral pain such as glossodynia may respond well to hypnosis as a primary treatment if there is a significant psychological component [57]. With organic disease, hypnosis may give temporary relief from pain.

Discomfort relief from herpes simplex is similar to that for postherpetic neuralgia (see below). A reduction in the frequency of recurrences of herpes simplex following hypnosis has also been reported [58]. In cases with an apparent emotional trigger factor, hypnotic suggestion may be useful as a complementary therapy for reducing the frequency of recurrence.

Hypnosis or autogenic training may be useful as adjunctive therapy for hyperhidrosis [59].

A 33 year old man with ichthyosis vulgaris which was better in summer and worse in winter began hypnotic suggestion therapy in the summer and was able to maintain the summer improvement throughout the fall, winter, and spring [60].

Pruritus and lesions of lichen planus may be reduced in selected cases using hypnosis [38,54].

Some cases of neurodermatitis have resolved and stayed resolved with up to 4 years of followup using hypnosis as an alternative therapy [61,62,63, 64].

Reduction of pruritus and resolution of lesions of nummular dermatitis has been reported with use of hypnotic suggestion [38,54].

Pain from herpes zoster and post-herpetic neuralgia can be reduced by hypnosis [38,58]. Hypnosis may be useful as a complementary therapy for postherpetic neuralgia.

Hypnosis may modify and lessen the intensity of pruritus [38]. A man with chronic myelogenous leukemia had intractable pruritus that was much improved with hypnotic suggestion [65].

Hypnosis and suggestion have been demonstrated to have a positive effect on psoriasis [66,67,68]. A 75 percent clearing of psoriasis was reported in one case using a hypnotic sensory-imagery technique [69]. In another case of extensive severe psoriasis of 20 years duration marked improvement occurred using sensory imagery to replicate the feelings in the patient's skin that he had experienced during sunbathing [70]. Another case of severe psoriasis of 20 years duration resolved fully with a hypnoanalytic technique [71]. Tausk and Whitmore [72] performed a small randomized double-blind controlled trial using hypnosis as adjunctive therapy in psoriasis with significant improvement only in the highly hypnotizable subjects and not in the moderately hypnotizable subjects. Hypnosis can be quite useful as a complementary therapy for resistant psoriasis, especially if there is a significant emotional factor in the triggering of the psoriasis.

The vascular blush component of rosacea has been reported to improve in selected cases of resistant rosacea where hypnosis has been added as complementary therapy [38,54].

Several reports of successful adjunctive treatment of trichotillomania have been published [73,74,75]. Hypnosis may be a useful complementary therapy for trichotillomania.

Two cases of urticaria responded to hypnotic suggestion in one study. An 11 year old boy had an urticarial reaction to chocolate that could be blocked by hypnotic suggestion so that hives appeared on one side of his face but not the other in response to hypnotic suggestion [76]. In 15 patients with chronic urticaria of 7.8 years average duration, hypnosis with relaxation therapy resulted within 14 months in 6 patients being cleared and another 8 patients improved, with decreased medication requirements reported by 80 percent of the subjects [77]. Hypnosis may be useful as complementary or even alternative therapy for selected cases of chronic urticaria.

Reports by Bloch [31] and Sulzberger [32] on the efficacy of suggestion in treating verruca vulgaris have since been confirmed numerous times to a greater or lesser degree [78,79,80,81] and failed to be confirmed in a few studies [82,83]. A recent study that showed negative results was criticized for using a negative suggestion of not feeding the warts rather than a positive suggestion about having the warts resolve [84]. Many reports confirm the efficacy of hypnosis in treating warts [85,86,87,88,89,90,91,92,93,94,95,96,97,98,99,100] One study [101] that tried to replicate the remarkable success reported in Lancet [102] of using hypnotic suggestion to cause warts to disappear from one hand but not the other in persons with bilateral hand warts was unsuccessful. A well conducted randomized control study resulted in 53 percent of the experimental group having improvement of their warts three months after the first of five hypnotherapy sessions, while none of the control group had improvement [103]. Hypnosis has been proved to be helpful as a complementary or alternative therapy for warts.

Vitiligo have improved using hypnotic suggestion as complementary therapy [38,54], but it is unclear whether the recovery was simply spontaneous. Hypnosis may be appropriate as a complementary supportive treatment for the psychological impact of having vitiligo.

MEDICAL HYPNOTHERAPY FOR REDUCING PROCEDURE ANXIETY

Hypnosis can reduce anxiety, needle phobia, and pain during cutaneous surgery, as well as reducing postoperative discomfort. Fick et al [104] used self-guided imagery content during nonpharmacologic analgesia on 56 nonselected patients referred for percutaneous interventional procedures in the radiology procedure suite. A standardized protocol and script was used to guide patients into a state of self-hypnotic relaxation. All 56 patients developed an imaginary scenario. The imagery they chose was highly individualistic. They concluded that average patients can engage in imagery, but topics chosen are highly individualistic, making prerecorded tapes or provider directed imagery likely to be less effective than self-directed imagery. I have used this technique with good success in dermatology patients [105].

Lang et al [106] conducted a larger randomized trial of adjunctive non-pharmacologic analgesia for invasive radiologic procedures consisting of three groups: percutaneous vascular radiologic intraoperative standard care (control group), structured attention, and self-hypnotic relaxation. Pain increased linearly with time in the standard and the attention group, but remained flat in the hypnosis group. Anxiety decreased over time in all three groups, but more so with hypnosis. Drug use was significantly higher in the standard group than in the structured attention and self-hypnosis groups. The hemodynamic stability was significantly higher in the hypnosis group than in the attention and standard groups. Procedure times were significantly shorter in the hypnosis group than in the standard group, with the attention group intermediate. Cost analysis of this study [107] showed that the cost associated with standard conscious sedation averaged $638 per case while the cost for sedation with adjunct hypnosis was $300 per case, making the latter considerably more cost-effective.

A meta-analysis of hypnotically induced analgesia found that hypnosis has been demonstrated to relieve pain in patients with headache, burn injury, heart disease, cancer, dental problems, eczema, and chronic back problems [108]. For most purposes light and medium trance is sufficient, but deep trance is required for hypnotic anesthesia for surgery [35]. Pain reduction mediated by hypnosis localized to the mid anterior cingulate cortex in a study [109] using a positron emission tomography (PET).

For hypnosis to be of benefit, patients must be mentally intact, not psychotic nor intoxicated; motivated, not resistant, and preferably medium or high hypnotizable as rated by the Hypnotic Induction Profile [29] or Stanford Hypnotic Susceptibility Scale and its variants. However, for self-guided imagery a moderate or high degree of hypnotizability is not critical to success. Letting the patient choose his or her own self-guided imagery allows most individuals to reach a state of relaxation during procedures.

SUBTLE ENERGY INTUITIVE TECHNIQUES

Subtle energy is an area that has been central to many non-western healing traditions. It has been called "chi" or "qi" in traditional Chinese medicine, "prana" in traditional Indian medicine, "ni" by Native American medicine men, "num" by African shamans, biofields by biologists, and morphic fields by physicists. It plays a role in the Chinese acupuncture meridians and in the Indian chakras or energy centers. Subtle energy can be positive or negative. One can sense it but not yet measure or isolate it. Some individuals are more sensitive and vulnerable to negative energy than others, leading in some cases to illness [110]. The complex and subtle relationships of the conscious and subconscious mind, the nervous system, endocrine system, immune system, and the rest of the body are the focus of medical research into why conventional western medicine sometimes fails to help while alternative paradigms of healing may succeed. The medical intuitive may obtain a diagnosis and treat effectively cases of chronic skin pain or pruritus or chronic inflammatory skin conditions that have not responded to western medicine. Belief that the treatment will help, the so-called placebo effect, is well documented to promote improvement or healing in a substantial percentage of people. Whether subtle energy is simply the placebo effect or something beyond it remains to be established.

REFERENCES

[1]   Chu D H, Haake A R, Holbrook K, Loomis C A: The structure and development of skin. In Freedberg, I M, Eisen AZ, Wolff K, Austen K F, Goldsmith L A, Katz S I editors, *Fitzpatrick's Dermatology in General Medicine* sixth edition, New York, McGraw-Hill, 2003 pp58-88.

[2]   Zane LT: Psychoneuroendocrinimmunodermatology: Pathophysiological mechanisms of stress in cutaneous disease. In Koo JYM, Lee CS editors, *Psychocutaneous Medicine*, New York, Marcel Dekker, 2003, pp 65-95.

[3]   Gupta MA, Gupta AK: Depression and dermatological disorders. In Koo JYM, Lee CS editors, *Psychocutaneous Medicine*, New York, Marcel Dekker, 2003, pp 233-249.

[4]   Levenson H, Persons JB, Pope KS. Behavior therapy & cognitive therapy. In: Goldman HH, editor. *Review of General Psychiatry*, 5th ed. New York; McGraw-Hill, 2000: 472.

[5]   Bär LHJ, Kuypers BRM. Behaviour therapy in dermatological practice. *Br J Dermatol* 1973; 88:591-598.

[6]   Fried RG. Nonpharmacologic treatments in psychodermatology. *Dermatol Clin* 2002; 20(1):177-185.

[7]   Jordan JM, Whitlock FA. Emotions and the skin: the conditioning of the scratch response in cases of atopic dermatitis. *Br J Dermatol* 1972; 86:574-585.

[8]   Jordan JM, Whitlock FA. Atopic dermatitis, anxiety and conditioned scratch responses. *J Psychosom Res* 1974; 18:297-299.

[9]   Thomas JR, Greene SL, Dicken CH. Factitious cheilitis. *J Am Acad Dermatol* 1983; 8:368-372.

[10]   Ferguson JM, Taylor CB, Wermuth B. A rapid behavioral treatment for needle phobics. *J Nerv Ment Dis* 1978; 166:294-298.

[11]   Hamilton JG. Needle phobia: a neglected diagnosis. *J Fam Pract* 1995; 41:169-175.

[12]   Ratliffe R, Stein N. Treatment of neurodermatitis by behavior therapy: a case study. *Behav Res Ther* 1968; 6:397-399.

[13]   Rosenbaum MS, Ayllon T. The behavioral treatment of neurodermatitis through habit-reversal. *Behav Res Ther* 1981; 19:313-318.

[14]   Ameen Sait M, Reddy BSN, Garg BR. Onychotillomania: 2 case reports. *Dermatologica* 1985; 171:200-202.

[15] Mortimer PS, Dawber RPR. Trauma to the nail unit including occupational sports injuries. *Dermatol Clin* 1985; 3(3):415-420.

[16] Stanley MA, Mouton SG. Trichotillomania treatment manual. In: Van Hasselt VB, Hersen M, editors: *Sourcebook of Psychological Treatment Manuals for Adult Disorders*. New York; Plenum Press, 1996:657-687.

[17] Dengrove E. Hypnosis. In: Dengrove E, editor: *Hypnosis and Behavior Therapy*. Springfield (IL); Charles C. Thomas, 1976:26-35.

[18] Sarti MG. Biofeedback in dermatology. *Clin Dermatol* 1998; 16:711-714.

[19] Panconese E, ed. *Lo stress, le emozioni, la pelle*. Milan: Masson, 1998: 94.

[20] Seikowski K, Weber B, Haustein UF. Zum einfluss der hypnose und des autogenen trainings auf die krankheitsverarbeitung bei patienten mit progressiver sklerodermie. *Hautarzt* 1995; 46(2):94-101.

[21] Freedman RR. Quantitative measurements of finger blood flow during behavioral treatments for Raynaud's disease. *Psychophysiol* 1989; 26(4):437-441.

[22] Middaugh SJ, Haythornthwaite JA, Thompson B et al. The Raynaud's treatment study: biofeedback protocols and acquisition of temperature biofeedback skills. *Appl Psychophysiol Biofeedback* 2001; 26(4):251-278.

[23] Piedmont RL. Relationship between hypnotic susceptibility and thermal regulation: new directions for research. *Percept Motor Skills* 1983; 56(2):627-631.

[24] Roberts AH, Kewman DG, Macdonald H. Voluntary control of skin temperature: Unilateral changes using hypnosis and biofeedback. In: Wickramasekera, editor: *Biofeedback, Behavior Therapy and Hypnosis: Potentiating the Verbal Control of Behavior for Clinicians*. Chicago; Nelson-Hall, 1976:139-149.

[25] Tausk FA. Alternative medicine: is it all in your mind? *Arch Dermatol* 1998; 134:1422-1425.

[26] Sime A. Case study of trigeminal neuralgia using neurofeedback and peripheral biofeedback. *J Neurother* 2004; 8: 59-71.

[27] Shenefelt PD. Using hypnosis to facilitate resolution of psychogenic excoriations in acne excoriée. *Am J Clin Hypn* 2004; 239-245.

[28] Shenefelt PD, Hypnosis in dermatology. *Arch Dermatol* 2000; 136: 393-399.

[29] Spiegel H, Spiegel D. *Trance and Treatment: Clinical Uses of Hypnosis*, 2nd ed. Washington, D.C.; American Psychiatric Publishing, 2004, pp 51-92.

[30] Lichtenberg P, Bachner-Melman R, Gritsenko I,Ebstein RP. Exploratory association study between catechol-o-methyltransferase (COMT) high/low enzyme activity polymorphism and hypnotizability. *Am J Med Genetics* 2000; 96(6):771-774.

[31] Bloch B. Über die heilung der warzen durch suggestion. *Klin Wchnschr* 1927; 6:2271-2275; 6:2320-2325.

[32] Sulzberger MB, Wolf J. The treatment of warts by suggestion. *Med Rec* 1934; 140:552-556.

[33] Marmer MJ. *Hypnosis in Anesthesiology*. Springfield (IL); Charles C. Thomas, 1959.

[34] Crasilneck HB, Hall JA. *Clinical Hypnosis*, 2nd ed, Orlando (FL); Grune & Stratton, 1985.

[35] Watkins JG: *Hypnotherapeutic Techniques*. New York; Irvington, 1987.

[36] Freeman R, Barabasz A, Barabasz M, Warner D. Hypnosis and distraction differ in their effects on cold pressor pain. *Am J Clin Hypnosis* 2000; 43:137-148.

[37] Faymonville ME, Laurys S, Degueldre C, DelFiore G, Luxen A, Franck G, Lamy M, Maquet P. Neural mechanisms of antinociceptive effects of hypnosis. *Anesthesiol* 2000; 92:1257-1267.

[38] Scott MJ. *Hypnosis in skin and allergic diseases*. Springfield (IL); Charles C. Thomas, 1960.

[39] Koblenzer CS. *Psychocutaneous Disease*. Orlando (FL); Grune & Stratton, 1987.

[40] Grossbart TA, Sherman C. *Skin Deep: A Mind/Body Program for Healthy Skin*, Revised ed. Santa Fe (NM); Health Press, 1992.

[41] Scott MJ. Hypnosis in dermatology. In Schneck JM (ed): *Hypnosis in Modern Medicine*, 3rd ed. Springfield (IL); Charles C. Thomas, 1963, pp 122-142.

[42] Scott MJ. Hypnosis in dermatologic therapy. *Psychosomatics* 1964; 5:365-368.

[43] Hartland J. Hypnosis in dermatology. *Brit J Clin Hypn* 1969; 1:2-7.

[44] Olness KN. Hypnotherapy in children. *Postgraduate Medicine* 1986; 79(4):95-100,105.

[45] Kaschel R, Revenstorf D, Wörz B. Hypnose und haut: trends und perspecktiven. *Experim Klin Hypn* 1991; 7:65-82.

[46] Hollander MB. Excoriated acne controlled by post-hypnotic suggestion. *Am J Clin Hypn* 1959; 1:122-123.

[47] Harrison PV, Stepanek P. Hypnotherapy for alopecia areata. (letter) *Br J Dermatol* 1991; 124:509-510.

[48] Twerski AJ, Naar R. Hypnotherapy in a case of refractory dermatitis. *Am J Clin Hypn* 1974; 16:202-205.

[49] Stewart AC, Thomas SE. Hypnotherapy as a treatment for atopic dermatitis in adults and children. *Br J Dermatol* 1995; 132:778-783.

[50] Mason AA. A case of congenital ichthyosiform erythroderma of Brocq treated by hypnosis. *Br Med J* 1952; 2:422-423.

[51] Wink CAS. Congenital ichthyosiform erythroderma treated by hypnosis. *Br Med J* 1961; 2:741-743.

[52] Schneck JM. Hypnotherapy for ichthyosis. *Psychosomatics* 1966; 7:233-235.

[53] Kidd CB. Congenital ichthyosiform erythroderma treated by hypnosis. *Br J Dermatol* 1966; 78:101-105.

[54] Tobia L: L'ipnosi in dermatologia. *Minerva Medica* 1982; 73:531-537.

[55] Chakravarty K, Pharoah PDP, Scott DGI, Barker S. Erythromelalgia--the role of hypnotherapy. *Postgrad Med J* 1992; 68:44-46.

[56] Jabush M. A case of chronic recurring multiple boils treated with hypnotherapy. *Psychiat Quarterly* 1969; 43:448-455.

[57] Golan HP. The use of hypnosis in the treatment of psychogenic oral pain. *Am J Clin Hypn* 1997; 40:89-96.

[58] Bertolino R. L'ipnosi in dermatologia. *Minerva Medica* 1983; 74:2969-2973.

[59] Hölzle E. Therapie der hyperhidrosis. *Hautarzt* 1994; 35:7-15.

[60] Schneck JM. Ichthyosis treated with hypnosis. *Dis Nerv Syst* 1954; 15:211-214.

[61] Kline M. Delimited hypnotherapy: the acceptance of resistance in the treatment of a long standing neurodermatitis with a sensory-imagery technique. *Int J Clin Exp Hypn* 1953; 1:18-22.

[62] Sacerdote P. Hypnotherapy in neurodermatitis: a case report. *Am J Clin Hypn* 1965; 7:249-253.

[63] Collison DR. Medical Hypnotherapy. *Med J Austr* 1972; 1:643-649.

[64] Lehman RE. Brief hypnotherapy of neurodermatitis: a case with four-year followup. *Am J Clin Hypn* 1978; 21:48-51.

[65] Ament P, Milgram H. Effects of suggestion on pruritus with cutaneous lesions in chronic myelogenous leukemia. *N Y State J Med* 1967; 67:833-835.

[66] Kantor SD. Stress and psoriasis. *Cutis* 1990; 46:321-322.

[67] Winchell SA, Watts RA. Relaxation therapies in the treatment of psoriasis and possible pathophysiologic mechanisms. *J Am Acad Dermatol* 1988; 18:101-104.

[68] Zachariae R, Oster H, Bjerring P, Kragballe K. Effects of psychologic intervention on psoriasis: a preliminary report. *J Am Acad Dermatol* 1996; 34:1008-1015.

[69] Kline MV. Psoriasis and hypnotherapy: a case report. *Int J Clin Exp Hypn* 1954; 2:318-322.

[70] Frankel FH, Misch RC. Hypnosis in a case of long-standing psoriasis in a person with character problems. *Int J Clin Exp Hypn* 1973; 21:212-130.

[71] Waxman D. Behaviour therapy of psoriasis--a hypnoanalytic and counter-conditioning technique. *Postgrad Med J* 1973; 49:591-595.

[72] Tausk F, Whitmore SE. A pilot study of hypnosis in the treatment of patients with psoriasis. *Psychother Psychosom* 1999; 495:1-9.

[73] Galski TJ. The adjunctive use of hypnosis in the treatment of trichotillomania: a case report. *Am J Clin Hypn* 1981; 23:198-201.

[74] Rowen R. Hypnotic age regression in the treatment of a self-destructive habit: trichotillomania. *Am J Clin Hypn* 1981;23:195-197.

[75] Barabasz M. Trichotillomania: a new treatment. *Int J Clin Exp Hypn* 1987; 35:146-154.

[76] Perloff MM, Spiegelman J. Hypnosis in the treatment of a child's allergy to dogs. *Am J Clin Hypn* 1973; 15:269-272.

[77] Shertzer CL, Lookingbill DP. Effects of relaxation therapy and hypnotizability in chronic urticaria. *Arch Dermatol* 1987; 123:913-916.

[78] Obermayer ME, Greenson RR. Treatment by suggestion of verrucae planae of the face. *Psychosom Med* 1949; 11:163-164.

[79] Ullman M. On the psyche and warts: I. Suggestion and warts: a review and comment. *Psychosom Med* 1959; 21:473-488.

[80] Dudek SZ. Suggestion and play therapy in the cure of warts in children: a pilot study. *J Nerv Ment Dis* 1967; 145:37-42.

[81] Sheehan DV. Influence of psychosocial factors on wart remission. *Am J Clin Hypn* 1978; 20:160-164.

[82] Clarke GHV. The charming of warts. *J Invest Dermatol* 1965; 45:15-21.

[83] Stankler L. A critical assessment of the cure of warts by suggestion. *Practitioner* 1967; 198:690-694.

[84] Felt BT, Hall H, Olness K, Schmidt W, Kohen D, Berman BD et al. Wart regression in children: comparison of relaxation-imagery to topical treatment and equal time interventions. *Am J Clin Hypn* 1998; 41:130-138.

[85] McDowell M. Juvenile warts removed with the use of hypnotic suggestion. *Bull Menninger Clin* 1949; 13:124-126.

[86] Ullman M, Dudek S. On the psyche and warts: II. hypnotic suggestion and warts. *Psychosom Med* 1960; 22:68-76.

[87] Vickers CFH. Treatment of plantar warts in children. *Br Med J* 1961; 2:743-745.

[88] Surman OS, Gottlieb SK, Hackett TP. Hypnotic treatment of a child with warts. *Am J Clin Hypn* 1972; 15:12-14.

[89] Ewin D. Condyloma acuminatum: successful treatment of four cases by hypnosis. *Am J Clin Hypn* 1974; 17:73-78.

[90] Clawson TA, Swade RH. The hypnotic control of blood flow and pain: the cure of warts and the potential for the use of hypnosis in the treatment of cancer. *Am J Clin Hypn* 1975; 17:160-169.

[91] Tasini MF, Hackett TP. Hypnosis in the treatment of warts in immunodeficient children. *Am J Clin Hypn* 1977; 19:152-154.

[92] Johnson RFQ, Barber TX. Hypnosis, suggestions, and warts: an experimental investigation implicating the importance of "believed-in efficacy". *Am J Clin Hypn* 1978; 20:165-174.

[93] Dreaper R. Recalcitrant warts on the hand cured by hypnosis. *Practitioner* 1978; 220:305-310.

[94] Straatmeyer AJ, Rhodes NR. Condyloma acuminata: results of treatment using hypnosis. *J Am Acad Dermatol* 1983; 9:434-436.

[95] Morris BAP. Hypnotherapy of warts using the Simonton visualization technique: a case report. *Am J Clin Hypn* 1985; 27:237-240.

[96] Spanos NP, Stenstrom RJ, Johnston JC. Hypnosis, placebo, and suggestion in the treatment of warts. *Psychosom Med* 1988; 50:245-260.

[97] Noll RB. Hypnotherapy of a child with warts. *J Dev Behav Pediatr* 1988; 9:89-91.

[98] Spanos NP, Williams V, Gwynn MI. Effects of hypnotic, placebo, and salicylic acid treatments on wart regression. *Psychosom Med* 1990; 52:109-114.

[99] Ewin DM. Hypnotherapy for warts (verruca vulgaris): 41 consecutive cases with 33 cures. *Am J Clin Hypn* 1992; 35:1-10.

[100] Noll RB. Hypnotherapy for warts in children and adolescents. *J Dev Behav Pediatr* 1994; 15:170-173.

[101] Tenzel JH, Taylor RL. An evaluation of hypnosis and suggestion as treatment for warts. *Psychosom* 1969; 10:252-257.

[102] Sinclair-Gieben AHC, Chalmers D. Evaluation of treatment of warts by hypnosis. *Lancet* 1959; 2:480-482.

[103] Surman OS, Gottlieb SK, Hackett TP, Silverberg EL.Hypnosis in the treatment of warts. *Arch Gen Psychiatry* 1973; 28:439-441.

[104] Fick LJ, Lang EV, Logan HL, Lutgendorf S, Benotsch EG. Imagery content during nonpharmacologic analgesia in the procedure suite: where your patients would rather be. *Acad Radiol* 1999; 6:457-463.

[105] Shenefelt PD. Hypnosis-facilitated relaxation during self-guided imagery during dermatologic procedures. *Am J Clin Hypn* 2003; 45, 225-232.

[106] Lang EV, Benotsch EG, Fick LJ, Lutgendorf S, Berbaum ML, Logan H, Spiegel D. Adjunctive non-pharmacological analgesia for invasive medical procedures: a randomised trial. *Lancet* April 29, 2000; 355:1486-1490.

[107] Lang EV, Rosen MP. Cost analysis of adjunct hypnosis with sedation during outpatient interventional radiologic procedures. *Radiology* 2002; 222:375-382.

[108] Montgomery GH, DuHamel KN, Redd WH. A meta-analysis of hypnotically induced analgesia: how effective is hypnosis? *Int J Clin Exp Hypn* 2000; 48: 138-153.

[109] Faymonville ME, Laureys S, Degueldre C, DelFiore G, Luxen A, Franck G, et al. Neural mechanisms of antinociceptive effects of hypnosis. *Anesthesiol* 2000; 92:1257-1267.

[110] Orloff J. *Positive Energy*. New York; Harmony Books 2001, pp 1-15.

In: Trends in Psychotherapy Research   ISBN 1-59454-373-9
Editor: M. E. Abelian, pp. 53-70   © 2006 Nova Science Publishers, Inc.

Chapter 3

INTEGRATIVE PSYCHOSOMATIC AND OTOLOGIC MODELS IN THE THERAPY OF CHRONIC TINNITUS

Gerhard Hesse[1], A. Laubert[2], H. Schaaf[1] and M. Almeling[1]*
[1]Tinnitus-Klinik Arolsen
[2]University of Witten/Herdecke

ABSTRACT

Chronic tinnitus has a very high prevalence in Europe and other industrialized countries. Latest studies found 4% of the German population with chronic tinnitus, almost 2 % suffering severely in their daily life. Because there is no curative therapeutic approach available, neither pharmacological nor surgical, the main focus lies on treatments enhancing the habituation of tinnitus. Habituation occurs in almost 50 % of the patients as a normal process, leading to a complete compensation. This is based on the ability of the auditory perception to habituate random noise and focus on important acoustic information.

However, habituation is impossible, if tinnitus is connected to hyperacusis, to fear of severe otologic disabilities such as impending deafness or to fear of brain damage, tumors or other diseases. With thorough audiological diagnosis these complications or basic causes of tinnitus can be found or excluded - counseling of the patients then can explain the symptom and thus facilitate the habituation process, often with the help of apparative therapy such as hearing aids or noise generators.

If tinnitus is held responsible for psychic disturbances such as lack of concentration, sleep disorders or manifest depressions, neither of these can be cured with psychotherapy alone, leaving aside the symptom tinnitus. On the other hand, tinnitus habituation is impossible without treating the psychosomatic imbalance. Therefore an integrative psychosomatic and otologic model is needed. This therapeutic approach combines hearing therapy based on proper knowledge about the individual's auditory abilities and psychotherapy, mostly cognitive and/or behavioral therapies. Retraining (TRT) alone is only sufficient for patients without psychosomatic symptoms and imbalance, whereas

---

* Tinnitus-Klinik Arolsen; Grosse Allee 1-3; 34454 Bad Arolsen; Germany; Tel.: +49-5691-896-727; Fax: +49-5691-896-700; e-mail: ghesse@Tinnitus-Klinik.de

integrative psychosomatic models provide tinnitus sufferers with self-competence and facilitate the habituation of tinnitus. Selected cases are presented to explain these models.

I. INTRODUCTION

I. 1. Prevalence of Chronic Tinnitus

The prevalence of chronic Tinnitus is actually higher then older studies indicated. Latest data from Germany found out that 25 % of the population experienced tinnitus for a short period of their life. 13.8% heard Tinnitus for a longer phase. About 4% of the population suffers from their tinnitus so much that they have to go under a special treatment. 1.5% are greatly affected in their daily life, 1% even in their occupation. This data, published by the German Tinnitus-League (DTL) (Pilgramm, Rychlick et al. 1999) is probably the same for all European and other industrialized countries. For Poland similar data have been published (Fabijanska, Rogowski et al. 1999). The main outcome of this study shows, that many people experience or suffer from tinnitus, but only a small part of them really do suffer enough to actually need treatment. This is certainly due to the normal habituation processes that lead to the fact that people have tinnitus, but they don't experience it disturbing anymore.

I. 2. Origins of Tinnitus

We must agree, that there still is no curative treatment for chronic tinnitus available. Neither medically nor surgically can the generators of tinnitus be influenced. We know from own clinical data (Hesse and Laubert 2001), that 90% of the tinnitus sounds are generated in the internal ear, mainly caused by damage of the outer hair cells (OHC). Noise or acoustic trauma may induce decoupling of the OHC from the tectorial or the basilar membrane. Ionic channels of the hair cells may tear off, virus-toxins or other toxic agents may influence stimulus transduction in the hair cells, and stimulus transmission may be disturbed at the synaptic level. Strain may cause spasms of the precapillary blood vessels, resulting in temporary malnutrition of the cochlea. Models for types of tinnitus generation have been proposed by (Zenner 1998).

At the present time this cannot be influenced by any medicine without destroying the sense of hearing completely. Optimization of cochlear blood flow and oxygen supply may be efficient in acute types of Outer Haircell (OHC) damage, esp. after acoustic trauma or sudden sensorineural hearing loss. Anti-arrhythmic agents like Lidocain can stop tinnitus in about 50% of the cases, but only temporarily for the time of infusion (Lenarz 1998). Side effects on the other hand are very serious and forbid longer application of this medicine.

There are approaches to implant special catheters, place them at the area close to the round window and try to apply medicine with a special dosage pump as a local therapy to the inner ear. Initial results, however, are not very promising (Schwab, Lenarz et al. 2004). So far the tested agents like vasoactive substances, steroids, Lidocain or Caroverin did not have any effect on the persistence of tinnitus, if applied locally (Lenarz 1999).

Surgical approaches, except of course surgery that treats mid ear diseases like otosclerosis and thus preserves or restores hearing as the main goal, are restricted to cutting the acoustic nerve with its known complications. But even in these cases more then 50% keep their tinnitus, due to central excitation of a primarily peripheral generated sound (Feldmann 1998).

Therefore with curative treatments far from being applicable, the focus of tinnitus therapy lies on habituation processes (Jastreboff and Hazell). This process works with the ability of the auditory system to change the perception of random noise, if its meaning is not connected to emotions like fear or anger. This ability of the auditory perception can be developed and trained even in older people by using the filter capacities of the efferent system with its effects on all parts of the auditory pathway, including the outer hair cells.

The theoretical background of this therapeutic approach is based on the understanding of the complete process of hearing.

I. 3. Hearing - Peripheral Hearing and Central Auditory Pathway

The function of the sound transfer in the middle ear as well as treatments of diseases set in that area are well known; now, even the mechanisms of the inner ear are better known because of new findings of function and structure of the hair cells (Zenner 1994) and the effective motor protein prestin (Zheng, Shen et al. 2000); but a correct and sound understanding of the function of the inner ear i.e. the sound transfer from hair cells to the acoustic nerve as well as the peripheral coding of signals are only known fragmentarily. Already the differentiation between afferent and efferent supply of the hair cells (Liberman 1988) shows the existence of complicated regulating loops controlling the entire auditory pathway with Corti's organ situated at the peripheral end. In the inner ear, sounds are mainly treated according to the principle of place (Tonotopy) and winding up of time, whereas in higher brain centers and auditory neurones more and more complex sound patterns are dealt with. Then, single neurones are specialised in certain characteristics; they are activated by certain pitches and blocked by others, they react to the increase or decrease of frequency or to the beginning or ending of sound impulses. Thereby, sound impulses are prepared for the further treatment within the auditory cortex by extracting certain characteristics: "Thereby, only the content of information is transported to the cortex, not the whole signal (Processing of information)." (Zenner 1997)

That kind of specialisation of cells is known as well as the anatomy of the whole afferent sound path: in the first neuron that ends in dorsal and ventral Nucleus cochlearis in the brain stem, the first binaural interaction takes place as each inner ear is connected with both brain half's. One part of the other neurones leads from the nucleus cochlearis to the nucleus olivaris superior of the same side, whereas the other part crosses over to the opposite side. In the further course, the same happens within the nuclei lemnisci laterales. In other stations of the sound paths via corpus geniculatum mediale and the radiatio auditiva, the auditory cortex is achieved.

The efferent paths descend from the auditory cortex down to the corpus geniculatum mediale. The colliculus inferior seems to have a major function in control of the efferent sound path and thereby of the function of enhancement and inhibition; it takes up descending paths from the cortex itself as well as from the corpus geniculatum mediale. From here, efferent fibres run to all subordinate brain centers which – in the end – reach again the outer hair cells of the inner ear. (Liberman 1991; Liberman 1993).

Besides the three-dimensional hearing, a major performance of such a complex sound procession is a hearing in high-noise areas or in disturbing sounds.

Function controls for these different sectors of the sound paths are not very common, specific microscopical and electro-physiological research-works are mainly based on findings with cats and rats (Eggermont and Kenmochi 1998), (Klinke and Galley 1974).

Research-works about the functions of major characteristics of psycho-acoustical hearing process are mainly based on Zwicker (Zwicker 1990); But they are – as already quoted above – not very common within general practices. Recently, the Binaural masking level difference test (BMLD), a psychoacoustic test differentiating the sound detection in unilateral and in bilateral broadband noise has been evaluated for clinical use (Hesse 2004).

Certain objective controlling methods with humans were tested according to the spirit of a brain-mapping; here, especially the working group around Hoke and Pantev (Pantev 1999), (Hoke and Hoke 1997) have achieved high merits mainly because of functional nuclear magneto graphic measurements.

Whereas the derivation of brain cortex potentials is mainly restricted to findings of frequency-specific sound limits, research-works about specific reactions of the sound processing as e.g. the Mismatch negativity (Naatanen and Excera, 2000), the Contingent negative variation (CNV) (Proefrock and Hoke 1995) or other processing potentials have not been sufficiently examined in their meaning for the diagnostics of the central hearing function.

But it is indisputable that the maturation of a healthy auditory pathway is achieved in a learning process that already starts during the development of the embryo (Matschke 1990). By latest research results and the results of the treatment with a Cochlea-Implant of deaf-borne children or of those who lost their hearing we know that an early stimulation may strongly influence the success of the therapy, i.e. the actual further improvement of a sound path. This implies as well that the development of the hearing ability depends on adequate stimulation – otherwise the sound path is either not installed or it recedes as is the case with the loss of hearing with adults. Also the auditive perception is decisively influenced by learning processes that are very intensive in the early childhood but that are changeable and extendable in later phases of life. The auditive perception is developed in three steps: modality specific, inter-modal and serial (Affolter 1972). When the development of the hearing perception is completed, each individual sound path is linked up with super ordinate brain centers, an acoustic memory is installed and speaking competence and comprehension are available.

So far, nothing has been said about the actual competence of the hearing (neither disturbed nor restricted). With selective ear training for example a musician is able to hear much more differentiated and analytical than an untrained person. Even here it has to be said that the stimulation of such abilities is more effective the earlier it starts. Especially the differentiated hearing within disturbing sounds may be improved enormously – the same is valid for the refinement in the distinction of frequencies and intensity.

So the actual shaping of auditive perception and the variety and ability of this perception is highly variable and certainly not only depending on learning processes but also on genetic predispositions.

When we propose to improve tinnitus and hyperacusis as well as dysacusis, by suitable treatments, this proposal is based on actual clinical experiences (Hesse 2000), that we made with patients where conventional therapies with medicines and equipments failed or did not bring decisive improvements.

I. 4. Tinnitus Habituation is Prevented by Psychosomatic Imbalance

We know that in most cases the process of (tinnitus) habituation works quite normally, leading to the fact that more than 75% of the people who experience tinnitus habituate this after the short period without any special therapy. But habituation is seriously prevented, when the person focuses on his tinnitus or the tinnitus itself is connected to severe emotions. Finally, if the person is in a psychosomatic state of instability, habituation processes are almost impossible. We have to look on tinnitus as a neuro-otologic and psychosomatic entity, because only in this combination, does the so-called state of decompensation, which means suffering and development of co-morbidity, start. This co-morbidity is seen as lack of concentration, lack of communication, sleep disorders and depressive syndromes. Co-morbidity is also anxiety: Fear of hearing-loss, of loss of communication or fear of brain strokes or even debility. In our own clinical data 72 % of the patients have a relevant psychological diagnosis (Nelting, Schaaf et al. 1999). This although, is a preselected patient's entity, in a normal tinnitus-clinic this percentage may be lower.

II. THERAPY

II. 1. Tinnitus Habituation Therapy (such as Retraining or TRT)

The first aspect of treating decompensated tinnitus therefore is proper counseling, based on a solid neurootological examination. Profound diagnosis leads to exclusion of diseases that may cause tinnitus and must be treated surgical or pharmacological like mid ear disease, acoustic neuroma, other brain tumors or inflammations like multiple sclerosis, infections or cardio-vascular diseases.

Therefore these examinations and exclusions also reduce fear in the patients, if explained and understood properly. Negative counseling of the patients must be strongly avoided.

With many patients suffering from chronic tinnitus, this counseling is sufficient to facilitate the habituation of tinnitus – no further treatment is necessary (12% of our outdoor patients).

Based on the audiological status further, especially apparative therapies might be useful; patients are supplied either with hearing aids or noise generators.

This combination of counseling and sound therapy has been proposed for the therapy of chronic tinnitus by Jastreboff and Hazell (Jastreboff and Hazell 1993) as tinnitus retraining therapy (TRT). Many tinnitus centers all over the world work very sufficiently with this method, based on Jastreboff's neurophysiological model. This model proposed by (Jastreboff 1990) is based on the understanding of the neuronal network of auditory perception, where each acoustic input is processed and connected to emotional and cognitive parts of the cortex and is either perceived and even focused or – if meaningless and not emotionally connected – habituated and not perceived any longer. This habituation process is the main aim of TRT. (Fig.:1)

Therefore TRT is not a curative therapy, because it does not influence the generators of tinnitus directly, but it helps reorganizing the auditory pathway: Tinnitus is then interpreted as "normal random noise". TRT is based on learning capacities of the patients and can only work, if the patient is willing to participate in the treatment.

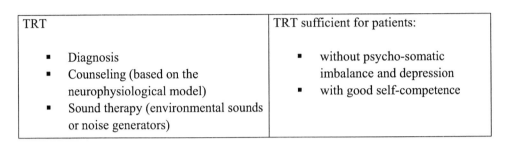

TRT	TRT sufficient for patients:
▪ Diagnosis ▪ Counseling (based on the neurophysiological model) ▪ Sound therapy (environmental sounds or noise generators)	▪ without psycho-somatic imbalance and depression ▪ with good self-competence

Figure 1. Tinnitus-Retraining-Therapy – TRT (Jastreboff & Hazell)

II. 2. Hearing Therapy Complements Habituation Therapy

An active hearing therapy has become a major approach for the treatment of tinnitus as well as oversensitivity to sound (hyperacusis) (Hesse 1999):

Active processes are taught that may drag the tinnitus into the background and supports the positive parts of the auditory perception so that the patient learns in time to suppress the disturbing noise of tinnitus. The hearing therapy may also intensify or enable the mechanical supply by hearing aids or noise generators. In a certain sense, this therapy is also a therapeutical base to restructure auditory abilities positively. (Schaaf and Hesse 1998).

A lot of patients - either with or without disturbing ringing of the ear - are very sensitive to noises. One of the major causes for this phenomenon certainly is the general acoustic strain in the daily life of industrial societies. On the other hand a lot of people show a hypersensitivity to sound since their childhood, especially and mainly when their hearing ability in general is good or even better than normal. In that case hypersensitivity to sound is almost always related to the fear that certain loud noises could damage the ear (Jastreboff and Hazell 1993); with children, this fear is certainly based in the unconscious. This fear for loud noises, often supported by well-meaning advisers, eventually even by doctors, enhances developing an attitude of sound protection, which means that noises are more and more avoided and the patients isolate themselves acoustically. But thereby, the sensitivity increases as the internal regulators turn to lower intensities (Anari, Axelsson et al. 1999).

With such patients, a hearing therapy has to have a de-frightening effect, the patients have to be guided back to a normal sound level, and simultaneously, the therapy should give them back the pleasure from hearing.

To carry out a hearing therapy, it is necessary to find out how the respective patient handles his hearing situation individually, and what his acoustic reality is like. For us, this means all sound experiences made during the life until present. On one side, those experiences consist of acoustic impulses processed individually and constitutionally and on the other side we find the reactions resulting from those experiences. Also the actual validation of sounds that may be different according to actual conditions and situations of life has an influence on the acoustic reality.

Even people with normal hearing show two different basic forms: one group handles the hearing with relish, those people are mostly communicative, and hearing is emphasized. They love communications, listen to music or play a musical instrument, and they love to develop thoughts and ideas within communications, in direct talks. Communication and hearing are seen as positive means. If those people suffer from hearing defects they often valuate this as a punishment. On the other hand, those people show well developed abilities of an auditory processing so that hearing deficiencies may be compensated or tinnitus can be quickly switched off. With those people, a hearing therapy is successful and quickly to be carried out.

On the other side, we find an introverted and calm person. He would prefer to communicate via letters or computer; he loves reading and his conversations will more-or-less be forced and short. Those people love silence and they are very much disturbed in their silence by a sudden hearing loss or especially by tinnitus.

For those people, a hearing therapy should provide that the hearing system receives as much information as possible and should improve the possibility of auditory processing.

It is clear that – in addition to these two standards – there are numerous intermediate stages and flowing transitions. But with all different kinds of hearing deficiencies such a classification can be made and has to be taken into account in the respective hearing therapy.

Before choosing a therapeutical method it has to be found out what kind of hearing problem we have at hand: is it a reduction of the hearing ability in the low-, middle- or high-tone section, is the loss of hearing uni- or bilateral, is it distinctive or only apparent in certain situations? This is very problematic for patients with a fluctuating auditory threshold, as with endolymphatic hydrops or Morbus Menière (Schaaf 1999). Those patients can hardly handle a present loss of hearing, they can hardly be supplied with hearing aids and additionally they have the problem that they cannot find regularities when the hearing is getting worse and when or why it is getting better. Especially patients with Tinnitus or hypersensitivity to sound have to be differentiated into people who are either hearing enthusiasts or calm and less auditive. When supplying hearing aids and respective exercises, the individual hearing situation of the affected person has to be taken into account.

III. METHODS OF HEARING THERAPY

> **The methods of hearing therapy show the following subjects:**
> 1. Exercises to sharpen perception
> 2. Improvement of the acoustic classification of tones and sounds
> 3. Teaching of a positive hearing perception
> 4. Focussing exercises in case of strong influence of disturbing noises
> 5. Special strategies for hearing with hearing aids
> 6. Integration from sounds and music

With each step, hearing therapy analyses the individual hearing problems of the patient. In a special way, it takes the individual hearing situation of the affected into account, who suffers from a sudden hearing loss or newly achieved tinnitus. Quite often, the therapy shows parallelisms to psychological stress situations that may have caused or keep up a special problem. In such situations it may be necessary to simultaneously consult a psychotherapist or to work on special subjects in psychotherapeutically visits. The auditive stimulation – explained by (Ding 1995) – mainly takes into account the acoustic influences of the environment which will then play the main role in the hearing therapy. This implies that at the beginning of each therapeutical hearing exercise an intensive individual dialogue is necessary in which the actual individual hearing situation of the affected is analysed and the respective therapeutical attempts are developed.

III. 1. Improvement of the Sensory Perception

"Being born deaf is worse than being born blind..." (Sacks, 1981).

Although everyone can understand this fact which is described in Oliver Sack's touching book about deafness, it is the optical sense that is very much overrated in our time. Although communication is hardly possible without hearing, the optical sense dominates our complete perception and deceives it, almost distracts it from the essential. According to its great variety and its innervation the audition is much more superior to the optical sense. Now, if the ability of the auditory sense should be stressed or improved, it is useful to "switch off" the optical sense first, i.e. to carry out hearing exercises with eyes being closed. Only then we realise how much the optical sense dominates our sensory perception. Also the improvement of other sensory perceptions such as smelling and feeling may well be a starting point and component of a specific hearing therapy. Exercises in blind guiding have proved well; here sounds of the environment are used for the orientation: smelling and feeling are very well trained with eyes being closed (at best in the open countryside). Such exercises in blind-guiding need an absolute trust in the situation and especially in the hearing therapist as a lot of people feel insecure with their eyes bandaged and they are not used to orientate themselves with their other senses. Therefore, the experience that this is successful is extremely important. Very often it is experienced that certain impressions of the senses are connected with feelings and that they provoke associations. Those impressions should always be discussed in after talks.

III. 2. Acoustic Classification of Sounds

In exercises emphasizing specific hearing situations, sounds have to be detected intentionally. Here also, results are best achieved with eyes being closed, when e.g. sound location are trained or direction and distance shall be determined. It is interesting that patients who suffer from tinnitus, almost no longer realise their disturbing ringing during that kind of exercise as their concentration is fixed on other sensual experiences and hearing sensations so that the Tinnitus falls into the background.

III. 3. Teaching of Positive Hearing Perception

One of the key aspects of hearing therapy is the teaching of positive hearing experiences. This is very well achieved with music, especially with pieces of music that the patient judges as harmonic and stimulating. But also in the open countryside, e.g. the sound of birds'voices or the gentle murmuring of the leaves may provoke positive associations. Even with dysacusis or tinnitus it may be sensed that the defective hearing function can still teach a positive perception. Especially for patients who think that an enjoyable hearing would no longer be possible because of a defective hearing, these experiences often become a turning point.

III. 4. Focussing Exercises with Influences of Disturbing Noises

In this dominant part of hearing therapy important acoustic information has to be separated from side- or background hissings. The patient has to concentrate on the most important stimulations to improve his defective "figurative-basic-perception" (Breitenbach 1995). In general, this exercise trains the ability to filter important information out of different sounds and to oppress unimportant things. Here, the improvement of differentiation between disturbing and useful sounds shall be trained. Before focussing exercises are carried out, the handling with silence should be defined for each patient individually. Here, the differences between the hearing in silence and the filtering out of disturbing sounds are experienced. The standardisation of individual handling of silence (as already explained above) is now specialised:

Whereas some patients are always looking for silence or mourn it, the others almost always try to permanently bring sounds to their ears, to almost numb them. During hearing therapy, an individual hearing hygiene has to be developed without any strain of the ear.

III. 5. Hearing Therapy with Hearing Aids

This new situation, i.e. the effect of intensification through hearing aids and simultaneously the new hearing of long-known sounds, has to be taught and guided. Additionally, there are special exercises of hearing tactiques as e.g. instructions for the behaviour in certain situations, for the sitting positions in a group, for the use of acoustic or optic means, for special strategies within the guidance of conversations and when using the phone. Those means, called hearing tactiques, are also part of a hearing therapy.

III. 6. Music

Music is very much suitable for hearing therapy, as it expresses the whole variety of auditive capabilities and simultaneously shows cultural and emotional experiences (Berendt 1989). Additionally, it develops and supports the differentiation of sounds. Receptive listening to music means to analyse and differentiate pieces of music from their emotional effect, to distinguish individual music instruments first and then let the sound have an effect.

The active playing a music instrument may train in a perfect way the ability to differentiate between frequency and intensity. Especially where children are involved, working with music has proved very effective (Lauer 1999).

IV. PSYCHOSOMATIC CO-MORBIDITY

However, if there is not enough self-competence or if the patient is psychologically unstable or severely depressive, TRT and hearing therapy alone are not sufficient – very often TRT destabilizes these patients more, when they become frustrated, because the therapy does not eliminate (switch off) their tinnitus.

Hearing loss	Tinnitus and hyperacusis
1. reduction of communication abilities 2. frightened to make mistakes 3. fear of loud surroundings and noise exposure (recruitment) 4. mistrust 5. social isolation	1. lack of concentration 2. insomnia 3. fear of possible diseases causing tinnitus 4. fear of deterioration 5. fear of personal failure 6. depressive symptoms 7. social isolation

Figure 2. Psychosomatic side effects and co-morbidity

Hearing loss alone provokes many psychosomatic reactions, tinnitus and hyperacusis even more.

> **The resulting decompensated tinnitus is a psychosomatic disease that requires an integrative neurootological and psychosomatic treatment, combining retraining and hearing therapy with psychotherapy like behavioural or cognitive therapy.**

V. CASE REPORTS

Some clinical cases shall demonstrate the necessity of differentiation and an additional psychological examination:

Patient H.G. had bilateral, high frequency tinnitus for 5 years. 1968 he had a noise trauma being exposed to machine-gun shooting without protection (army). Resulting with a high-frequency hearing loss and tinnitus for 3 months, which afterwards habituated. Examinations (Fig.3) revealed no other reasons for tinnitus, his problem was increasing aggressiveness and nervousness due to his tinnitus.

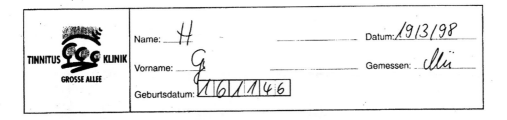

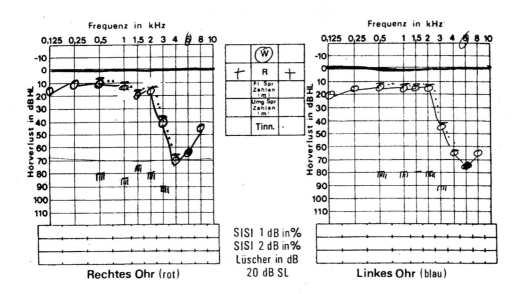

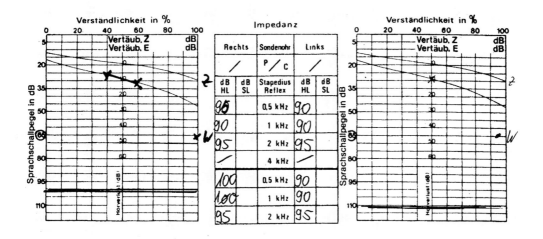

Figure 3. Pat. H.G.: bilateral, high frequency hearing loss, tinnitus 4000 Hz, bilateral, tonal. Speech discrimination and mid-ear function normal

For this patient TRT was perfect, he was supplied with open fitted hearing aids. The hearing-loss was much more disturbing for the patient than the actual tinnitus – the patient discovered this only after his hearing improved due to the hearing aid. After 9 month of TRT his tinnitus was not a problem any more, after one-year habituation was achieved and tinnitus noticed only in times of strain and emotional imbalance.

Patient S.S. suffered from a unilateral, high frequency tinnitus and a severe hyperacusis. It started after a noise trauma in a discotheque 1996, hyperacusis war progressive and intolerable since 1 year with an over sensitivity to all sounds, escape tendencies and increasing social isolation. Everyday fitness could only be achieved with permanent ear protection, leading to further isolation. Audiometric findings (Fig. 4) revealed perfect hearing thresholds, DPOAE showed signs of hyperactivity of outer hair cells (increased emissions and steep growth functions, described by (Janssen, Kummer et al. 1998) and (Hesse, Masri et al. 1999).

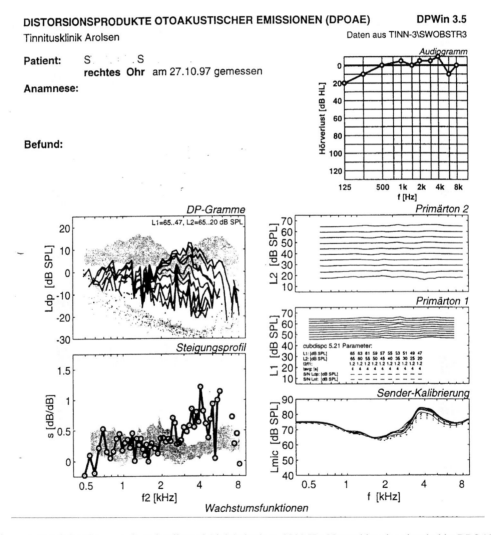

Figure 4. Pat. S.S.: Hyperacusis and unilateral (right) tinnitus, 3800 Hz. Normal hearing thresholds; DPOAE: high emissions and increased growth functions between 2 and 6 kHz

Therapy with this patient started with examinations and counseling, based on the neurophysiological model. Noise generators were fitted. The patient however refused to wear the instruments, afraid of further "damage" to his ears. Intensive psychosomatic stabilization was necessary to build up a good therapeutic relation. Only then the patient could slowly begin to expose himself to sound and – protected by the hearing therapist – overcome his social isolation. Noise generators were used after 6 weeks. In this case TRT started only after intensive psychosomatic therapy – after 16 month with very good success and hyperacusis minimized to very rare occasions.

Patient N.P. complained about progressive, bilateral hearing loss and bilateral low-frequency tinnitus, starting in 1988 with progressive tendencies. As an infant he was a stutterer after a traumatic experience. Together with commencing hearing loss and tinnitus he developed more communication problems and social anxiety. There was a great overexertion at work and an increasing disability to communicate.

Audiometric findings revealed a pantonal hearing loss of 40-50 dB and tinnitus of 700 Hz. However, Mid-ear reflex and BERA was normal and DPOAE showed completely normal inner ear function except a mild high frequency hearing loss (Fig.5).

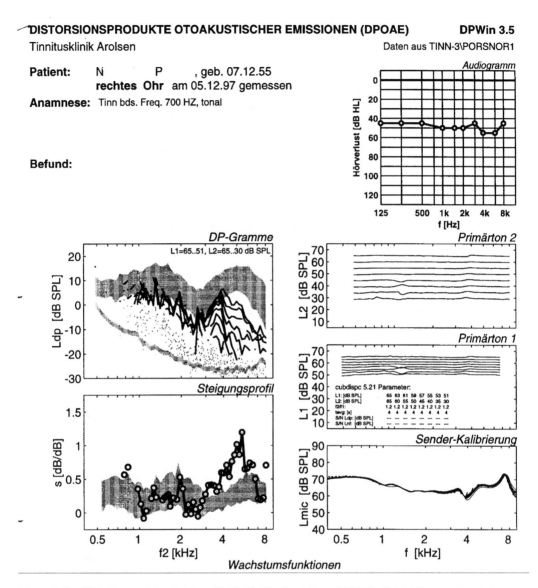

Figure 5. Pat. N.P.: Pantonal hearing loss 40-50 dB, Tinnitus bilateral 700 Hz. DPOAE: normal emissions and growth function in low and middle frequencies, slight hypofunction in high frequencies

According to objective audiometric findings, this patient had only a minimal high frequency hearing loss; the diagnosis therefore was psychogenic deafness. Treatment here was only psychotherapy, revealing the causes and internal barriers that lead to the auditory dysfunction. It lasted less than 6 month of therapy to stabilize the patient; after that his subjective hearing was almost normal again.

Integrative Psychosomatic and Otologic Models

These cases demonstrate that the TRT methods of diagnosis, counseling and sound therapy are very helpful. In some cases however, they are not sufficient. If the patient has psychosomatic reasons for focussing on his tinnitus, if the tinnitus and/or the hearing loss stands for a symptom of sensual and emotional over excitation, than it is not primarily the tinnitus that has to be treated. If tinnitus is made responsible for other problems, mainly for depressive symptoms, the tinnitus has to be treated by means of hearing therapy, means of training and developing the auditory perception. But this therapy must be accompanied by psychosomatic, psychotherapeutic interventions to stabilise the patient and must find out the real cause for the psychological symptoms or the depression.

VI. RESULTS OF INTEGRATIVE THERAPY

Most scientific evaluations in tinnitus therapy lack valid control groups and – more important – solid criteria to measure tinnitus annoyance and improvement. There are some evaluated questionnaires in English (Hallam, Jakes et al. 1988), (Sweetow and Levy 1990) as well as in German language (Greimel, Leibetseder et al. 1999), (Goebel and Hiller 1998). These however, do not measure hyperacusis, and they are still subjective instruments. Simply using visual analogue scales (VAS), very common in tinnitus therapy, is not reliable enough to fulfil scientific standards.

Therefore any study about outcome of tinnitus therapy must be critically reviewed, especially when results promise "80% (or more) improvement", measuring improvement of life quality (Mc Kinney, Hazell et al. 1999).

We can subjectively measure the degree of tinnitus perception, but nevertheless this is not profound statistical data.

According to our own results with 240 outdoor patients, we had only 17 % with normal hearing, 65 % with inner ear hearing loss and 18 % other hearing disturbances. Tinnitus frequency was a mean of 5700 Hz (700-14000 Hz), minimal masking level (MML) 10-15 dB above the hearing threshold.

75 % of our patients, treated by TRT alone, improved their tinnitus perception, whereas 18 % deteriorated during TRT. 7 % did not experience any changes. According to the Tinnitus-Questionnaire (TF) (Goebel/Hiller/Hallam) there was significant improvement (7 points) (Repik, Rienhoff et al. 2000).

With our indoor patients (n=1304) results were more remarkable: according to the TF, improvement was 13.1 points. More than 50% of the patients were severely or very severely suffering from chronic tinnitus before therapy. We found in only 5% of our indoor patients normal hearing (Hesse, Rienhoff et al. 2001). This indicates that the hearing loss is much more dominant than tinnitus. Patients, however, emphasize more on their tinnitus. The best post therapeutic results and stabile improvement is very much dependant on treatment of hearing loss (Nelting, Schaaf et al. 1999), e.g. wearing of hearing aids or improving hearing tactics.

VII. CONCLUSION

Modern tinnitus therapy has to help reorganising the functions of all components of the network of acoustic perception. One of the main aspects is the separation of tinnitus perception from its emotional components and thereby change the psychological importance of the phantom sound.

Initially this can be achieved by methods of habituation therapy, if the patient is collaborating and if his psychosomatic status reveals enough stabilization. If there is a psychological co-morbidity, integrative psychosomatic models are required to

- stabilize the tinnitus sufferer
- provide the patients with self-competence
- and facilitate the habituation of tinnitus.

REFERENCES

Affolter, F. (1972). "Entwicklung visueller und auditiver Prozesse." Schweiz.Zeitschrift f. *Psychologie* 31: 207-293.

Anari, M., A. Axelsson, et al. (1999). "Hypersensitivity to sound." *Scand. Audiol.* 28: 219-30.

Berendt, J.-E. (1989). Ich höre, also bin ich. Freiburg, Bauer.

Breitenbach, E. (1995). "Material zur Diagnose und Therapie auditiver Wahrnehmungsstörungen." Würzburg: *Ed. Bentheim.*

Ding, H. (1995). Aurale Rehabilitation Hörgeschädigter. Berlin Heidelberg New York, *Springer.*

Eggermont, J. J. and M. Kenmochi (1998). "Salicylate and quinine selectively increase spontaneous firing rates in secondary auditory cortex." *Hear Roes* 117(1-2): 149-60.

Fabijanska, A., M. Rogowski, et al. (1999). Epidemiology of tinnitus and hyperacusis in Poland. Sixth international Tinnitus Seminar, Cambridge.

Feldmann, H. H. (1998). Tinnitus: Grundlagen einer rationalen Diagnostik und Therapie. Stuttgart, New York, *Thieme Verlag.*

Goebel, G. and W. Hiller (1998). Tinnitus-Fragebogen (TF). Ein Instrument zur Erfassung von Belastung und Schweregrad bei Tinnitus (siehe Anlage tinnitus Fragebogen). Göttingen, Bern, Toronto, Seattle, *Hogrefe Verlag für Psychologie.*

Greimel, K. V., M. Leibetseder, et al. (1999). "Ist Tinnitus messbar? - Methoden zur Erfassungen tinnitusspezifischer Beeinträchtigungen." HNO 47: 196-201.

Hallam, R. S., S. C. Jakes, et al. (1988). "Cognitive variables in tinnitus annoyance." *Brit. J. Clin. Psychol.* 27: 112 - 118.

Hesse, G. (1999). Hörtherapie. Retraining und Tinnitustherapie. G. Hesse. Stuttgart, New York, *Thieme:* 60-69.

Hesse, G. (2000). Retraining und Tinnitustherapie. Stuttgart, New York, *Thieme.*

Hesse, G. (2004). "Hörgeräte im Alter." HNO 52: 321-328.

Hesse, G. and A. Laubert (2001). "Tinnitus-Retraining-Therapie - Indikationen und Behandlungsziele." *HNO* 49: 764-779.

Hesse, G., S. Masri, et al. (1999). Hypermotility of outer hair cells: DPOAE findings with hyperacusis patients. Proceedings of the sixth international Tinnitus Seminar. *J. Hazell. Cambridge:* 342 - 344.

Hesse, G., N. K. Rienhoff, et al. (2001). "Ergebnisse stationärer Therapie bei Patienten mit chronisch komplexem Tinnitus." *Laryngo-Rhino-Otology* 80: 503-508.

Hoke, M. and E. S. Hoke (1997). " Wandel in Diagnostik und Therapie: Auditorische reiz- und ereigniskorrelierte Potentiale und Magnetfelder in der audiologischen Diagnostik." Deutsche Gesells. *Hals-Nasen-Ohrenheilkunde:* 176-217.

Janssen, T., P. Kummer, et al. (1998). " Growth behavior of the 2 f1 - f2 distortion product otoacoustic emission in tinnitus." *J Acoust Soc Am* 103(6): 3418-30.

Jastreboff, P. J. (1990). "Phantom auditory perception (tinnitus): mechanisms of generation and perception." *Neuroscience Research* 8: 221-254.

Jastreboff, P. J. and J. W. P. Hazell (1993). " A neurophysiological approach to tinnitus: Clinical implications." *British J Audiology:* 7-17.

Jastreboff, P. J. and J. W. P. Hazell (1996). "Treatment of tinnitus based on a neurophysiological model." *Internetpräsentation:* 1-19.

Klinke, R. and N. Galley (1974). "Efferent innerration of vestibular and auditory receptors." *Physiol. Rer.* 54: 316-374.

Lauer, N. (1999). Zentral-auditive Verarbeitungsstörungen im Kindesalter - Grundlagen - Klinik - Diagnostik - Therapie. Stuttgart, *Thieme.*

Lenarz, T. (1998). Medikamentöse Therapie. Tinnitus. H. Feldmann. Stuttgart, New York, *Thieme:* 111-124.

Lenarz, T. (1999). "Tinnitus. Leitlinien der Deutschen Gesellschaft für Hals-Nasen-Ohren-Heilkunde, *Kopf- und Hals-Chirurgie.*" HNO 47: 14-18.

Liberman, M. C. (1988). " Physiology of cochlear efferent and afferent neurons: direct comparisons in the same animal." *Her Res* 34(2): 179-91.

Liberman, M. C. (1991). " Central projections of auditory-nerve fibers of differing spontaneous rate, I. Anteroventral cochlear nucleus." *J Comp Neurol* 313(2): 240-58.

Liberman, M. C. (1993). " Central projections of auditory nerve fibers of differing spontaneous rate, II. Posteroventral and dorsal cochlear nuclei." *J Comp Neurol* 327(1): 17-36.

Matschke, R. G. (1990). Untersuchungen zur Reifung der menschlichen Hörbahn. Stuttgart, *Thieme Verlag.*

Mc Kinney, C. J., J. W. P. Hazell, et al. (1999). An evaluation of the TRT method. Proceedings of the sixth international Tinnitus Seminar. *J. Hazell.* Cambrige: 99-105.

Nelting, M., H. Schaaf, et al. (1999). Katamnesis-study (1 or 2 years after in-patient treatment). Proceedings of the sixth international Tinnitus Seminar. *J. Hazell.* Cambrige: 558 - 559.

Pantev, C. (1999). Plastische Veränderungen im Hörcortex des Menschen. Vortrag auf der 2.Jahrestagung der Deutschen Gesellschaft für Audiologie München.

Pilgramm, M., R. Rychlick, et al. (1999). Tinnitus in the Federal Republik of Germany: A representative epidemiological study. Proceedings of th sixth international Tinnitus Seminar. *J. Hazell.* Cambrige: 64 -67.

Proefrock, E. and M. Hoke (1995). Contingent magnetic variation (CMV) studied with stimuli close to the hearing threshold in normal subjects and tinnitus patients. Biomagnetism: Fundamental Research and Clinical Applications. L. Deecke, C. Baumgartner, G. Stroink and S. J. Williamson. Amsterdam, *Elsevier:* 234-239.

Repik, I., N. K. Rienhoff, et al. (2000). "Ergebnisse der ambulanten Tinnitus-Retraining-Therapie." *Z Audiol* 39: 32-39.

Schaaf, H. (1999). Die kochleäre Endolymphschwankung. Retraining und Tinnitustherapie. G. Hesse. Stuttgart, New York, *Thieme:* 84-87.

Schaaf, H. and G. Hesse (1998). "TRT Tinnitus Retraining Therapie." *Psychomed* 10/3.

Schwab, B., T. Lenarz, et al. (2004). "Der Round Window μCath zur Lokaltherapie des Innenohres - Ergebnisse einer plazebokontrollierten, prospektiven Studie bei chronischem Tinnitus." *Laryngo-Rhino-Otol* 83: 164-172.

Sweetow, R. W. and M. C. Levy (1990). " Tinnitus severity scaling for diagnostic/therapeutic usage." *Hearing Instruments* 41(2): 20-21.

Zenner, H. (1994). Physiologische und biochemische Grundlagen des normalen und gestörten Gehörs. Oto-Rhino-Laryngologogie in Klinik und Praxis, Band 1 Ohr. H. H. H. Naumann, J; Herberhold, C; Kastenbauer E;. Stuttgart, New York, *Thieme:* 81-230.

Zenner, H. P. (1997). "Das Tor zu Sprache und Geist." *HNO Informationen* 3: 55-58.

Zenner, H. P. (1998). "Eine Systematik für Entstehungsmechanismen von Tinnitus." *HNO* 46: 699-711.

Zheng, J., W. Shen, et al. (2000). "Prestin is the motor protein of cochlear outer hair cells." *Nature* 405: 149-155.

Zwicker, E. u. F., H. (1990). Psychoacoustics - Facts and Models. Berlin, *Springer*.

In: Trends in Psychotherapy Research
Editor: M. E. Abelian, pp. 71-96

ISBN 1-59454-373-9
© 2006 Nova Science Publishers, Inc.

Chapter 4

CORRELATES OF SUICIDE ATTEMPTS AND COMPLETIONS AND THE CLINICIAN'S RESPONSE TO A PATIENT'S SUICIDE

*Sharon M. Valente**

Research and Education, Department of Veterans Affairs
11301 Wilshire Blvd. Rm 6235 #118R
Los Angeles, California 90073
University of Southern California
Los Angeles, California 90033-9999

ABSTRACT

A patient's death by suicide constitutes a common but rarely examined occupational hazard in psychiatry and nursing. Clinicians need to determine patients' risk for suicide to manage suicidal patients, prevent suicide, estimate stability for discharge and cope with the aftermath if their preventive efforts fail. Evaluating and differentiating suicide attempters from completers are a serious clinical challenge; miscalculation of risk and inadequate vigilance can have lethal consequences.

When preventive efforts fail, clinicians feel poorly prepared to cope with the aftermath of suicide even though bereavement is a universal human response. Losing a patient to suicide may trigger ongoing distress and/or promote the clinician's professional growth. The clinician may experience various feelings including sadness, guilt, and doubt about suicide prevention skills and may also threaten the clinician's health and work performance until tasks of grief and mourning are accomplished.

This retrospective study compared suicide attempters (SA) and completers (SC) and examined the clinician's response to the suicide of a patient. Suicide messages and distressing symptoms were examined among a matched cohort of suicide completers (SC) (n=25) and suicide attempters (SA) (n=25) at a Veterans Administration Medical Center. Although the clinicians documented and reported patients' clear, direct, and

---

* 346 N. Bowling Green Way; Los Angeles, California 90049-2818; sharon.valente@med.va.gov; 310 472-4495 (phone/fax); 310 478 3711 x49442 (bus); 310 268-4038 fax

frequent messages about suicide, patients were still able to complete their suicide. Themes within psychiatric patients' suicide messages and the number of documented suicide messages helped differentiate SA s from SCs. SCs were more likely to have a fear of being killed, hopelessness, and perceived symptom distress. SA s (28.6%) typically made a contract with staff not to commit suicide in the hospital while no SCs did so. Over 50% of the suicide messages were clear and directly referred to suicide. Indirect or unclear messages about suicide are more likely to be overlooked or discounted. In a secondary analysis of suicide messages using Leenaars' categories (1992), completers' and attempters differed in their messages about unbearable psychological pain and dissatisfaction with interpersonal relationships. The SCs who completed suicide after hospital discharge, did so within 6 weeks of discharge; during this time patients face high risk and require careful follow-up.

To examine the aftermath of suicide, primary clinicians were interviewed about their interactions with the patient and their response to the SC patient's suicide. They experienced their own grief as well as their lack of omnipotence over suicide, and the fear of their colleagues' responses. Understanding bereavement and factors influencing bereavement after suicide may help therapists process their own grief more effectively.

Key Words: Suicide, suicide messages, suicide risk, psychiatric diagnosis, bereavement after suicide

Suicide is a complex social, biological and psychological response to an intolerable life situation and not the result of a single isolated or impulsive act. It is the eighth leading cause of preventable death in the United States. Suicide is defined as an intentional, self-inflicted death. Many indicators of suicide risk have emerged from retrospective studies. Many factors including the individual's life history, experiences and relationships can contribute to suicide. Psychodynamic theory would suggest that suicide is a result of an individual's responses to intolerable psychological distress and unmet needs. When compared with general population norms (13 suicides/100,000), psychiatric patients have suicide rates that are 4-6 times higher (Litman, 1998; Maris, Berman, Maltzberger, & Yufit, 1998; Roy, 2001). Associations have been well documented among suicide, affective disorders, psychiatric disorders, chemical dependency (Maris, Berman, Maltzberger, & Yufit, 1998). However, these lists of high risk factors do not help differentiate those who attempt from those who complete suicide and they do not highlight the acute indicators of suicide risk.

Clinicians estimate suicide potential after considering a person's risk factors, suicidal ideas and plans, and observations, and history. However the ability to predict imminent suicide is currently limited. It is difficult to evaluate risk because some populations have low rates of completed suicide, research on preventing suicide is scant, and assessment guidelines do not differentiate potential attempters from completers and lack empirical testing (Maris et al., 1998; Shneidman, 2001). Empirical data verifying risk indicators such as suicide messages and symptom distress may improve evaluation and risk management (Maris et al., 1998). When patients are questioning the value of their lives, they need education and emotional support and advocacy. Shneidman suggests that suicidal impulses stem from an emotional pain called psychache, and that psychache deserves the same evaluation and treatment as physical pain (2001).

Suicide is both a stigmatized and sensitive issue and suicidal individuals represent the most stressful emergency situations for clinicians. Stigma may prompt clinicians to expand the social distance between themselves and the patient. The general public warns others of their suicide attempts but it is unclear whether psychiatric patients warn others in clear messages. No thorough analysis of suicide messages of psychiatric patients during or after hospitalization was found in the published literature. Patients who are receiving psychiatric treatment evoke considerable anxiety, fear, and guilt among clinicians when they attempt or commit suicide (Litman, 1998; Valente & Saunders, 2000; Valente, 2003).

The purpose of this paper is threefold:

1. to highlight the literature on suicide among psychiatric patients and clinician's bereavement after a patient's suicide
2. to describe a retrospective study examining correlates of suicide attempters and completers among veterans with a psychiatric diagnosis. Potential indicators of suicide risk such as suicide messages were examined. Interviews with primary clinicians explored their responses to the suicidal patients.
3. to examine interviews with clinicians after a patient's suicide. The themes from interviews of clinicians describing their response to patient's suicide are reported.

BACKGROUND AND LITERATURE REVIEW

This review examines the literature about suicide attempters and completers, selected correlates of suicide risk, and the aftermath of a patient's suicide on the clinician.

Suicide Attempters and Completers

According to Maris (Maris et al., 1998), suicide attempters and completers are overlapping populations. Attempters are those who survive a potentially fatal attempt; completers are those whose attempts end in death – so it is the outcome of the action that differentiates the populations. The overlapping group includes those attempters who subsequently become completers and end their lives by suicide. The challenge for clinical staff is to evaluate potential lethality so they can discharge to outpatient care those who are least likely to become completers. Researchers have not identified the psychological characteristics depicting the risk that differentiates attempters from completers. In one study, suicide completers tended to have previous serious suicide attempts, and have poorer social support and use multiple suicide methods (Johnsson, Ojehagen, & Traskman-Bendz, 1996). The highest risk period for suicide post-hospitalization, is within the first year or two after discharge. Research identifying correlates that differentiate serious and nearly lethal suicide attempters from completers and the aftermath of suicide can make a significant contribution to the literature (Hawton, 2001).

Although suicidal intent is the most common reason for admitting a person to a psychiatric inpatient setting, no randomized clinical trials have been conducted to explore the deterrent effect of hospitalization of high risk persons (Institute of Medicine, 2003). Threats of self harm account for a large percentage of hospital admissions for adults and geriatric populations. Typically treatment revolves around psycho pharmacy to treat psychiatric disorders and electroconvulsive therapy for moderate to high suicidal risk. Approximately 5-

6% of suicides occur during hospitalization (Institute of Medicine, 2003). Unfortunately assessment tools do not adequately determine acute suicide risk or predict when person will attempt or complete suicide.

Retrospective Review of Chart Records

Archival research uses already existing information to answer research questions (Cosby, 1993). The researcher does not actually collect the original data but analyzes these data that are part of a record or, in this case, the patient's clinical record. The retrospective review of clinical chart records is a rich source of data for examining issues related to clinical practice. These records form the basis of the information about a patient and the foundation for clinical decisions about the treatment and management of the patient. Although these data were not originally gathered for research purposes, they constitute the working document for clinicians. When staff members record information in the clinical record, they record what they deem important for the care and evaluation of the patient. Suicidal behavior is categorized as a sentinel event by the Institute of Medicine and the Surgeon General and, as such, staff members are expected to chart the details related to any suicidal comments or behavior. These clinical records have been deemed relevant and used extensively for research purposes (Allport, 1942).

Content analysis is the systematic analysis of existing documents such as archival or clinical records. In content analysis, the researcher devises a coding system that raters use to quantify the information contained in the documents (Cosby, 1993). The raters are trained to use the coding system and methods are used to verify the consistency of coding. The researcher defines categories based on the narrative texts in the clinical records. The use of archival data allows researchers to study important issues that might not be open to study by other methods. While archival methods are a valuable approach to data collection and analysis, the major problems include the difficulty of obtaining the desired records or records maybe incomplete or destroyed. In addition, the researcher cannot be sure of the completeness and accuracy of the information collected by the clinician (Cosby, 1993).

Correlates of Suicide Risk: Suicide Messages

Communication of suicidal intent is a high risk factor that has preceded 80% of completed suicides, but authorities have disagreed about whether psychiatric patients communicate their suicide risk clearly (Leenaars, 1998; Shneidman, 1998, 2001; Wolk-Wasserman, 1987). Communications include documented entries in the clinical chart about the patient's suicidal comments and behaviors and suicide notes. Many writers have conducted thematic analyses of suicide notes (Leenaars, 1988; Shneidman and Farberow, 1957). Shneidman and Farberow used content analysis to examine 717 suicide notes to understand the writer's cognition, affect, and attitudes toward life and death. In a retrospective study of 119 suicides using psychological autopsy, Robins reported that most subjects (65%) used more than one form of communication and reported their suicidal thoughts to at least 2 groups of individuals (Robbins, 1981). Although 85% of these people had recently expressed or intensified suicidal ideas, 25% of the friends and professionals who heard these threats concluded they were not genuine (Robbins, 1981). Most suicidal people warn from one to 4 others of their suicide risk, and 60-80% of older adults forewarn their health care provider before they commit suicide (Drake, Gates, Whitaker, & Cotton, 1985). Themes identified in suicidal communications include intolerable psychological pain, relationship problems, cognitive constriction (Leenaars, 1998). Some researchers argue that psychiatric patients do not give clear or understandable suicide communications but give covert communications that must be decoded (Wolk-Wasserman, 1987). Suicide messages are defined as verbal or written comments about intent to die by suicide and wishes to be dead. Despite the importance of suicidal communications as warning indicators, few researchers have examined the psychiatric patient's suicide messages.

Leenaars conducted an analysis of suicide notes and identified categories or patterns including: unbearable psychological pain, interpersonal relationship problems, inability to adjust, and cognitive constriction. From an extensive analysis of 1,200 suicide notes, Leenaars classified the themes, psychodynamics and potential differences in the messages and tested this logical, empirical and theoretical method for comparing suicide notes. Following Carnap's procedures (1959), both theoretical formulations about suicide and suicidal notes were translated into protocol sentences. Independent judges who were professional psychologists established inter-rater reliability with coefficients of concordance ranging from .57 to .88 (at the level of .05-.01 confidence). The protocol sentences differentiated actual and simulated suicide notes. Cluster analysis reduced the protocol sentences into discrete patterns.

Correlates of Suicide Risk: Symptom Distress

Suicidal patients have reported significantly more distressing physiological and psychological symptoms than non suicidal controls. Most suicide completers (70%) had diagnosed physical illnesses than suicide attempters (Beisser & Blanchette, 1967; Drake et al., 1985). Some patients may communicate their suicidal intent by reporting their distress about their physical symptoms. Chronic, serious diseases are associated with an increased risk of suicide (Hughes & Kleespies, 2001).

Correlates of Suicide Risk: Violence

Violence plays an important but poorly understood role in suicide (Freud, 1917; Hendin 1987). Beisser & Blanchette (1961) retrospectively reviewed 71 suicidal psychiatric patients' clinical records in a state hospital and concluded that isolation prompted violent assaultive patients to turn their violent tendencies on themselves. Further exploration of violence is needed to determine if it helps identify risk and differentiate attempters from completers.

AFTERMATH OF A SUICIDE

Suicidal patients are often the most stressful and frequent emergency situation facing clinicians in psychiatry. Although it is reasonable to anticipate that some high risk patients would commit suicide, the literature is on clinicians' responses to a suicide is scant (Gitlin, 1999; Kleespies et al., 1993) Suicides occur among about 1 in 5 or more patients in psychotherapy with psychiatrists or residents. Few clinicians have a foundation in their professional education to prepare them for their response to a patient's suicide (Bongar et al., 1998; Valente & Saunders, 2002). Hence, clinicians often feel unprepared for their own, often intense, grief reactions after suicide (Midence, Stanley, Gregory, & Stanley, 1996). Clinicians report that they are stunned and numb when they first hear that a patient has committed suicide and then they fear repercussions from the family and they fear the loss of respect from colleagues.

Scant research examines the clinician's reactions to a patient's suicide. Clinicians have a pivotal role not only in detecting risk of suicide and in reducing the barriers to treatment, forming an empathic alliance and offering education, treatment, and referrals. Therapeutic interventions and social support can often lessen psychiatric disorders and suicidal impulses. Regardless of experience, most clinicians are vulnerable to the aftermath of a suicide or to the disruptive impact of a patient's suicide on their belief systems, self confidence, and practice (Rae, 1998).

Clinicians may feel overburdened with guilt, responsibility, and self blame for failure to prevent suicide. Initial reactions often include shock, numbness, denial and disbelief and then a sense of depersonalization, shame, guilt, and self recriminations (Gitlin, **1999;** Worden, 1991). A patient's suicide evokes turmoil, whether the patient was new or well known. Clinicians often agonize over the details, circumstances, and meaning of the suicide and examine their personal responsibility for preventing the suicide.

Such feelings can influence the emotional quality and course of the professional's development. Consulting with supportive colleagues and supervisors, particularly those who have had a patient commit suicide is particularly helpful. Clinicians may lose confidence in their professional competence and role performance, may fear recriminations from the family and professional colleagues, and worry about the risk of legal action. As Shneidman (Shneidman, 2001) noted,

> "The person who commits suicide puts his psychological skeleton in the survivor's emotional closet – he sentences the survivor to deal with many negative feelings and, more, to become obsessed with thoughts regarding his actual or possible role in having precipitated or failed to abort the suicide (p. 30). "

Often this leads to soul searching and questions about one's competence, power to prevent suicide, and professional responsibilities. The bereaved clinician may expect to manage their own affect, clinical duties, and provide leadership but this may be complicated by personal responses to grief. Little support exists for therapists who have lost a client to suicide. It is as if the psychotherapist becomes the hidden or "invisible" mourners after a patient's suicide. However, research is scant about the grief's lasting impressions on the therapist. Clinicians can process the impact of suicide by relating a narrative to supportive colleagues or supervisors (Gitlin, 1999; Kleespies, Penk, & Forsyth, 1993). Storytelling or narratives offer a chance for reflection and healing. In the author's experience, "narratives are a dynamic process in which the self is constructed through language and telling the story to an empathic listener. In telling the story (e.g., what happened, how it happened, how I felt, what I thought and how I responded), meaning is constructed during the narration" (Valente, 2003).

Therapists have recounted their experiences, feelings, and distress when a patient committed suicide. Gitlan (1999) reports his feelings of shock, embarrassment, and distress when a patient died by suicide. He eloquently describes his fears and concerns about how his colleagues would respond. Valente (2003) describes unrealistic anger at others who had treated the patient and who had not prevented the suicide.

Theoretical Framework

The conceptual model used to examine correlates of completed and attempted suicide in this study suggests that variables (e.g., suicide messages, symptom distress) provide a significant reflection of suicide risk and emerge from theoretical models. Psychological theory suggested that communications about suicide were common, frequent and critical indicators of potential suicide. Physiological theory suggested that direct communication may be impaired among some psychiatric patients with disorders such as schizophrenia who may indirectly communicate their suicide impulses by their behavior or distress about their symptoms.

Purpose of the Study

This retrospective study compared psychiatric patients' suicide messages, symptom distress, and psychological characteristics that differentiated suicide attempters from completers and examined clinicians' response to a patient's suicide.

Hypotheses

1. In clinical records, suicide completers will have communicated more suicide messages than suicide attempters.
2. In clinical records, suicide completers will have different content in their suicide messages than attempters.
3. Suicide completers will give clear and understandable messages.
4. More suicide completers have documented reports of symptom distress than attempters.

DESIGN AND METHODS

This descriptive and comparative study of suicide attempters and completers study used a post-hoc, descriptive and comparative design to examine clinical records of completed and attempted suicides at a Veterans Affairs Health Care System in a large metropolitan area. Allport (Allport, 1942) established that the importance of personal documents and records in psychological research outweighed the fact that they were not originally collected for research purposes. Allport also argued that regardless of their defects, these records are critically important because they form the basis for clinical decisions about the patient.

The aim of the study was to compare the clinical records regarding psychological characteristics and factors of suicide completers and suicide attempters. The sample was veterans who were males with a psychiatric diagnosis and military service. Although not created for research, the clinical records serve as the foundation for clinical, social, and treatment decisions regarding the patient. One limitation with this design is that using the clinical notes as a primary source of data to indicate the prevalence/frequency of suicide messages means that the comparison reflects the recording of the suicide messages. The recording may not accurately reflect how often suicide messages were made. However, these constitute the records and data base that clinicians use to manage these patients. Although we verified the records in interviews with the primary staff assigned to these patients, this does not quantify the accuracy of recording suicide messages. In addition, clinicians who had served as primary caregivers for the patient were interviewed to verify the clinical records and to examine the patient-clinician relationship. The goal was to explore any disruptions or separations in the clinician-patient relationship, the clinicians' positive or negative feelings about the patient, and expressions that the patient felt rejected if the clinician was on leave.

A secondary analysis of the suicide messages examined the usefulness of Leenaars (1992) method of analysis for suicide notes The suicide messages of attempters and completers in the current study were examined using Leenaars' classification (See Table 4). Suicide messages from clinical records were randomly organized by the Principal Investigator who deleted identifying data. Independent raters who were blind to whether the suicide message came from a completer or attempter categorized the messages according to Leenaars' classification. The unit of analysis was a chart notation in the clinical record that typically contained short sentences quoting the patient but occasionally included long, run-on sentences without punctuation. A suicide message (e.g., "I really want to die and I don't know how to do anything") was considered in relationship to each pattern and its definition. Most messages fit under a single pattern.

A multidisciplinary judge panel of mental health experts with experience in suicidology reviewed the categorization of suicide messages under Leenaars' patterns and offered consultation on goodness of fit. When messages potentially matched two patterns, a consensus of the judges decided the best placement. Next, the messages were relabeled as attempters or completers' messages.

Interviews with Staff

Because the clinical records did not contain indications or descriptions of the staff-patient relationship, data about this variable – the clinician's perspective of the patient and separations from the patient when the clinician was on leave, the PI conducted interviews with the primary clinicians for patients who committed suicide. These interviews also provided data that verified other data reported in the clinical charts. Themes in the interviews with the primary clinicians of those who had committed suicide included responses, communication lapses, collaborative errors, and unrecognized risk.

SAMPLE

All clinical records of psychiatric patients with suicide (n=25) as a mode of death registered in the Veterans Administration from 1978-1991 were matched with suicide attempters (n=25) for age, gender, and psychiatric diagnosis. Suicide attempters had at least two previous, potentially lethal suicide attempts. Matching reduced the potential confounding effect of selected variables. After institutional approval was received, all clinical record data were coded to protect confidentiality and to blind researchers to the status of the patient (attempter or completer). Attempters were operationally defined as having two or more serious episodes of potentially lethal self destructive behavior with intent to die recorded on the clinical records. Completers were operationally defined as having a clinical record that officially recorded death by suicide. Two attempters and two completers were dropped from analysis because their clinical records had major areas of incomplete or missing information for the data collected in this study. The demographic and clinical characteristics of these cases were not significantly different from the subjects who were retained for analysis.

Table 1. Demographic Data of Suicide Completers and Attempters

Demographic Data	Category	Completers	Attempters
		Percentage	
Yearly Income	Less than 5K	73.3	62.1
Branch of Service	Army	60	57.1
Military Discharge	Honorable	95	97
Rank in Service	Private/Corporal	39.5	58.8
	Sargeant/Chief	38.9	20.6
	Captain	16.7	20.6

Demographic Data

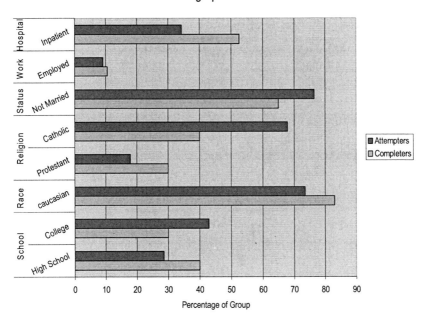

Subjects ranged in age from 26-63 years of age (Table 1). Most subjects were Catholic, married, army veterans, and unemployed. No significant group associations were found in alcohol abuse, loss of loved ones, employment, finances, and years in the military, death of a parent, or family history of suicide. No significant differences were found between completers and attempters based on sociodemographic characteristics.

Instruments

The investigator designed three data collection instruments for this study. The major instrument was a demographic and clinical characteristic tool (DCCT) that gathered demographics, hospitalizations, military history, family history, and psychiatric treatment data, suicide history (e.g., suicidal ideas, attempts, threats, and behaviors) from the medical records. Other variables on the DCCT included perceived symptom distress, staff-patient relationships, suicide messages, and violence. Suicide messages included the patient's written, verbal, or behavioral indications of helplessness, and suicide or death wishes. In the absence of a established, valid, and published method to evaluate the clarity of suicide messages, the investigator designed one 4-point likert scale to rate the clarity and understandability of the message, and a second 4-point likert scale to measure how directly the message related to suicide (See Table 5). The investigator trained research assistants (RA) who achieved 98% accuracy on abstracting data from the clinical records to the DCCT. To document inter-rater reliability on chart abstraction, RAs compared their DCCT data entry on every third chart. Data collectors were blind to whether the subject was an attempter or completer and to the study hypotheses. The Principal Investigator also verified a random 30% of RA's DCCTs with the original clinical record to check accuracy. Accuracy was also verified in semi-structured interviews with two staff members who had primary responsibility for the patient and knew the patient well.

Because many patients have large clinical records, the second instrument, a Personal Profile (PP) was compiled for each suicide completer and attempter by abstracting the clinical record data. The PP contained a synopsis of military service, mental status, current situation, history, physical examination, presenting complaints, treatment, discharge plans, medications, and problem list. The PP summarized the demographic and clinical data for each patient and was given to two independent raters who standardized the psychiatric diagnosis using DSMIIIR criteria (American Psychiatric Association, 1987). Inter-rater reliability on the major psychiatric diagnosis was 100%. Psychiatric diagnoses were standardized to eliminate the influence of the changes in DSM diagnostic changes during the study. A licensed clinical psychologist and psychiatrist who were blind to the study hypotheses and the outcomes (attempted or completed suicide) of each patient, reviewed the PP and assigned DSMIIIR (American Psychiatric Association, 1987) diagnoses to each PP. Their inter-rater reliability was $r=.98$.

A third instrument, a Semi-Structured Staff Interview Guide (SSIG) with 20 open-ended questions was designed to verify the accuracy of the clinical data on the DCCT and PPs and to examine two primary staff members' reports of relationships with the patient. Items included relationship with the patient, staff members' perceptions of the patient, impact of the patient's suicide (for completers), events leading up to the suicide, suicide messages or communications, staff members' thoughts or psychological reactions after the suicide, staff with close relationships to the patient.

The PI conducted all interviews. Staff members who knew the same patient were interviewed separately and agreed not to discuss their interview with colleagues. Data collection, training procedures, and instrument reliabilities were refined during a pilot study. Finding primary staff members who knew the patient well over a period of time was not difficult because staff members at Veterans Hospitals typically work for this agency more than 30 or 40 years.

DATA ANALYSIS

Data were obtained from clinical records of subjects in both groups, verified, and analyzed using the Statistical Package for the Social Sciences computer program (SPSS) after subjects were coded as completers or attempters. The PI analyzed the quantitative data from the clinical records using descriptive statistics, t-tests, cross tabulation, statistical cluster analysis. Alpha was established at $p<.05$. All written narrative comments regarding suicide messages, symptom distress, and violence were entered verbatim into Word, a word processing program. Following Wilson's (Wilson, 1989) procedures, we analyzed comments in words (e.g., "fear"), phrases (e.g., "Tried to hang self"), or sentences (e.g., "I just want to go to sleep and never wake up") that conveyed a unified idea (Downe-Wamboldt, 1992; Morse, 1994). These data were coded so that the researchers did not know which comments came from attempters or completers.

The data analysis team was experienced masters and doctorally prepared mental health clinicians with expertise in suicidology from nursing, psychology and social work. After the narrative data were entered in the computer and verified; a team approach to data analysis was used to increase credibility and dependability of analysis (Lincoln & Guba, 1985). All transcriptions were read independently by two researchers. Initially, substantive coding categories were developed from concepts that arose from the data. The coding categories were discussed by the research team who then reached consensus on categories. Consensual agreement was reached on the final coding.

After the suicide messages were abstracted from the clinical records and recorded on the DCCT, content analysis was used to evaluate the clarity and directness of these messages. A doctorally prepared , licensed, clinical psychologist and a suicidologist independently rated each suicide messages. To rate clarity and directness of suicide messages, each rater who was unaware of whether the message came from an attempter or completer, independently assigned a two digit score to each message. Messages were reviewed in random order. The first digit rated the clarity or ease of understanding the suicide message on a 0-3 point scale (0= no message, 1= very clear; 3= not clear); the second digit rated directness, or precision with which the message related to suicide on a 0-3 point scale. The raters initially achieved >90% agreement on the scores and resolved the discrepancies by consensus.

FINDINGS

Hypothesis 1: Suicide completers will have more documented suicide messages than suicide attempters was supported. Suicide completers had significantly more suicide messages than attempters. The mean number of suicide messages for completers was 4.727 (SD=4.63); suicide attempters had 1.914 (SD= 1.946). suicide message (t=2.7, df=25.7, p<.012). Suicide completers gave between 0 to 13 messages which ranged from messages of nonspecific distress, to threats or actions to kill the self and others; three (15%) gave no messages and were gravely disabled or confused. Common themes in these messages included: action to kill self, denies suicide, affect, hopelessness, and violence (see Table 2). Attempters gave from 0-9 suicide messages and 20% gave no messages. The few who gave no messages are of great concern and a challenge to clinicians as the documentation reflects that they apparently gave no warnings. One patient left the unit while he was wearing pajamas. He said, "I don't like this hotel much" and walked out. Another patient's only message was "I don't feel wanted by others." Significantly more completers than attempters gave highly lethal threats, reported hopelessness, and gave affective and fear of being killed messages than attempters (Table 3).

Table 2. Suicidal Themes in Suicide Messages of Completers and Attempters

Themes in Messages	Examples
Action to Kill Self	"Took one bottle of pills to kill self" "If you send me home, I"ll kill myself"
Thoughts/Wishes	"Thought of suicide for 1 ½ months after losing job" "Thought of suicide today, but no plan"
Wish/Threat to Kill Others	"I'm going to kill myself and my wife"
Affect	"I feel hopeless, angry at self; too hopeless to stay alive"
Perceived symptom distress	I've been suffering for 2 years with headaches; can't stand the pain any longer; wish I were dead"
Violent threats/behavior	"I'll be violent and don't care; if this keeps up, I'm going to hurt someone" "Threatens to blow up RNs car; no one cares"
Low Lethality Threats	"Just want to go to sleep and never wake up" no plan.
High Lethality Threats	"Thinking of blowing brains out – wants to shoot self with gun"
Denies Suicide Risk	"I went to the pier to jump off; but didn't; I'm a coward. Now, I'm not suicidal"
Will not Kill Self in Hospital	"Attempted suicide because life was shit; does not want to kill self in hospital"
Non Lethal Attempts	Slashed wrists; superficial lacerations
Lethal Attempts	Jumped from roof
No Hope	"fears he will never be well; I want to die"
Lethal Plan	"will shoot self with gun"

Adapted from Valente

Table 3.

Suicidal Themes in Messages

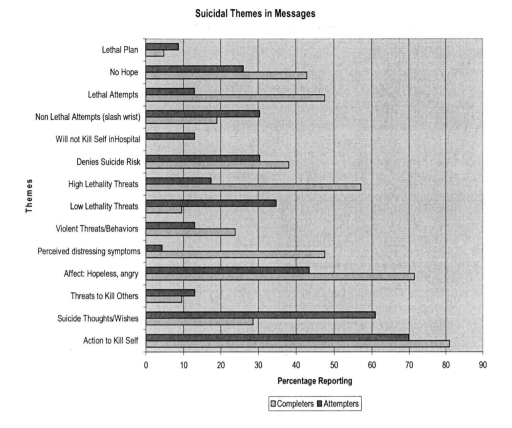

Hypothesis 2: Suicide completers will have different content to their documented suicide messages than attempters. Significantly more completers than attempters gave messages that included highly lethal threats, reported hopelessness, affect (e.g., anger, frustration) and fear of being killed (p=.05). Attempters were more likely to promise not to kill themselves during hospitalization. Three suicide completers who gave no documented suicide messages were gravely disabled and/or severely disorganized. In a secondary analysis, completers and attempters gave different themes in their messages that described unbearable psychological pain and problems and unsatisfactory interpersonal relationships but no differences emerged in the patterns of inability to adjust.

Hypothesis 3: Suicide completers will give clear and understandable messages. Half of the completers and attempters gave clear messages; 25% of these messages gave clear warning of suicide intent (see Table 5). The themes of these messages included intent to suicide, denial of suicide, non-specific distress.[1] Those who show intent to suicide, gave direct messages about self killing or suicide. One patient said, "I'm going to kill myself and my wife." Patients who deny or discount suicide do so by saying that they did not really mean

---

[1] Although it may seem contradictory to emphasize both the intent and denial of suicide, some patients communicate their intent to suicide and then subsequently deny it. Often, they argue later that they did not "mean it" but were motivated to threaten suicide to gain admission to the hospital or attention.

it when they threatened or attempted suicide. Hence their behavior is contradictory, and staff members may not know whether the original statement or behavior or the subsequent denial was more credible. For instance, one patient denied a threatened and attempted hanging by saying he did not really mean it. A few patients had no suicide messages but indicated non-specific distress with vague words or behavior. One patient said, "I want relief from physical and emotional pressure; I feel dead inside."

Table 4. A Comparison of Patterns and Examples of Completers' and Attempters' Suicide Messages

Pattern	Completers' Message	Attempters' Message
Unbearable psychological pain		
Flight from pain, other motives, emotional states. Suicide solves urgent problems of injustice	"I am depressed. I have a fear of the future; I feel down and will kill myself" "I want to be dead; sleep –never wake up I want relief from physical and psychological pressure."	I feel hopeless; fell like hurting someone. I'd be better off dead." "I feel defeated, hopeless, and I look for places to hang myself."
Problem and dissatisfactory interpersonal relationships		
Unresolved problems, needs, and frustrations are obvious and overwhelming	"I've seriously considered cutting off my hand to kill myself and make amends for causing my wife's abortion."	"I feel hopeless, wish I were dead; I set fire to my bed to burn and die; no one would care if I burned"
Inability to adjust		
Sees self as weak, inferior, unable to adapt	"I want to end it all because I can no longer handle everyday problems." I can't go on any longer	"He (e.g., I) is homosexual and is going to kill himself because he can't deal with being me. Life is garbage; I'm a black cloud – at the bottom of the heap – a failure;
Cognitive constriction		
Evidence of adult trauma; intoxicated by emotions, constricted logic and perceptions	"If you send me home, I'll kill myself." I'd be better off dead. I've plans to slit my wrists."	"I plan to overdose on heroine; I tried to slit my throat with a razor blade; I wanted to kill myself." I thought I heard a voice say, "Find a way to kill yourself."

From Valente (1994). Messages of psychiatric patients who attempted or committed suicide. Clinical Nursing Research 3(4), 316-333.

Table 4. Messages Illustrating Distressing Symptoms

Patient A:

These headaches keep getting worse. The many medications I've had don't help. Nothing helps. It makes me feel like I want to blow up. I fear I'll never get well. I see a bad end for myself. I see little hope; I have so much pain. I've been suffering with these headaches for 2 years and can't stand the pain any longer. I've felt hopeless for 14 years. Please give my things to my family.

Patient B:

I tried to jump out the window and off a building because the voices were getting to be too much. I pray someone will make them go away. I can't stand them anymore.

Table 5. Clarity and Directness of Suicide Messages

Messages (quotations)	Clarity	Directness
Want to kill myself and my wife.	1	1
I'll be violent .. if this keeps up, I'm going to hurt someone. I feel like I'm going to kill myself.	1	1
Feel hopeless, life is not worth living.	1	2
I'm going to die in a few weeks; concerned about dying.	1	2
Wants suicide status; fears he is going crazy.	2	2
I went to the pier to jump but did not have courage.	3	2

Scoring

Clarity of Suicide Intent

0 = message denies suicide, disqualifies or contradicts itself

1 = message is understandable and does not disqualify, deny or contract itself and is based on reality (e.g., I want to kill myself).

2 = message is partially or moderately unclear

3 = message is not understandable.

Directness

0 = message denies suicide, disqualifies or contradicts itself .

1 – message refers directly to suicide.

2 = message is partially or moderately direct.

3 = message is indirect and does not relate to suicide.

(e.g., these terrible nightmares will kill me).

Source: Author

Hypothesis 4. Suicide completers will have more symptom distress than attempters was supported. Significantly more suicide completers perceived they had symptom distress than attempters X^2 (1, N=55) = 115.73, p <.0007. Suicide completers (45.5%) and attempters (2.9%) reported symptom distress, which included the patient's distress about physical symptoms (e.g., headaches and pain). Examples of symptom distress were reports such as "I can't tolerate these headaches any more" or "If I don't get relief from this pain, I won't be able to go on." Staff did not document their responses to the patient's complaints such as interventions to relieve the distress and the results of the interventions.

Other Factors

Although several lists of risk factors indicate that suicidal patients have high rates of family suicide and early death of a parent, these risk factors did not characterize this sample (Bongar et al., 1998a; Bongar et al., 1998b; Maris et al., 1998). When post-hospital discharge records were examined, all the patients who died by suicide after discharge did so within six weeks after leaving the hospital. This finding suggests that need for careful weekly or monthly follow up during the high risk time after discharge.

Completers gave messages that indicated (1) cognitive rigidity; (2) self perception as a powerless victim of external events; (3) poor logic and (4) poor problem solving skills. They had more complaints of symptom distress and their messages included themes of hopelessness and fear of being killed.

Secondary Analysis of Suicide Messages

In the category of unbearable psychological pain, completers and attempters differed on hope for the future, the possibility of help and whether suicide was the only outcome or just one outcome (See Table). The completers mentioned feelings of depression, discouragement, hopelessness and fear of the future. Messages indicated a desire to be dead and escape their despair, hopelessness and fear. Completers were exhausted from suffering and tired of life. Attempters expressed some thoughts or hope that help could reduce their suicidal urges. They suggested they "would" be better off dead; this indicated suicide was a possibility and risk and not a foregone conclusion. Few patients reported they sought opportunities to share their feelings with clinicians. Most patients were in treatment prior to suicide; some hoped that the treatment would reduce their despair.

Under the category of interpersonal relations, both completers and attempters mentioned disturbed relationships and unsatisfied or frustrated needs for relationships where they felt valued. For many patients, staff members replaced their family as significant others. Without love and loving relationships, patients expressed little reason to live. Patients did not mention any problem solving approaches to improving relationships.

No differences emerged between completers and attempters in the pattern, inability to adjust" that emphasized problems handling "being me" and coping. Suicidal people saw themselves as weak or inferior and unable to overcome difficulties and saw life as bitter, hard, and hopeless. The category of cognitive constriction concerned evidence of adult trauma and control by emotions, distorted perceptions or limited, narrow reasoning.

Interviews with Primary Staff - Staff members reported their responses to the patient who committed suicide, their perspective of any primary staff members' absences and the impact on the patient, their collaborative errors, communication lapses, and reactions in the aftermath of suicide.

Responses to the Patient

Staff members recalled the patients promptly, knew them well, and could describe the patient's positive attributes and challenging behaviors. Staff members generally liked the patients and knew about the patient's dreams and wishes and family issues. In one instance, the primary staff and physician did not know the patient well because he was a new patient who was admitted on a weekend and committed suicide shortly after admission.

Collaborative Errors

Often, the different primary staff members (e.g., psychologist, social worker, nurse) had conflicting perspectives of the patient's suicide risk prior to the suicide. For one patient, the psychologist thought his risk of suicide was lowered when he expressed his anger outwardly. Although some theorists in the last century have suggested that anger outward can lessen suicide risk, currently theory suggests that anger outward and suicide risk can coexist and the patient can be a danger to self an others simultaneously. In contrast, the nurse perceived the patient as very high risk and described him as "always holding his suicide over us as a threat;

he would say, if you don't do this, then I can always kill myself". These staff members did not collaborate and compare their perspectives of the risk of this patient and did not debate his suicide risk given their different ways of viewing the data.

Communication Lapses

The LVN who was primary staff worried that he just did not act like himself before he was discharged. Typically this patient was outgoing, friendly, and socially interacted with her. She was worried that he was much more withdrawn and isolative, but she did not communicate this perception to other staff members who could have evaluated the risk of suicide before this man left the unit and killed himself. Other staff focused on discharge plans and helping this homeless patient find housing and lost sight of his high suicide risk.

Aftermath of Suicide

Primary staff engaged in ongoing self-reflection about patients who committed suicide and asked what they could have done to prevent the suicide. After an initial shock and numbness, they experienced a wide array of feelings with anger, self blame, guilt and grief predominating. In some instances, staff members were very distressed. For instance, one social worker asserted that she would never again admit a suicidal patient to the unit, although this goal is unrealistic. Most staff felt isolated and reported that other professionals ignored or avoided them in the aftermath of a suicide. Those who attended the patient's funeral reported that it was a good way to share their grief, support the family, and achieve some sense of closure.

One nurse remained distressed that after the patient's suicide in the evening, she had not received "enough" support from administration and felt overwhelmed with the responsibility of managing the patients on the unit as well as coping with the paperwork and duties after a patient's death.

Fear of repercussions was a prominent theme. Staff worried that the families might be angry or might sue them for failure to prevent suicide. They also worried about their professional reputations and they worried that colleagues might not view them as competent clinicians.

DISCUSSION

Typically, patients' documented suicide messages indicated their open, frequent, and direct comments of suicide intent and lethality. Hence, clinicians must pay serious attention to suicide communications and listen for the themes these messages. This study provides valuable data regarding the open and direct communications of suicidal intent of many patients. A higher frequency of suicide messages may suggest that this patient is on a trajectory toward ongoing suicide attempts with high lethality and more likely to become a completer. According to Benner, staff members may differ in their skill development and their ability to recognize patterns such as suicide messages that reflect suicide risk (Benner, Tanner, & Chesla, 1992)

This confirms Leenaars (Leenaars, 1988, 1998) findings that suicide messages are potent indicators of risk. While all suicide communications are important and require documentation, evaluation of both attempters and completers is essential, the data suggest that clinicians who contemplate discharging suicide attempters should exercise caution and weigh suicide messages as an important factor in estimating the risk of completed suicide after discharge and in improving the patient's connection to outpatient follow up.

Data about suicide messages offered useful indicators of suicide risk. The number of documented suicide messages were a robust indicator that differentiated suicide completers from attempters, but presence of a lethal plan did not. As the number of documented suicide messages increased, suicide risk increased. In contrast to the findings of Briere and Astrachan and Wolk Wasserman (who believed that psychiatric patients did not give clear messages of suicide, the findings of this study indicate that half of psychiatric patients give clear messages of suicide risk and these deserve serious consideration. Other patients who give clear messages of suicide risk at one time but may later contradict or deny their suicide risk, tend to confuse staff members who may reduce their surveillance because they credit the denials of suicide risk, or discount all messages because of the contradictions, and forget the ambivalence associated with suicide. As suggested by Leenaars (1988, 1998) and Drake the content of suicide messages deserves serious attention, documentation and monitoring from clinical staff (Drake et al., 1985).

The analysis of suicide messages using Leenaars' categories highlighted patterns common among completers and attempters. Differences emerged in unbearable psychological pain, when attempters gave messages of hope and tentative suicide plans, and completers expressed hopelessness. Other patterns illustrated commonalities between completers and attempters and suggest that they may be more alike than different in inability to adjust

The suicide completers demonstrated suicide messages that tended to show more cognitive rigidity (e.g., the use of restricted thinking styles characterized by lack of alternative or positive solutions to problems). Hence these findings support the work of others who found cognitive rigidity among suicide completers. Using this cognitive style, suicide completers describe themselves as powerless victims of external events, and they do not employ logic or problem solving skills (Schotte & Clum, 1987; Weishaar & Beck, 1998) Completers suggest that suicide is their only response to distressing external events and hence could benefit from cognitive behavioral interventions and improved assistance with problem solving. Suicide attempters' messages did not show such a rigid, direct link between solving problem with a solution of suicide. Although previous studies found that suicide risk is high from weeks to 2 years after psychiatric hospital discharge, the suicides of this group occurred in the first 2 months after hospital discharge. This again suggests that outpatient follow up after hospital discharge is a high priority.

Given the complexities and idiosyncrasies present in interpersonal communication, the ways that different people communicate a "suicide message" can vary. Not all people will communicate their suicide messages in the same way. However, clinical psychiatric staff have education and experience in listening and using therapeutic approaches to encourage communication. They are also educated to record the patient's communications about death wishes and suicide.

Some patients reported distress about physical symptoms such as pain, headaches, medication side effects and diverse psychological symptoms such as fear or hallucinations (e.g., the new patient has a knife and will kill me; he beat me up beforc), loss of impulse control and a feeling of going to pieces. Distress about physical symptoms were predominantly reported by patients with diagnosis of schizophrenia. Although these various symptoms were repeatedly recorded in clinical notes, the nature or type of staff response to these symptoms was not noted. Although pharmacological interventions were documented (e.g., giving a medication to relieve side effects), no psychiatric interventions were described. The clinical staff did not indicate whether they discussed the distress with the patient, intervened to relieve symptoms, or taught ways to relieve symptoms. One patient wrote several notes to the psychiatrist saying, "I have never in my life begged anyone for anything, but I'm begging you to please try to do something because I can't stand these pains in my head any longer but staff members did not report their clinical response. Headaches are listed on the problem list but no plan exists for the patient's distress. Unfortunately, the clinical emphasis on pain as the 5th vital sign emerged after this study. Symptom distress may serve as a cry for help and a warning of hopelessness or suicide (Beisser & Blanchette, 1967). According to Shneidman (Beisser & Blanchette, 1967; Shneidman, 2001), suicidal episodes are characterized by psychache, a distress in the mind. If the patient expresses this distress verbally or symptomatically, it deserves evaluation, concern and treatment. Shneidman asserts that clinicians need to address and help relieve this distress however it is displayed.

Interviews with primary staff examined whether disruptions in the staff-patient relationship existed prior to the death by suicide and explored the staff's perception of the patient. In the completed suicide group, primary staff were absent in 80% of the cases before the death, but staff disagreed about whether these absences had any important impact on the suicide. Although staff did not believe their absence was important, they perhaps did not explore the patient's vulnerability to a new loss (staff absence) in light of prior unresolved losses. One staff member thought (in retrospect) that the staff absences might have had more impact than was previously recognized.

Limitations of the Study

The data reported here need to be viewed with caution pending further research confirmation. The limits of a post-hoc, comparative study are well documented. The population examined in this study are veterans who are primarily males with combat training receiving health care treatment from the Department of Veterans Affairs. Data reflect those obtained from the clinical records which were created for the purpose of managing the patient and not for research. In some instances, staff members may have failed to document a patient's suicidal comment. The documented suicide messages reported in this study reflect what the staff members perceived as important and recorded in the clinical record. This study looked at suicides across diagnoses, it may also be useful to examine suicides within a diagnostic category.

CONCLUSIONS

Suicide messages from a retrospective study of 25 completers and a matched cohort of attempters at a Veterans affairs Medical center were examined with content analysis and Leenaars' classification method. Evaluating and differentiating suicide attempters from completers is a serious clinical challenge; miscalculation of risk can have lethal consequences. Paying serious attention to the clear, open, and direct messages of suicide and including these in risk estimation can improve management of suicide risk. Clinicians need to thoroughly consider and clarify the patterns, feelings, plans, and thoughts linked with each message. Themes within psychiatric patients' suicide messages were as important as the number of messages. Themes that helped differentiate SA s from SCs deserve serious consideration. SCs were more likely to have a fear of being killed, hopelessness, and perceived symptom distress. SA s (28.6%) typically made a contract with staff not to commit suicide in the hospital while no SCs did so. Contrary to Breier and Astrachan's (1984) findings that patients failed to communicate clear suicide message, we found that schizophrenics (50%) and depressed patients (50%) gave clear suicide messages. However, some patients in this study also later contradicted these messages by denial or discounting their suicidal thoughts. Discrepant messages about suicide may reflect ambivalence (Valente, 1994). All patients who committed suicide after discharge from the hospital did so in the first 6 weeks after discharge. Hence increased monitoring and consistent contact to connect the patient with outpatient services are needed during this vulnerable time. Supervision of suicidal patients that include suicide precautions should include vigilant attention to suicide messages and their themes (Cheung, 1992; Green & Grindel, 1996).

One of the serious questions raised by these data is that staff members reported and documented the patient's clear and open suicidal intent and yet these data did not deter some patients from completing suicide while in treatment. When staff members decreased their vigilance about suicide risk, it is unclear whether this reflected their assessment that the patient's behavior improved and suicide impulses lessened, or reflected their assessment that the suicide messages were manipulative or attention getting rather than serious.

Of interest was the suicide attempters' implications that suicide would occur if help, symptom relief, or effective treatment were not forthcoming. Attempters' tentative "if only " and If…then" messages invite therapeutic intervention. Clinicians need to reduce symptoms increase hope, and improve patient-staff collaboration and monitor patients' perceptions of hope and helplessness.

Although 50% of patients clearly express their suicide risk, clinicians must detect indirect expressions of risk (e.g., denied, discounted, or derided suicide messages). Staff members who believe a suicidal patient's denial of suicide plans run the dangerous risk of failing to validate the messages against the behavior and failing to adequately monitor risk (Bongar et al., 1998b). Patterns in suicide messages are useful indicators of risk (Leenaars, 1998). The presence of messages should alert a clinician to evaluate risk; as the number of messages increase, risk is heightened (Leenaars, 1998). Clinicians cannot afford to subscribe to the misconception that psychiatric patients do not communicate suicide risk. Clinicians who detect and explore themes in suicide messages can estimate and take measures to reduce low self esteem, provide safety, and improve problem solving skills.

Indirect, contradictory or confusing suicide messages deserve exploration and clarification. Staff members may be perplexed by patients who threaten and then deny or discount their suicide plans and staff who may be tempted to discount these messages require education about the ambivalence and risk of suicide. Danger increases when clinicians focus on part of the suicide message, particularly denial. Clinicians need to remain suspicious of the intent behind contradictory or indirect suicide messages (Leenaars, 1998; Shneidman, 2001). Staff members also need to compare notes about patients' suicide messages. Evaluation of suicide risk is most accurate when all messages are detected, documented, and themes examined.

More research and longitudinal studies are needed to evaluate suicide risk, interventions, and prevention. Greater knowledge of suicide messages will help predict increases in suicide risk and documentation of interventions. Since clinical records did not have notes about staff responses to patients' complaints of symptom distress, other data sources need to be examined to identify and evaluate these. Further study is needed to determine if the cluster and differentiating characteristics found in this study actually predict risk. Follow-up interventions need to be evaluated for potential to nurture patients through the high risk period following discharge from in-patient status. Replicating this study with a larger population in each major psychiatric disorder would help examine the themes in specific diagnostic categories.

A study examining the barriers clinicians encounter in hearing and being present when patients express suicidal messages and physical symptoms would be useful. Further examination of the clinician's role in patient education about problem solving, alternate solutions, coping strategies, and methods to reduce hopelessness and suicidal urges would be helpful.

SAMPLE PATIENT PROFILE A

Current Situation

This 58 year old Caucasian is married and resides with his wife. They have 3 children. He reports he is retired and unemployed. Navy service dates are listed. He is discharged to outpatient status.

Mental Status

Depressed, not psychotic, psychological testing shows normal intelligence, depression, and anxiety.

History, Physical Exam

Non contributory. He has had almost two decades of history of serious depression with numerous electroconvulsive therapy (ECT) treatments, manic depressive episodes, long hospitalizations, and one attempt to hang himself. His wife has reported she feared he might be violent. Trials of psychotherapy, family therapy, and family group therapy have not resulted in sustaining a recovery. He was readmitted in an immobilized state when pharmacotherapy, family therapy, and individual therapy were initiated.

Presenting Complaints

Withdrawn behavior, anxiety and increasing depression for five weeks. As depression increases, he sleeps more. He finds it difficult to explore problems relating to others and tends to project his feelings of hopelessness and disgust on others. He wants to be dead and never wake up. In response to conflict, he feels worthless and assumes the blame for family altercations. Despite his anger, he remains passive in tone and immobilized for fear that his wife will abandon him.

Treatment

Patient was placed on increasing doses of antidepressant because of his past response to this specific drug but medication was not effective. He was placed on Dalmane 30 milligrams at night which was somewhat effective in reducing sleep problems. His depression became increasingly severe and was compounded by family disruption after he told his wife of his own past infidelities at a time when her own father was dying. This drastically changed the family equilibrium by decreasing her commitment to the marriage and it increased the patient's depression. He had been suicidal numerous times and was placed on suicide status. Finally in view of his past response to ECT, he was given 12 ECT treatments in January but without substantial improvement.

Discharge Plan

He was discharged with a prescription for an antidepressant in doses increasing to 250 milligram at bedtime and Dalmane 30 mg. at bedtime. As he and wife requested, he was to be followed in outpatient psychotherapy, family group therapy, and pharmacotherapy.

Summary of Problems:

Depression (lack of energy, low mood, decreased concentration), facial acne, impotence, family conflicts, unemployed, dental disease, anger, anxiety, suicidal status.

Suicide Messages

"He has made vague reference to suicide but says he is not suicidal ...

Discouraged and feels he is getting worse...

Talking about suicide, feeling hopeless, angry at self and wife...

Tried to hang self.

Thought about suicide today but it was just a thought; I have no plan

Went to garden to try to hang myself – I used my bathrobe belt but it broke; that didn't work. I gave up...

Work: I just gave up. I couldn't even do that right...

I just want to go to sleep and never wake up...

I want relief from physical and emotional pressure ...

SAMPLE PATIENT PROFILE B

Military

Honorable Discharge from Army

Current Situation

This 62 year old unemployed Caucasian man has been treated in the same inpatient psychiatric unit for the past year and a half. He has a college degree and worked 12 years in operations. He is married and has daughters. Because placement in a nursing home was unacceptable to the patient when discharge was considered, he resides with his wife and has a live in companion to supervise his care.

Mental Status

Anxiety, compulsivity, depression, insomnia, suicidal thoughts, history of manic behavior, history of cross dressing episodes and nearly lethal suicide attempts. Low self esteem no self confidence. Psychological testing shows depression, anxiety, poor self esteem, and marked concerns about the ability to function in a satisfactory way. Evidence shows the patient is seriously troubled and frightened by the way he experiences himself at present. Self blame and worry about past and future poor performance. Impatient with present state and feels strong need to take action in a way that relieves his predicament. Deep desires for attention and affection from others. Seeks reassurance and reinforcement from others but is shy and reluctant to express these desires lest others perceive him as too demanding.

History, Physical Exam

Status, post operative from acoustic neuroma recurrent with residual cerebellar damage. Tumor, etiology uncertain, probably related to lithium carbonate use or possibly cerebellar lesion.

Presenting Complaints

Discharge in July was followed by a nearly fatal overdose and readmission. Initially, the patient was admitted because of a suicidal driving episode under bizarre circumstances with the patient being drunk and dressed in women's clothes.

Treatment

Therapy included individual, family and group therapy. Trials on medication, ECT, neuroleptics, various antidepressants all the left the patient worse or slightly better but with debilitating side effects. The optimal combination of medications provided to be Lithium Carbonate, 300 mg qid, Sinaquan, 75 mg hs, Sherry wine, 120 cc bid (recommended by neurologist), valium 2 mg bid. Course of illness throughout hospitalization has been extremely rocky. The patient frequently demonstrated worrisome behavior. He opened a car door when his wife was driving on the freeway; he talked about suicide on the top floor of the hospital building and other alarming incidents together with explicit worries about suicide. Lengthy treatment ensued over the past year and a half with pharmacologic support and there has been substantial ground gained with this man's lifelong depression. This man is a high suicide risk and has been refractory to treatment plans of ECT and pharmacology.

Discharge Plan

Patient will continue with family therapy and medications on outpatient basis.

Summary of All Problems on Problem List

Compulsivity, anxiety, depression, insomnia, s/p removal of acoustic neuroma, depression, suicidal ideas, marital conflict, confused and impulsive, dental problems, cold symptoms,, vomiting, rapid pulse due to extra pyramidal symptoms, suicidal status, anorexic, hand tremors, anger

REFERENCES

Allport, G. W. (1942). The Use Of Personal Documents In Psychological Science. *Social Science Research Counseling Bulletin, 49*(Xix), 210.

Beisser, A. R., & Blanchette, J. E. (1967). A Study Of Suicides In A Mental Hospital. *Diseases Of The Nervous System, 22*, 365-369.

Benner, P., Tanner, C., & Chesla, C. (1992). From Beginner To Expert: Gaining A Differentiated Clinical World In Critical Care Nursing. *Advances In Nursing Science. 14(3):13-28*

Bongar, B., Berman, A., Maris, R. W., Silverman, M. M., Harris, E. A., & Packman, W. (1998a). *Risk Management With Suicidal Patients.* New York: Guilford.

Busch, K.A., Fawcett ,J., & Jacobs, D.G. (2003). Clinical Correlates Of Inpatient Suicide. *Journal Of Clinical Psychiatry, 64*(1):14-9

Carnap (1959). Physical Language. In A. Aymer (Ed). Logical Positivism. New York: *Free Press*

Cosby, P.C. (1993). Methods In Behavioral Research. (5th Ed). London, England: *Mayfield* Pp. 66-69.

Cheung, P. (1992). Suicide Precautions For Psychiatric Inpatients: A Review. *Australian And New Zealand Journal Of Psychiatry, 26*(4), 592-598.

Dhossche, D.M., Meloukheia, A.M., & Chakrovorty, S. (2000). The Association Of Suicide Attempts And Co Morbid Depression And Substance Abuse In Psychiatric Consultation Patients. *General Hospital Psychiatry* 22(4), 281-8.

Douglas, J., Cooper, J., Amos, T., Webb, R., Guthrie, E., & Appleby, L. (2004). "Near-Fatal" Deliberate Self-Harm: Characteristics, Prevention And Implications For The Prevention Of Suicide. *Journal Of Affective Disorders,*79(1-3):263-8

Downe-Wamboldt. (1992). Content Analysis: Method, Applications, And Issues. *Health Care For Women International, 13*, 313-321.

Drake, R. E., Gates, C., Whitaker, A., & Cotton, P. G. (1985). Suicides Among Schizophrenics: Who Is At Risk? *Journal Of Nervous And Mental Disease, 172*, 613-617.

Fagiolini A, Kupfer DJ, Rucci P, Scott JA, Novick DM, Frank E. (2004). Hopelessness, Depression, Substance Disorder, And Suicidality--A 13-Year Community-Based Study. *Journal Of Clinical Psychiatry, 65,* 509-514.

Fawcett, J. (2004). Suicide Risk Assessment. Psychiatric Annals, 34(5), 339-342.

Freud, S. (1916./1949). Mourning And Melancholia. *In Collected Papers 4.* London: *Hogarth Press*

Gitlin, M. (1999). A Psychiatrist's Reaction To A Patient's Suicide. *American J. Psychiatry, 156*(10), 1630-1634.

Green, J. S., & Grindel, C. G. (1996). Supervision Of Suicidal Patients In Adult Inpatient Psychiatric Units In General Hospitals. *Psychiatric Services, 47*(8), 859-873.

Hawton, K. (2001). Studying Survivors Of Nearly Lethal Attempts: An Important Strategy In Suicide Research. *Suicide And Life Threatening Behavior, 32*(1 Supple), 76-84.

Hughes, D., & Kleespies, P. (2001). Suicide In The Medically Ill. *Suicide And Life Threatening Behavior, 31*(1), 48-59.

Institute Of Medicine, (2002). Reducing Suicide. *National Academies Press*

Johnsson, F. E., Ojehagen, A., & Traskman-Bendz, L. (1996). A 5-Year Follow Up Study Of Suicide Attempts. *Acta Psychiatrica Scandinavica, 93*(3), 151-157.

Kleespies, P. M., Penk, W. E., & Forsyth, J. P. (1993). The Stress Of A Patient's Suicidal Behavior During Clinical Training: Incidence, Impact, And Recovery. *Professional Psychology: Research And Practice., 24*(3), 293-303.

Kuo, W.H., Gallo, J.J., Eaton, W.W. (2004). Hopelessness, Depression, Substance Disorder, And Suicidality--A 13-Year Community-Based Study. *Social Psychiatry Psychiatric Epidemiology,*39(6):497-501.

Leenaars, A. (1988). *Suicide Notes*. New York: *Human Sciences Press.*Washington DC

Leenaars, A. (1998). Suicide Notes, Communication And Ideation. In R. W. Maris & A. Berman & J. T. Maltzberger & R. I. Yufit (Eds.), *Assessment And Prediction Of Suicide* (Pp. 337-361). New York: Guilford.

Lincoln, Y. S., & Guba, E. G. (1985). *Naturalistic Inquiry*. Newbury Park: *CA: Sage.*

Litman, R. E. (1998). Predicting And Preventing Hospital Suicides. In R. W. Maris & A. Berman & J. T. Maltzberger & R. I. Yufit (Eds.), *Assessment And Prediction Of Suicide* (Pp. 448-466). New York: *Guilford.*

Maris, R. W., Berman, A., Maltzberger, J. T., & Yufit, R. I. (1998). *Assessment And Prediction Of Suicide*. New York: *Guilford.*

Midence, G., Stanley, K., Gregory, S., & Stanley, R. (1996). The Effects Of A Patient Suicide On Nursing Staff. *Journal Of Clinical Nursing, 5*(2), 115-120.

Morse, J. M. (1994). *Critical Issues In Qualitative Research Methods*. Thousand Oaks, *CA: Sage.*

Robbins, E. (1981). *The Final Months: A Study Of The Lives Of 134 Persons Who Committed Suicide*. New York: *Oxford University Press.*

Roy, A. (2001). Consumers Of Mental Health Services. *Suicide And Life Threatening Behavior, 31*(4), 60-83.

Schotte, D. E., & Clum, G. A. (1987). Problem Solving Skills In Suicidal Psychiatric Patients. *Journal Of Consulting And Clinical Psychology, 55*(1), 49-54.

Shneidman, E. S. (1998). Conspectus Of Suicide. In R. W. Maris & A. Berman & J. T. Maltzberger & R. I. Yufit (Eds.), *Assessment And Prediction Of Suicide*. New York: *Guilford.*

Shneidman, E. S. (2001). *Comprehending Suicide*. Washington: American Psychological Association.

Shneidman, E.W. & Farberow, N. (1957). Clues To Suicide. New York: *Mcgraw Hill*

Stone, G. (1999). Suicide And Attempted Suicide. New York *Carroll & Graf*

Suominen, K., Isometsa, E., Suokas, J., Haukka, J., Achte, K., & Lonnqvist J. (2004). Completed Suicide After A Suicide Attempt: A 37-Year Follow-Up Study,161(3):562-3.

Valente, S. M. (1994). Analysis Of Suicide Messages Of Psychiatric Patients. *Clinical Nursing Research, 3*(4), 316-320.

Valente, S. M., & Saunders, J. M. (2000). Oncology Nurses' Difficulties With Suicide. *Medicine And Law, 19*(4), 793-814.

Valente, S.M. (2003). Aftermath Of A Patient's Suicide. *Perspectives In Psychiatric Care.* 39, 1, 17-22.

Weishaar, M. E., & Beck, A. T. (1998). Clinical And Cognitive Predictors Of Suicide. In R. W. Maris & A. Berman & J. T. Maltzberger & R. I. Yufit (Eds.), *Assessment And Prediction Of Suicide.* New York: *Guilford.*

Wilson, H. S. (Ed.). (1989). *The Craft Of Qualitative Analysis. In H.S. Wilson (Ed). Research In Nursing (2nd Ed).* Menlo Park, CA: *Addison Wesley.*

Wolk-Wasserman, D. (1987). Some Problems Connected With The Treatment Of Suicide Attempt Patients. *Crisis, 8,* 69-82.

Worden, J. (1991). *Grief Counseling And Grief Therapy.* New York: *Springer Pub*

Wrobleski, A. & McIntosh, J.L. (1987). Problems of suicide survivors: a survey report. *Israel Journal of Psychiatry & Related Sciences. 24(1-2):137-42..*

In: Trends in Psychotherapy Research
Editor: M. E. Abelian, pp. 97-120

ISBN 1-59454-373-9
© 2006 Nova Science Publishers, Inc.

Chapter 5

FORMERLY ADOLESCENT MOTHERHOOD AND CHILD PHYSICAL ABUSE: THE ROLE OF IDENTITY FORMATION

Tracie Olfrey Afifi[1]* and Douglas A. Brownridge[2]

[1] Department of Community Health Sciences, University of Manitoba,
Winnipeg, Canada, R3E 3N4
[2] Department of Family Social Sciences, University of Manitoba,
Winnipeg, Canada, R3T 2N2.

ABSTRACT

It is well established in the child abuse literature that children born to adolescent mothers are at a heightened risk for the perpetration of child abuse. However, little is known about the extent to which this relationship persists among those who became mothers as adolescents but are now within adulthood. Such knowledge is important since adolescence is a relatively short period in the lifecycle, but is one that sets the stage for a lifetime of parenting, including abusive parenting. Applying Erikson's theory, it is argued that impaired identity resulting from adolescent parenthood will increase the risk of child abuse. The purpose of this study is to investigate the manner in which variables that serve as proxies for identity formation, namely education, employment, and self-esteem, operate in the production of child abuse for formerly adolescent mothers (FAMs). Using a representative sample of 4,387 Canadian mothers, both descriptive and logistic regression analyses are conducted. The results demonstrate that children of FAMs are, indeed, more likely to be abused than children of non-FAMs. With few exceptions, the identity variables operate as hypothesized. However, the multivariate analyses show that identity formation alone is an insufficient explanation for the higher likelihood of child abuse for children of FAMs. Not only do the results suggest that Erikson's theory is inadequate as an explanation of the heightened risk of child abuse of children born to FAMs', but the analyses also imply that a more holistic approach is needed to fully

* Department of Community Health Sciences; PZ-430 PsycHealth Centre; 771 Bannatyne Avenue; University of Manitoba; Winnipeg, MB; Canada. R3E 3N4; Phone: (204) 787-5084; Fax: (204) 787-4972; E-mail: t_olfrey@umanitoba.ca

comprehend is phenomenon. The paper concludes with a proposed holistic framework for understanding FAMs higher likelihood of child abuse.

Research has shown that adolescent mothers are at a heightened risk for child abuse (Bolton, Laner, & Kane, 1980; Connelly & Straus, 1992; De Paul & Domenech, 2000; Miller, 1984; Straus, Gelles, & Steinmetz, 1980). It has been estimated that between 36% and 51% of all reported cases of abuse in the United States are perpetrated by mothers who are currently within adolescence or who first gave birth during that period of their lives (Bolton, 1990). However, why this relationship exists and how it evolves with time is not well understood. An examination of the course of this relationship over time, indeed, is an understudied phenomenon in the research on child abuse.

The purpose of this research is to determine if the increased likelihood of child abuse that has been found for children born to adolescent mothers continues after the mother make the transition into adulthood and, if so, to contribute to an understanding of why this is the case. To investigate this question, the risk of child physical abuse for a child born during a woman's adolescence (referred to here as formerly adolescent mothers: FAMs) will be compared to the risk of child abuse for a child born within a woman's adulthood (adult mothers).

There is no single agreed-upon definition of physical abuse among researchers. Therefore, the use of the term in the present study must be clarified. The Health Canada (2001) definition will be used. It states that physical abuse is "the deliberate application of force to any part of a child's body, which results or may result in a non-accidental injury. It may involve hitting a child a single time, or it may involve a pattern of incidents" (p. 5). This definition of physical abuse includes physical punishment, reflecting the notion that physical abuse includes a continuum of acts ranging from levels of lesser to greater severity.

The majority of empirical research has demonstrated that a positive relationship between adolescent motherhood and child abuse does exist (Benedict, White, & Cornely, 1985; Bolton & Laner, 1981; Bolton et al., 1980; Chaffin, Kelleher, & Hollenberg, 1996; Connelly & Straus, 1992; Creighton, 1985; De Paul & Domenech, 2000; Haskett, Johnson, & Miller, 1994; Herrenkohl & Herrenkohl, 1979; Miller, 1984; Schloesser, Pierpont, & Poertner, 1992; Straus et al., 1980). For example, Garcia Coll, Hoffman, Van Houten, and Oh (1987) found that adolescent mothers compared to adult mothers used more physical punishment with their children. Using child abuse potential scores, DePaul and Domenech (2000) found that risk of child abuse was significantly higher in adolescent mothers compared to adult mothers.

No studies have found a negative relationship between adolescent motherhood and child abuse. However, there are a few studies that either do not find a significant relationship between adolescent motherhood and child abuse (Cadzow, Armstrong, & Fraser, 1999; Earp & Ory, 1980; Gil, 1970; Massat, 1993; Murphy, Orkow, & Nicola, 1985), or find inconclusive results (Sherman, Evans, Boyle, Cuddy, & Norman, 1983). The inability to detect a relationship or inconclusive findings may be due to problems related to conceptualizing adolescent motherhood. It is possible that studies finding no relationship between adolescent motherhood and child abuse are confounded by a short phase of adolescence, ending at age 20. That is, child abuse resulting from the circumstances found among adolescent mothers may not manifest itself until the women are adults.

Very few researchers identify FAMs in adolescent motherhood-child abuse studies. However, when this group was included, Bolton et al. (1980) found that 36.5% of the sample of child abuse cases (n = 4,851) were perpetrated by mothers who gave birth within adolescence, including mothers currently within adolescence and FAMs. The data were collected in 1978, when only 14% of the general population in the United States were adolescents (Adams, Gullotta, & Markstorm-Adams, 1994). Similar findings emerged from a study conducted in the UK; at a time when adolescents accounted for approximately 10% of the general population in the United Kingdom, 35.9% of reported cases of child abuse were perpetrated by mothers currently within adolescence or had given birth during adolescence (Creighton, 1985).

Overall, the weight of scientific evidence suggests that adolescent motherhood is related to child abuse. However, confirming the existence of this relationship does not explain why it exists. The age of a woman when she becomes a mother may not be the only factor that contributes to her increased likelihood of child abuse. Many developmental challenges accompany the stage of adolescence that may contribute to the adolescent motherhood-child abuse relationship (Adams et al., 1994). As the process of moving from adolescence to adulthood is a developmental one, Erikson's psychosocial theory can provide a framework for understanding this process.

THEORETICAL FRAMEWORK

Adolescent mothers are within adolescence for only a short period before they move into adulthood, yet they remain parents for a lifetime. Little, however, is known about the course of the relationship between adolescent motherhood and child abuse risk over time, as these mothers move into and through a new developmental stage. Therefore, a developmental approach may help to illuminate this relationship. Erikson's (1963) stage theory may be particularly helpful, as it addresses the role of developmental crises and their resolution in personality functioning and psychological well being. Erikson proposes that the inability to resolve a developmental crisis will be carried into the next life stage and hinder the completion of future developmental tasks.

The stage in Erikson's theory that corresponds to adolescence is "identity versus role confusion." According to Erikson, if the adolescent is unable to form a healthy identity during adolescence, the resolution of future developmental tasks will be impaired. Erikson (1963) states that educational attainment, occupational goals, and beliefs about others' perceptions of oneself are fundamental for the formation of a secure identity during adolescence.

The additional task of parenting during adolescence creates role collision by forcing the development of parenting skills and responsibilities that are not typically required at this life stage. It could be argued that the untimely occurrence of motherhood within adolescence in Western industrial societies can interfere with the development of a strong identity because of the collision of roles, which, in turn, leads to role confusion. If motherhood occurs during adolescence, education and occupational goals may be interrupted and the negative perceptions of others may threaten the development of positive self-esteem. Eriksonian theory would predict that the resulting role confusion will end in crisis and create an impaired identity. This impaired identity is predicted to manifest itself in an inability to manage the demands of parenthood, hampering the mother's ability to recognize and meet the child's needs, and increasing the likelihood of child abuse.

Identity Variables

When applying Erikson's theory, education, occupational goals, and self-esteem become identity variables. It is necessary to discuss these variables in more detail to understand how they function and how they are theorized to continue to function over time.

Education

Following Erikson's theory, becoming a mother within adolescence may disrupt the attainment of educational goals and contribute to role confusion. Pregnancy during adolescence has indeed been associated with an increased likelihood of dropping out of high school (Freeman & Rickels, 1993). Freeman and Rickels (1993) compared adolescents who chose to have an abortion to adolescents who chose to continue the pregnancy. Two years later, 93% of the abortion group had completed high school compared to 69% of the delivery group.

Further, it has been found that abusing populations have lower educational attainment than non-abusing populations (Benedict et al., 1985; Cadzow et al., 1999; De Paul & Domenech, 2000; Schloesser et al., 1992). Benedict et al. (1985) found the mean completed years of education for an abusing sample to be 10.5 years. Therefore, a higher level of education is associated with a lower risk of child abuse. Education, at the very least, is hindered or delayed with the event of parenting within adolescence, thereby increasing the risk of child abuse.

With respect to FAMs, the question becomes, will the risk of child abuse evolve as the adolescent mother becomes an adult mother? Erikson's theory would lead one to argue that lower educational attainment within adolescence will impair identity formation due to role confusion and will be carried into adulthood. Since adolescent motherhood has been shown to increase the likelihood of high school drop out (Freeman & Rickels, 1993), it is reasonable to assume that educational attainment for FAMs will be lower than for adult mothers. Therefore, it can be predicted that education will continue to be relatively low for FAMs; thereby increasing their risk of child abuse for children born to adolescent mothers compared to adult mothers.

Occupational Goals

Although occupation and employment choices are not settled within adolescence, it is during this period that various choices are explored. Adolescent mothers, compared to their non-parenting counterparts, may have less opportunity to investigate and pursue occupational interests due to the additional pressures and responsibilities of parenting. The inability to explore occupational options may translate into increased unemployment or decreased employability.

A longitudinal study by Furstenberg, Brooks-Gunn, and Morgan (1987) compared adolescent mothers and non-parenting classmates. The results of the study indicate that after six years those who had become parents in adolescence were less likely to be employed.

In comparison to non-abusive populations, abusive populations tend to have considerably higher rates of unemployment (Christoffersen, 2000; Creighton, 1985; Gillham et al., 1998; Kotch & Thomas, 1986). For example, Christoffersen (2000) found that lack of vocational training and long term maternal unemployment were more likely in abusive families compared to non-abusive families. Therefore, the risk of child abuse increases with unemployment or decreased employability.

With the constrained opportunity to achieve occupational goals and explore employment choices that comes with adolescent motherhood, role confusion may develop creating an impaired identity and, thereby, increasing the risk of child abuse. On the basis of Eriksonian theory, it can be predicted that role confusion rooted in the continuing inability to explore occupational choices and form a healthy identity will continue into adulthood, along with decreased employment or employability and the continuation of heightened risk for child abuse.

Self-Esteem

According to Erikson, belief about others' perceptions of oneself influence the formation of a healthy identity. Believed perceptions of others that become internalized, labelled by C. H. Cooley as the "looking glass self" (Felson, 1993), affect our self-esteem (Bishop & Inderbitzen, 1995; Burnett, 1996; Burnett & McCrindle, 1999). Self-esteem has been defined as "the global evaluative dimension of the self" (Santrock, 1996, p. 384) and has been found to be a good indicator of identity formation (Hurlbut, McDonald Culp, Jambunathan, & Bulter, 1997).

How peers communicate their appraisals of the adolescent changes the adolescent's self-perceptions and self-esteem (Felson, 1993). Becoming a mother during adolescence may heighten a young woman's exposure and sensitivity to others' negative judgments and harm her self-esteem. The resulting negative view of herself may interfere with the development of a strong identity.

Research comparing the self-esteem of pregnant and non-pregnant adolescents has resulted in inconsistent findings. Some research has determined that there is a correlation between low self-esteem and adolescent pregnancy (Elkes & Crocitto, 1987; Held, 1981; Lineberger, 1987). The crisis of pregnancy during adolescence may lead to feeling overwhelmed, inadequate, unworthy, creating poor self-esteem (Zongher, 1977). Other research has been unable to confirm such a finding (McCullough & Scherman, 1991; Robinson & Frank, 1994).

Despite this discrepancy across studies, it has been demonstrated that adolescent females who experience many transitions, compared to those who do not experience many transitions during adolescence may develop lower self-esteem (Simmons, 1987). Motherhood during adolescence would create more transitions and place the adolescent mother at risk for lower self-esteem than non-parenting adolescents (Hurlbut et al., 1997). For example, Herrmann, Van Cleve, and Levisen (1998) found a significant drop in self-esteem for adolescent mothers between birth of the child and six months. Furthermore, low self-esteem of adolescent mothers has been found to predict an inability to understand the child's perspective, lack of empathy, unrealistic developmental expectations, and approval of corporal punishment, all of which may increase the likelihood of child abuse (Hurlbut et al., 1997).

Some empirical findings lend support to this prediction. In a representative sample of 644 families reported for child abuse, low maternal self-esteem was associated with child abuse (Brown, Cohen, Johnson, & Salzinger, 1998). Other research also confirms this relationship (Anderson & Lauderdale, 1982; Friedrich & Wheeler, 1982; Steele, 1987). It has been suggested that people who have low self-esteem may become abusive towards their children because they see the child as a reincarnation of their own "bad self" and, therefore, punishment of the child, in their eyes, becomes justified (Steele, 1997). Following Erikson, if self-esteem is low in adolescence due to an impaired identity it will continue to be low in adulthood, thereby maintaining an increased risk of child abuse among FAMs.

According to Erikson's theory, it could be predicted that the identity formation of FAMs will remain impaired and the adolescent motherhood-child abuse relationship will persist with increasing age. Children of FAMs will continue to have higher risk of child abuse than adult mothers. This research will determine if FAMs and adult mothers differ on the identity variables of education, employment, and self-esteem and, therefore, determine if impaired identity due to role confusion persists into adulthood for FAMs. Also, this research will detect if the existence of impaired identity can account for the increased risk of child abuse for children of FAMs. Erikson's theory would predict that if impaired identity formation occurs for adolescent mothers and increases the likelihood of child abuse, then the continuing impaired identity formation will account for the heightened risk of child abuse for children of FAMs'.

This research contained three hypotheses. First, it was hypothesized that children of FAMs would be more likely to be abused than children of adult mothers. Second, it was hypothesized that FAMs would score lower than adult mothers on the three measures of adolescent identity: educational attainment, employment status, and self-esteem. Finally, it was hypothesized that lower levels of education, employment status, and self-esteem would increase the likelihood of the occurrence of child abuse and these identity variables would account for the higher odds of child abuse for children of FAMs.

MATERIALS AND METHODS

The dataset used for this research was Statistic's Canada National Longitudinal Survey of Children and Youth (NLSCY) cycle three.[2] In 1998-99, approximately 32,000 families were contacted to answer a questionnaires providing information with regard to the family, household, and child. The sample was comprised of women who are biological mothers of children aged 10 to 15 years who responded to the self-completed questionnaire, from which the child abuse variable is drawn. Based on this selection, the sample size for this research was 4,387 including 4,250 adult mothers and 137 FAMs.

Measurement

Motherhood Status

Mothers were classified as either FAMs or adult mothers on the basis of their responses to an item, which asked for the mother's year of age at the birth of the target child (child responding to the self-completed questionnaire). All mothers nineteen years and younger at the time of the birth of the target child were considered FAMs. All mothers aged 22 or older at the time of birth of the target child were considered adult mothers. The three-year age

---

[2] Data used in the analysis were obtained by special agreement with Statistics Canada to access the NLSCY master file. The analyses are the sole responsibility of the authors. The opinions expressed do not represent the views of Statistics Canada.

spread between the two groups was designed to provide a clear differentiation between mothers who were adolescents when their child was born and those who had their child after they had entered adulthood.

Child Abuse

Children aged 10 to 15 years who participated in cycle three of the NLSCY were asked to answer a self-completed questionnaire in the privacy of their own homes while the interviewer waited. On this questionnaire, children were asked to state the frequency in which they are hit or threatened to be hit. [3] Frequencies were rated on a five-point scale: never, rarely, sometimes, often, and always. Children's responses to this item were collapsed to create a dichotomous variable with the categories of "yes" or "no" indicating that child abuse did or did not occur. This decision was made on the basis of a preliminary examination of the distribution of responses to this variable, which indicated that frequencies across the hitting categories were too few in number to allow reliable comparisons among these groups, particularly when they were further distributed across two categories of motherhood status.

Measures of Identity

Mothers' resolution of their adolescent identity crises (Erikson, 1963) was measured in three ways: educational attainment, employment status, and self-esteem. Maternal educational attainment is determined by mothers' responses to two questions. For descriptive analysis, the question used asked for the mother's highest level of educational attainment with categories less than high school, high school, some post secondary, and diploma or university degree. For multivariate analysis, the actual number of years of education was used.

Maternal employment status was assessed by mothers' responses to an item, which asked them to provide their current working status with categories collapsed into employed and unemployed.

According to Erikson (1963), what is critical to the formation of adolescent identity is other's perceptions of oneself. In the present study, maternal self-esteem was measured an item, which asked, "How often have you felt or behaved this way during the past week?: I felt that people disliked me." Low self-esteem was defined as feeling disliked some or a little of the time to most of the time within the past week. High self-esteem was defined as feeling disliked rarely or none of the time within the past week. For multivariate analysis, the mean days in one week they felt disliked was used.

Control Variables

Control variables for this research were number of children and marital status. Number of children has been selected because the two comparison groups consisted of women who have children in different life stages. This means women having children in adolescence have a large window of opportunity to have more children compared to women who have children later in adulthood. More children has been associated with an increased risk of child abuse and, therefore, could contribute to increased risk of abuse for FAMs. By controlling for number of children, if FAMs have more children than adult mothers any additional risk of

---

[3] Although the threat of violence is a form of psychological abuse, it has been stated that psychological abuse is embedded in all forms of child abuse and, therefore, is appropriate to be included within this study's measure of child abuse (Garbarino, Gutterman, & Seeley, 1986; Hart, Brassard, & Karlson, 1996)

increased child abuse due to having more children has been adjusted for and a better test of the theory is permitted. Number of children was measured by a variable that asked for the number of children under 17 who live in the household.

Marital status was also controlled for in this research. Marital status is one way of understanding possible living environments. If the mother is married or living common law, it is likely that support both financially and within the household is, at the very least, somewhat better than for mothers who are single, separated, divorced, or widowed. Therefore, marital status can provide a modest understanding of contributors within the household and account for possible economic and social support that is likely to decrease child abuse. Past research has found that adolescent mothers are more likely to be single (Leadbeater & Way, 2001) and that being single is associated with increased risk of child abuse (Murphey & Braner, 2000). In theory, FAMs are more likely to be single and, therefore, less supported. Controlling for marital status will account for this difference among comparison groups and allow for a more accurate test of the theory.

Marital status of the mother was determined by a question, which asked for the marital status with options collapsed into married or common law (including the living with partner) and single (including single never been married, widowed, separated, and divorced).

Methods of Data Analysis

The data analysis was conducted in two stages. To understand the differences between the comparison groups and to test hypothesis one and two, descriptive analysis techniques were used. The relationships between categorical variables were tested using cross-tabulations with chi square tests of significance. In addition to chi square tests of significance, Mann Whitney-U was also used to test the relationship between and ordinal and categorical variables. For multivariate analysis, multiple logistic regressions were used. This analysis was conducted in two phases. First, multiple logistic regression was conducted on FAMs and adult mothers separately to understand how the variables operate for each group of women. Second, a sequential analysis was used to determine the extent to which children of FAMs heightened risk of child abuse relative to children of adult mothers is accounted for by the identity and control variables.

RESULTS

Descriptive Analysis

Child Abuse by Motherhood Status

The results of the cross-tabulation of the occurrence of child abuse by motherhood status in the present study are presented in Table 1. The results have shown that, while the majority of children are not abused, 33% of children of FAMs compared to 22% of children of adult mothers were abused. Hypothesis one, in which children of FAMs compared to children of adult mothers were expected to be more likely to be abused was confirmed with these results.

Table 1. Child Abuse and Motherhood Status (%)

	Adult Mothers	FAMs
Child Abuse***		
Occurrence	22.2	32.8
Non-Occurrence	77.8	67.2

***p < .01

Identity Variables by Motherhood Status

Table 2 contains results of each identity variable cross-tabulated with motherhood status. FAMs (24%) compared to adult mothers (10%) were more likely to have less than a high school education. Furthermore, FAMs (16%, 25%, and 35% respectively) compared to adult mothers (19%, 29%, and 42% respectively) were less likely to have graduated high school, have some post secondary education or trade school, and a community college diploma or university degree. These results supported the education aspect of hypothesis two, which stated that FAMs would have less education than adult mothers.

Education is an ordinal level variable and, therefore, a Mann Whitney-U test was also used. The results indicate that the mean rank for FAMs compared to adult mothers' mean rank differed significantly (p = .00) and, therefore, the educational attainment level for each group of women was different. This finding was consistent with the results of the cross-tabulation of motherhood status by educational attainment and provided further support for the educational portion of hypothesis two.

Table 2. Identity Variables by Motherhood Status (%)

	Adult Mothers	FAMs
Education***		
Less than high school	10.4	23.9
High school	18.6	15.9
Some post secondary	29.1	25.4
Degree or diploma	41.9	34.8
Employment ***		
Unemployed	21.1	31.4
Employed	78.9	68.6
Self-Esteem		
Low	7.9	9.5
High	92.1	90.5

***p < .01

With regard to employment status, FAMs (31%) compared to adult mothers (21%) were more likely to be unemployed. This finding supported the employment portion of hypothesis two, stating that FAMs compared to adult mothers were expected to be more likely to be unemployed.

Also as expected, lower self-esteem was more predominate in FAMs (10%) compared to adult mothers (8%). Even though the direction of the relationship was consistent with the hypothesis, the self-esteem aspect of hypothesis two was not fully supported because the difference between the two groups was insignificant.

Control Variables by Motherhood Status

Table 3 contains the results of both control variables cross-tabulated with motherhood status. The number of children of FAMs and adult mother were quite similar. FAMs compared to adult mothers were only slightly more likely to have one, three, or four or more children. Adult mothers were slightly more likely to have two children compared to FAMs. However, the minor differences between the two groups of women were insignificant. According to this cross-tabulation, FAMs were not more likely to have larger families compared to adult mothers.

Table 3. Control Variables by Motherhood Status (%)

	Adult Mothers	FAMs
Number of children		
1 child	19.5	19.9
2 children	47.3	44.1
3 children	24.6	27.2
4 or more children	8.5	8.8
Marital Status***		
Single	15.1	29.9
Not Single	84.9	70.1

***p < .01

In terms of marital status, FAMs (30%) compared to adult mothers (15%) were twice as likely to be single.

Multivariate Analysis

Separate Logistic Regressions for FAMs and Adult Mothers

Table 4 provides the results of the logistic regressions on child abuse of children of FAMs and children of adult mothers taken separately. The results indicated that when adjusting for all other variables in the model, as hypothesized education was negatively associated to the abuse of children of FAMs and children of adult mothers. So, as the level of education increased the odds of child abuse decreased. However, the impact of each additional year of education was more than four times greater for FAMs. For every additional year of maternal education, the odds of abuse for a child of FAMs' were reduced by 18%. For each additional year of maternal education for adult mothers, odds of child abuse for these children were reduced by only 4%, but did not reach statistical significance. Therefore, it seems that the level of mother's education had a larger impact on the odds of child abuse for children of FAMs.

Table 4. Results of Logistic Regression of Child Abuse and Motherhood Status

Variables	Adult Mothers n = 4204 Odds Ratio	FAMs n = 137 Odds Ratio
Education	0.958	0.821*
Employment Unemployed	1.039	0.692
Employed	1.000	1.000
Self-Esteem	1.111**	1.196
Number of Children	1.035	1.521**
Marital Status Single	1.336***	1.876*
Not single	1.000	1.000
Constant	0.414**	1.426
-2 log-likelihood	4377	234
X^2	19	17

*p < .10; **p < .05; ***p < .01

With regard to the hypothesis that unemployment would lead to increased occurrence of child abuse, the direction of the relationship indicate that this was only true for adult mothers. Unemployment status for adult mothers increased the odds of child abuse by a mere 4%, but was not statistically significant. Contrary to this, unemployment status for FAMs decreased the odds of child abuse but also did not reach statistical significance.

The hypothesis that low self-esteem would increase the risk of child abuse was partially supported. Low self-esteem increased the risk of child abuse by 20% for FAMs (but did not reach statistical significance likely due to a small n) and by 11% for adult mothers. It must be stated, however, that the impact of low self-esteem for FAMs compared to adult mothers was almost twice as high, suggesting that self-esteem does play a more important role in child abuse for children of FAMs.

Having more children in the family increased the odds of child abuse for children for FAMs only. For each additional child, the odds of child abuse increased by 52% for children of FAMs. Clearly, the impact of having a large family was much higher for FAMs compared to adult mothers.

Single marital status also increased the odds of child abuse for children for both FAMs and adult mothers. Being single created 88% increased odds of child abuse for children of FAMs and a 34% increase for children of adult mothers. The impact of being single was more than two times greater for FAMs compared to adult mothers. Generally, the identity and control variables operate in a similar way for FAMs and adult mothers. However, for each comparison there was a much larger impact on the odds of child abuse for children of FAMs than children of adult mothers.

Logistic Regression for FAMs and Adult Mothers Combined

To understand the extent to which identity variables account for child abuse for children of FAMs and adult mothers, sequential logistic regressions were run. To do this, the variables were divided into two blocks, one for identity variables and one for control variables.

Table 5 contains the results of the sequential logistic regressions. The first model in table 5 provides the motherhood status variable without any controls. Consistent with the descriptive analysis, the odds of child abuse were significantly higher for children of FAMs compared to children of adult mothers. Children of FAMs have 71% higher odds of being abused than children of adult mothers.

Table 5. Results of Sequential Logistic Regression on Child Abuse

	FAMs/ Adult mothers n =4387	Identity Variables n =4341	Control Variables n =4387	Full Model n =4341
Variables	*Odds Ratio*	*Odds Ratio*	*Odds Ratio*	*Odds Ratio*
FAM/ Adult mothers				
FAMs	1.713***	1.614**	1.624***	1.550**
Adults	1.000	1.000	1.000	1.000
		BLOCK 1		BLOCK 1
			BLOCK 2	BLOCK 2
Constant	0.286***	0.586	0.236***	0.461**
-2 log-likelihood	4677	4620	4663	4610
X^2	8	21	22	31

**p < .05; ***p < .01

The difference in odds ratios of these two groups of women was statistically significant ($\underline{p}$ < .01). The second model in table 5 controls for identity variables. When controlling for identity variables, the odds of child abuse for children of FAMs compared to children of adult mothers were reduced by 10% and, although the significance of the difference was reduced, the odds ratio remained statistically significant ($\underline{p}$ < .05). The third model in table 5 includes only the control variables. When only these variables are controlled, the odds of child abuse did not decrease as much as when the identity variables were controlled. The difference between FAMs and adult mothers decreased by 9% and, of course, remained statistically significant ($\underline{p}$ < .01). The final model in table 5 is the full model containing all of the independent variables in the study. When all the variables in the model are controlled, the odds of child abuse for children of FAMs compared to children of adult mothers were reduced by 16%. In other words, controlling for all variables in the model, children of FAMs still had a 55% higher odds of child abuse compared to children of adult mothers. The results from the logistic regression determine that hypothesis three was only partially supported. While taken separately, the identity variables and control variables were important for explaining children of FAMs higher odds of child abuse; it is evident that the combination of the identity and control variables provides the greatest reduction of odds. Further, although the significance of the odds ratio was reduced from .01 to .05, it was evident that neither the identity nor the control variables fully account for children of FAMs significantly higher prevalence of child abuse.

DISCUSSION

Past research has demonstrated that adolescent mothers are at increased risk of abusing their children (Benedict et al., 1985; Chaffin et al., 1996; Creighton, 1985). The findings of the present study have demonstrated that this risk of child abuse for children of FAMs continues with time, as the adolescent mother becomes a FAM. The continuation of this relationship into adulthood highlights the importance of identifying FAMs in research.

In short, this research determines that children born to adolescent mothers continue to be at a greater risk for child abuse compared to children born to adult mothers. According to Erikson's theory, this increased risk may be attributable to poor identity formation, as reflected in mothers' levels of education, employment status, and self-esteem.

Identity Variables and Motherhood Status

Educational Attainment

On the basis of previous research on adolescent parenting populations (De Paul & Domenech, 2000; Freeman & Rickels, 1993), it was hypothesized that educational attainment would be lower among FAMs than among adult mothers. The present findings support this hypothesis. Even though women can continue their education after having a child within adolescence, their rate of progress or achievement is lower compared to women without such a disruption. The present findings suggest that completing high school is likely to be more challenging for individuals who have the responsibility of childrearing.

Erikson's theory predicts that lower levels of education will interfere with the formation of a secure identity. It was hypothesized that this situation would increase the likelihood of child abuse (Benedict et al., 1985; Cadzow et al., 1999; Schloesser et al., 1992). Lower levels of educational attainment did not have a large impact on the odds of child abuse for adult mothers. Yet, the impact of lower education on the risk of child abuse was considerably greater for children of FAMs. Each additional year of maternal education reduced of the odds of the occurrence of child abuse by 18% for children of FAMs. A possible explanation as to why education impacted the odds of child abuse for children of FAMs but not for children of adult mothers may be found within the framework of Erikson's theory. According to this theory, education may be especially important for FAMs because, according to Erikson's theory, it helps to form a secure identity and it is the ill formed identity that increases the risk of child abuse. Adult mothers' education during adolescence is not interrupted by motherhood and, consequently, the formation of a secure identity is more likely. Additional years of education for FAMs may help to increase the likely of forming a secure identity and, therefore, have a greater impact on decreasing the odds of child abuse for children born to these women.

The results of this research indicate that education accounts for some of the increased likelihood of child abuse for children of FAMs. The impact of education is great for FAMs and, therefore, it should be included in future research on FAMs and child abuse.

Employment Status

Previous research conducted in the United States has determined that adolescent mothers have high rates of unemployment (Leadbeater & Way, 2001). It was predicted that FAMs would have higher rates of unemployment than adult mothers. The present findings demonstrate that the rate of unemployment continues to be higher for FAMs than for adult mothers, supporting this hypothesis. Higher rates of unemployment for FAMs may be based on lower levels of education, inability to explore employment options, and/or decreased employability because of additional responsibilities of childrearing commencing in adolescence. It is possible that FAMs are more likely than adult mothers to decide to be stay-at-home mothers, rather than hold low quality employment positions.

Interestingly, even though statistical significance was not reached, the relationship between employment status and child abuse was different for children of FAMs and adult mothers. While being unemployed decreased the odds of child abuse for children of FAMs, it appears that employment status did not have a large impact on the odds of child abuse for children of adult mothers. Therefore, employment status may not be a relevant variable for adult mothers in terms of their likelihood to abuse their children.

Surprisingly, unemployment status of the FAMS did produce a negative relationship with child abuse for their children (but not statistically significant likely due to a small n). Such a finding should not necessarily be taken to suggest that unemployment is a desirable status for FAMs. Instead, this result may help to understand the conditions of FAMs who do work. Traditionally, a woman's responsibility was within the home attending to the household and childcare and it was the man's role to work outside the home and make financial contributions to the family (Klein & White, 1996). The modern family has deviated from this tradition, as women have entered the work force and created the situation of dual career households. Yet, even though women are in successful careers, it is common for the majority of household and childcare responsibilities to still be the responsibility of women (Lero, 1996). Therefore, the finding that employment increased the odds of child abuse may highlight the unequal distribution of household and childcare responsibilities among men and women. This, however, does not explain why the risk of child abuse for unemployed women only applies to children of FAMs.

The present findings may suggest that unemployment status decreased the odds of child abuse for children of FAMs. An explanation as to why this may be the case can be speculated. What this research is unable to determine is if the type or quality of job is a more important factor than employment status. It may be the case that FAMs hold employment positions that are not equal to those of adult mothers in terms of autonomy, creativity, and the possibility to be promoted. Therefore, it may not be employment status that provides the best prediction of child abuse, but rather, the quality of the job or how satisfied a woman is with her job.

Alternatively, if a woman is dissatisfied with her employment situation, a healthy identity formation may be more likely if she becomes unemployed and is able to securely identify herself as a mother and, thus, the abuse of her children may be less likely. Therefore, poor identity formation may still lead to the abuse of children, but it may not simply be employment status that allows for a secure identity to be formed. The results from this research suggest that more information than just employment status is needed to accurately understand the role of employment in the formation of a secure identity and its impact on child abuse.

Self-Esteem

It was predicted that FAMs would have lower self-esteem than adult mothers. According to the present findings, this does not appear to be the case; there was no difference in the self-esteem scores of the two groups. Past research on self-esteem and adolescent parenting has resulted in inconsistent findings and difficulty in understanding how self-esteem operates. Obtaining accurate measures of such aspects of personality is not an easy task, and may contribute to the inconsistency of findings.

Alternatively, it may be the case that, with time, the FAM will adjust to her role as mother and low self-esteem will increase to normative levels. Time and the acceptance of a mothering role will not increase levels of educational attainment or increase employability, but may have a positive impact on self-esteem. As a result, self-esteem may function differently than the other identity variables.

The present research demonstrates that low self-esteem is associated with child abuse. This finding is in accordance with previous research (Brown et al., 1998). Individuals with low self-esteem may create internal working models of the self as being unworthy, inadequate, and incompetent (Harter, 1998). When these feelings occur in conjunction with childrearing challenges, such as irritable children, difficult child behaviours, or simply parent-child conflict, the mother with low self-esteem may feel she is not equipped to deal with the problem. Consequently, the mother may resort to aggressive disciplinary techniques such as hitting the child, to terminate the immediate difficult childrearing situation; potentially creating a pattern of child abuse.

Interestingly, the increased odds of child abuse for children of FAMs with low self-esteem are almost two times that for children of adult mothers with low self-esteem (although statistical significance was not reached likely due to a small n). While FAMs are not more likely to have low self-esteem than adult mothers, the fact that low self-esteem may have a larger impact for FAMs suggests that different mechanisms are functioning in the two groups of women. In other words, it may be that the root or cause of low self-esteem is different for the two groups of women. For example, FAMs' low self-esteem may be directly related to their mothering role because of exposure to negative judgements of their early parenthood. Therefore, FAMs may associate poor feelings of themselves with parenting and, more specifically, their children, contributing to an increased risk of abusive parenting behaviour. It may be that adult mothers are able to separate their feelings about themselves from their feelings about their children because adult mothers' low self-esteem may be unrelated to their parenting role. Therefore, the adult mother's ability to cognitively separate her low self-esteem from parenting may be a preventative factor for this group.

To summarize the discussion of identity variables, this research demonstrates that FAMs differ from adult mothers on most identity variables. Therefore, the fundamental aspects required to form a healthy identity may be impaired for FAMs. In other words, it seems that the collision of adolescent and adult roles may result in confusion, which, in turn, precipitates impaired identity for FAMs.

Control Variables and Motherhood Status

Number of Children

The present research demonstrates that, in Canada, FAMs do not have more children than adult mothers. This result contradicts past research from the United States that finds women who give birth in adolescence have more children than women who give birth in adulthood (Connelly & Straus, 1992). This finding may suggest that it is not the number of children that differs between FAMs and adult mothers, but rather, when the children are conceived. It has been found that repeat pregnancies soon after the first birth are very high for adolescent mothers (Leadbeater & Way, 2001). Therefore, it may be that adolescent mothers have children close together in adolescence, but do not continue to give birth at this rate in adulthood. Consequently, when comparing these women later in life, FAMs and adult mothers will not differ in family size, but rather, the life stage in which they gave birth.

In this study, it was found that the number of children increases the odds of child abuse for children of FAMs. This finding partially supports previous research on child abuse and family size (Straus et al., 1980).[4] More children have been noted to increase the stress in the household and, therefore, represent a risk marker for child abuse (Kotch et al., 1995). As the number of members of the family increases, generally the resources become limited, creating a stressful environment conducive to child abuse.

According to the present findings, FAMs were not more likely than adult mothers to have more children but having more children had a much larger impact on child abuse for children of FAMs than children of adult mothers. Children of FAMs were at a 52% increased likelihood of child abuse for each additional child in the family. Since the increased odds of child abuse for children of adult mothers was very low and statistically insignificant ($p = .385$), family size did not have an impact on the risk of child abuse for these families; suggesting that adult mothers may be better equipped than FAMs to manage the demands of more children. More children in the household inevitability increases stress by requiring emotional and financial contributions for the fulfilment of the children's needs, which may be more challenging for FAMs. FAMs may have fewer effective resources to handle complex parenting circumstances created by the presence of increased numbers of children. Indeed, past research has shown that adolescent mothers are more reliant than adult mothers on physical means of discipline (Garcia Coll, Hoffman, Van Houten, & Oh, 1987; Stevens-Simon & Nelligan, 1998). Clearly, since the number of children in the household impacts FAMs, this variable is important for understanding the abuse of children of FAMs.

Marital Status

The present findings confirmed that, in Canada, FAMs are more likely than adult mothers to be single and supports previous research conducted in the United States demonstrating that adolescent mothers are less likely to be married (Leadbeater & Way, 2001). Adolescent women who become pregnant are less likely now than in previous decades to marry the father of the unborn child simply because of the pregnancy (Leadbeater & Way, 2001). In the United States in 1955, 85% of teenage women who became pregnant married the father,

---

[4] Straus (1980) suggests that the risk of child abuse increases with increasing number of children in the family up to five and then families with more that five are at a decreased level of risk. Since few families in Canada have

compared to 28% in 1992 (Moore, Miller, Glei, & Morrison, 1995). Nevertheless, a FAM who does not marry the father may have a difficult time finding an alternate partner to marry because of the challenges of developing a serious relationship while raising children, such as limited time and opportunities to meet a compatible mate willing to take on the responsibility of her children. These challenges may increase the likelihood that many FAMs will remain single.

Being single increases the odds of child abuse for children of both FAMs and adult mothers. Therefore, children of a single mother, regardless of her age, may be more likely to be abused because of the stress of being a single mother and surviving on one income compared to dual earner families. Having less income and less support may increase the odds of child abuse. However, the increased odds of child abuse were considerably higher for children of single FAMs than for children of single adult mothers. This finding may reflect a qualitative difference in single status between these two groups of women. In the present study, single status included those who were single (never married), widowed, divorced, and separated. It may be the case that adult women tend to become single mothers due to divorce or separation while FAMs may be more likely to have never been married. If this is the case, single adult mothers may be more likely to have financial contributions from their former partners. If the FAMs are divorced or separated, they also may receive financial compensation from their former husbands. However, these husbands are likely to be formerly adolescent fathers and, therefore, financial contributions are likely to be lower compared to those from adult fathers. It is also more likely that single adult mothers are more emotionally prepared for childrearing compared to single adolescents who are likely to become pregnant by accident and are dependent on others to support their child. Therefore, a qualitative difference in single status between these two groups of women may contribute to the difference in odds of child abuse.

The Odds of Child Abuse for FAMs Relative to Adult Mothers

Results of the sequential regressions provide an understanding of the impact of each group of variables on the higher odds of child abuse for children of FAMs. Not surprisingly, the risk of child abuse for children of FAMs is the strongest when no variables are controlled. When identity variables are controlled, the risk of child abuse is reduced by a small margin. When only the control variables are controlled, the higher risk of child abuse for children of FAMs is again reduced by a small margin, but to a slightly lesser extent in comparison to the identity variables. It is when both identity and control variables are added to the model that the odds of child abuse are reduced to the greatest extent. Unexpectedly, however, even when all variables in the model are included, the odds of child abuse for children of FAMs relative to adult mothers are still very high.

Drawing from Erikson's theory, identity variables should, for the most part, account for the increased likelihood of child abuse for children of FAMs; impaired identity formation due to role confusion should largely explain children of FAMs' heightened risk of child abuse. Controlling the identity variables does reduce the odds of child abuse for children of FAMs.

---

five children or more (Statistics Canada, 1996), the focus of this discussion will be restricted to families with up to five children.

The greater impact of the identity variables on the likelihood of child abuse for children of FAMs clearly demonstrates the validity of their inclusion in an explanation of the relationship between FAMs and child abuse, yet the explanatory value of these variables is very limited. The identity variables certainly do not fully account for the increased likelihood of child abuse for children of FAMs. Therefore, even though impaired identity formation appears to be greater among FAMs than adult mothers, it does not completely explain why children of FAMs are more likely to be abused. Erikson's theory offers only limited explanatory value for understanding the FAM-child abuse relationship.

The findings of the present study, therefore, suggest that Erikson's theory is inadequate as a stand-alone explanation of why children of FAMs are more likely to be abused than children of adult mothers. In a very modest capacity, identity variables aid understanding of child abuse if they are among other variables within a larger framework. The present findings suggest that a more holistic approach needs to be used to fully understand this relationship.

IMPLICATIONS

This research confirms that difficulties of adolescent motherhood continue into adulthood for FAMs and designates these women as an at-risk population. It should be clarified that being within an at-risk population does not indicate that all members of the group will fall victim to the at-risk behaviour. Therefore, being an adolescent or FAM does not inevitability mean that she will be a "bad" mother. Instead, membership to an at-risk population can help society understand who is more vulnerable and, therefore, who requires attention. This implies that FAMs comprise a special group of women requiring a special response to their needs as mothers. The ultimate goal is to supply these mothers with appropriate supports so that they will be able to provide a thriving environment for their children without exposing them to abuse.

To begin with, education is undoubtedly an important factor in the reduction of the risk of child abuse for children of FAMs. This research implies that keeping adolescent mothers in school will help to reduce their odds of child abuse later in adulthood. Therefore, programs need to be developed and maintained to enable these women to complete high school and provide them with an opportunity to continue a post secondary education. Adolescent parenting programs in Canada do exist but are not well developed or widely available.

The findings on employment have uncertain implications. This research is only able to speculate and not accurately understand and confirm why children of employed FAMs were more likely to be abused and, thus, detailed suggestions for improvement cannot be made at this time. It is likely however, that if children of FAMs experience greater odds of child abuse because of the quality of the mothers' employment, then an investment in the skills of these women needs to be made to increase their ability to find jobs that they find satisfying. Without further research on employment and child abuse for children of FAMs compared to children of adult mothers, such changes can only be viewed as suggestions in preliminary stages of development.

The implications of the findings on self-esteem were also difficult to interpret.

Recall that there is little difference between FAMs and adult mothers levels of self-esteem. Based on the possibility that this finding could be due to a poor measure of self-esteem, as a cautionary step, this variable should still be included in future investigations of the relationship between FAMs and child abuse. Moreover, this research demonstrates that low self-esteem increased the odds of child abuse. Increasing levels of self-esteem and positive feelings of self-worth are likely to reduce the risk of child abuse. A program that encourages the development of parenting skills, coping strategies, creates a support network, and validates the importance of their parenting role may contribute to the increase of self-esteem and, consequently, have positive ramifications on the reduction of child abuse.

The control variables in this research also contribute to our understanding of child abuse for children of FAMs and have implications. Even though FAMs according to this research were not more likely to have more children than adult mothers, they seem to be less well equipped to handle more children. The implication of this finding is that FAMs need to be taught more effective parenting skills and coping strategies to handle the complexity of raising more than one child. Also, as a preventative measure, adolescent mothers should be informed of the stressors of having additional children.

Single marital status increased the odds of child abuse significantly more for children of FAMs compared to children of adult mothers. According to this research, adult mothers compared to FAMs seem to be better at handling childrearing without a partner. Therefore, efforts need to be made to equip FAMs with the means of more effective parenting skills to increase their ability to raise children in the absence of a partner.

Viewing these implications collectively provides an initial sketch of some elements that need to be included in a proactive program focused on the prevention of child abuse by FAMs in Canada. It is very apparent, however, that more research is needed to determine what accounts for the remaining unexplained risk of child abuse for children of FAMs relative to children of adult mothers. Such research needs to include a more holistic framework for analysis that can encompass the variables identified in this research, yet include other variables that will account for more of the risk of child abuse for children of FAMs.

A PROPOSED HOLISTIC APPROACH

The contexts of the ecological model include the broader context, immediate interaction context, and developmental-psychological context (Belsky, 1993). It is argued that the variables within all contexts of the ecological model and the interactions of these variables can predict child abuse. The benefit of the multiple domains of the model is that they can incorporate and become adapted to many living circumstances. The ecological model can be applied to FAMs illuminating the sociocultural context to which these families belong.

Based on gains from the present research, it has been proven that variables of education, employment, self-esteem, number of children, and marital status should be included in the ecological framework, as well as the inclusion of other variables. Variables can be organized into each context of the ecological model creating a framework to study FAMs and child abuse. The variables discussed in the holistic approach is not an exhaustive list of all the important variables to consider, but provides future direction for research on FAMs and child abuse from an ecological perspective.

Within the broader context are demographic variables as well as variables incorporating aspects of society, culture, and ethnicity. Based on the present research, number of children or family size should be included in this context. In addition to these variables, past research has identified income as an important component for understanding the heightened risk of child abuse for FAMs. Many studies have determined that low-income families have higher rates of child abuse (Brown et al., 1998; Gelles, 1989). Adolescent mothers tend to have very low income because of limited education and employment (Cadzow et al., 1999; De Paul & Domenech, 2000) and, therefore, income may be a useful variable in FAM-child abuse research.

Another variable that may be useful in future research on adolescent motherhood and child abuse is ethnicity. In Canada, the rate of adolescent pregnancy is four times higher among Aboriginal teens compared to non-Aboriginal teens (Health Canada, 1999). Similarly, in the United States, African Americans teens give birth four times the rate of Caucasian teens (National Center for Health Statistics (NCHS), 1993). As well, childrearing practices can be influenced by ethnic beliefs and, therefore, the inclusion of this variable in future research may contribute to our understanding of why some women abuse and others do not.

Within the immediate context is marital status, which in this research is a loose measure of social support. Even though these variables may be related, ideally they should be studied separately. This research has found that marital status has some explanatory power for understanding the increased risk of child abuse for children of FAMs and, therefore, should be included in future models. In addition to the support of a partner, other support networks should also be investigated. Past research has found that low perception of social support has placed young adolescents at risk for child abuse (Haskett et al., 1994). Support networks may function differently for adolescent and adult mothers and, therefore, should be included in future models. Along with marital status and social support is parenting style. Parenting behaviours associated with increased risk of child abuse are commonly found to be typical of adolescent mothers (Baranowski, Schilmoeller, & Higgins, 1990; Garcia Coll et al., 1987; Luster & Rhoades, 1989; Stevens-Simon & Nelligan, 1998).

The developmental-psychological context includes education, employment, and self-esteem, which have proven in this research to contribute to some degree to the understanding of the increased likelihood of child abuse for FAMs. As well as the aforementioned identity variables, maternal health and alcohol abuse could be added to the variables within the developmental-psychological context. Past research has demonstrated that health problems are associated with child abuse (Lahey, Conger, Atkeson, & Treiber, 1984). Adolescent mothers may be at a greater risk for health problems due to the competing nutritional needs of the still growing mother and fetus, resulting in birth complications for the child and stunted growth for the adolescent (Hechtman, 1989). If maternal health problems persist for FAMs this variable may contribute to the increased risk of child abuse. Previous research has determined that alcohol abuse may contribute to increased likelihood of child abuse (Tarter, Hegedus, Winsten, & Alterman, 1984). Since this variable has been useful in the prediction of child abuse it may also be useful in determining if alcohol consumption is different for FAMs and adult mothers and, as a consequence, increases the risk of child abuse.

In conclusion, this research has identified a new perspective on the study of adolescent motherhood and child abuse. We now know that the risk of child abuse does continue into adulthood for women who give birth during adolescence. Ideally, the present research will stimulate others to see the importance of the issue of FAMs and child abuse. Giving birth within adolescence does not inevitably create unfit mothers or the occurrence of child abuse. However, children born to these women have a greater risk of being abused and, therefore, it is our hope that this research will contribute to the knowledge base needed to support these women so they are able to raise their children in a thriving environment.

REFERENCES

Adams, G. R., Gullotta, T. P., & Markstorm-Adams, C. (1994). *Adolescent life experiences* (third ed.). Pacific Grove, CA: Brooks/Cole Publishing Company.

Anderson, S. C., & Lauderdale, M. L. (1982). Characteristics of abusive parents: A look at self-esteem. *Child Abuse & Neglect, 6,* 285-293.

Baranowski, M. D., Schilmoeller, G. L., & Higgins, B. S. (1990). Parenting attitudes of adolescent and older mothers. *Adolescence, 25* (100), 781-790.

Belsky, J. (1993). Etiology of child maltreatment: A developmental-ecological analysis. *Psychological Bulletin, 114*(3), 413-434.

Benedict, M. I., White, R. B., & Cornely, D. A. (1985). Maternal perinatal risk factors and child abuse. *Child Abuse & Neglect, 9,* 217-224.

Bishop, J. A., & Inderbitzen, H. M. (1995). Peer acceptance and friendship: An investigation of their relation to self-esteem. *Journal of Early Adolescence, 15* (4), 476-490.

Bolton, F. G. (1990). The risk of child maltreatment in adolescent parenting. *Advances in Adolescent Mental Health, 4*, 223-237.

Bolton, F. G., & Laner, R. H. (1981). Maternal maturity and maltreatment. *Journal of Family Issues, 2* (4), 485-508.

Bolton, F. G., Laner, R. H., & Kane, S. P. (1980). Child maltreatment risk among adolescent mothers: A study of reported cases. *American Journal of Orthopsychiatry, 50* (3), 489-504.

Brown, J., Cohen, P., Johnson, J. G., & Salzinger, S. (1998). A longitudinal analysis of risk factors for child maltreatment: Findings of a 17-year prospective study of officially recorded and self-reported child abuse and neglect. *Child Abuse & Neglect, 22* (11), 1065-1078.

Burnett, P. C. (1996). Children's self-talk and significant others' positive and negative statements. *Educational Psychology, 16,* 57-67.

Burnett, P. C., & McCrindle, A. R. (1999). The relationship between significant others' positive and negative statements, self-talk, and self-esteem. *Child Study Journal, 29* (1), 39-49.

Cadzow, S. P., Armstrong, K. L., & Fraser, J. A. (1999). Stressed parents with infants: Reassessing physical abuse risk factors. *Child Abuse & Neglect, 23* (9), 845-853.

Chaffin, M., Kelleher, K., & Hollenberg, J. (1996). Onset of physical abuse and neglect: Psychiatric, substance abuse, and social risk factors from prospective community data. *Child Abuse & Neglect, 20* (3), 191-203.

Christoffersen, M. N. (2000). Growing up with unemployment: A study of parental unemployment and children's risk of abuse and neglect based on national longitudinal 1973 birth cohorts in Denmark. *Childhood: A Global Journal of Child Research, 7* (4), 421-438.

Connelly, C. D., & Straus, M. A. (1992). Mother's age and risk for physical abuse. *Child Abuse & Neglect, 16,* 709-718.

Creighton, S. J. (1985). An epidemiological study of abused children and their families in the United Kingdom between 1977 and 1982. *Child Abuse & Neglect, 9,* 441-448.

De Paul, J., & Domenech, L. (2000). Childhood history of abuse and child abuse potential in adolescent mothers: A longitudinal study. *Child Abuse & Neglect, 24* (5), 701-713.

Earp, J. A., & Ory, M., G. (1980). The influence of early parenting on child maltreatment. *Child Abuse & Neglect, 4,* 237-245.

Elkes, B. H., & Crocitto, J. A. (1987). Self-concept of pregnant adolescents: A case study. *Journal of Humanistic Education and Development, 25,* 122-135.

Erikson, E. H. (1963). *Childhood and Society* (second ed.). New York, NY: W. W. Norton & Company, Inc.

Felson, R. B. (1993). The (somewhat) social self: A developmental affect self-appraisals. In J. Suls (Ed.), *Psychological perspectives on the self* (Vol. 4, pp. 1-26). Hillsdale, NJ: Erlbaum.

Freeman, E. W., & Rickels, K. (1993). *Early Childbearing.* Newbury Park, CA: Sage Publications.

Friedrich, W. N., & Wheeler, K. K. (1982). The abusing parent revisited: A decade of psychological research. *Journal of Nervous and Mental Disease, 10,* 577-587.

Furstenberg, F. F., Brooks-Gunn, J., & Morgan, P. S. (1987). *Adolescent mothers in later life.* New York, NY: Cambridge University Press.

Garbarino, J., Gutterman, E., & Seeley, J. (1986). *The psychologically battered child.* San Francisco, CA: Jossey-Bass.

Garcia Coll, C. T., Hoffman, J., Van Houten, L. J., & Oh, W. (1987). The social context of teenage childbearing: Effects on the infant's care-giving environment. *Journal of Youth and Adolescence, 16* (4), 345-360.

Gelles, R. J. (1989). Child abuse and violence in single-parent families: Parent absence and economic deprivation. *American Journal of Orthopsychiatry, 46,* 492-501.

Gil, D. G. (1970). *Violence against children: physical child abuse in the United States.* Cambridge, MA: Harvard University Press.

Gillham, B., Tanner, G., Cheyne, B., Freeman, I., Rooney, M., & Lambie, A. (1998). Unemployment rates, single parent density, and indices of child poverty: Their relationships to different categories of child abuse and neglect. *Child Abuse & Neglect, 22* (2), 79-90.

Hart, S. N., Brassard, M. R., & Karlson, H. C. (1996). Psychological maltreatment. In L. Briere, J. Berliner, J. A. Bulkley, C. Jenny, & T. Reid (Eds.), *The APSAC handbook on child maltreatment* (pp. 72-89). Thousand Oaks, CA: Sage Publications.

Harter, S. (1998). The development of self-representations. In W. Damon, I. E. Sigel, & K. A. Renniger (Eds.), *Handbook of child psychology* (5th ed., Vol. 4, pp. 553-617). New York, NY: Wiley.

Haskett, M., E., Johnson, C., A., & Miller, J., W. (1994). Individual differences in risk of child abuse by adolescent mothers: Assessment in the perinatal period. *Journal of Child Psychology, 35* (3), 461-476.

Health Canada. (1999). *A second diagnostic on the health of First Nations and Inuit people in Canada.* Ottawa, ON.

Health Canada. (2001). A conceptual and epidemiological framework for child maltreatment surveillance, *Child Maltreatment Section* (pp. 79). Ottawa, ON.

Hechtman, L. (1989). Teenage mothers and their children: risks and problems: A review. *Canadian Journal of Psychiatry, 34,* 569-575.

Held, L. (1981). Self-esteem and social network of the young pregnant teenager. *Adolescence, 16,* 905-912.

Herrenkohl, E. C., & Herrenkohl, R. C. (1979). A comparison of abused children and their nonabused siblings. *Journal of American Academy of Child and Adolescent Psychiatry,* 18, 260-296.

Herrmann, M. M., Van Cleve, L., & Levisen, L. (1998). Parenting competence, social support, and self-esteem in teen mothers case managed by public health nurses. *Public Health Nursing, 15* (6), 432-439.

Hurlbut, N. L., McDonald Culp, A., Jambunathan, S., & Bulter, P. (1997). Adolescent mothers' self-esteem and role identity and their relationship to parenting skills knowledge. *Adolescence, 32* (127), 639-654.

Klein, D. M., & White, J. M. (1996). *Family Theories.* Thousand Oaks, CA: Sage Publications.

Kotch, J. B., Browne, D. C., Ringwalt, C. L., Stewart, P. W., Ruina, E., Holt, K., Lowman, B., & Jung, J. W. (1995). Risk of child abuse or neglect in a cohort of low-income children. *Child Abuse & Neglect, 19,* 1115-1128.

Kotch, J. B., & Thomas, L. P. (1986). Family and social factors associated with substantiation of child abuse and neglect reports. *Journal of Family Violence, 1* (2), 167-179.

Lahey, B. B., Conger, R. D., Atkeson, B. M., & Treiber, F. A. (1984). Parenting behaviors and emotional status of physically abusive mothers. *Journal of Consulting and Clinical Psychology, 52,* 1062-1071.

Leadbeater, B. J. R., & Way, N. (2001). *Growing up fast.* Mahwah, NJ: Lawrence Erlbaum Associates, Inc., Publishers.

Lero, D. S. (1996). Dual-Earner Families. In M. Lynn (Ed.), *Voices: Essays on Canadian families* (pp. 19-53). Toronto, ON: Nelson Canada.

Lineberger, M. R. (1987). Pregnant adolescents attending prenatal parent education classes: Self-concept, anxiety, and depression levels. *Adolescence, 22,* 179-193.

Luster, T., & Rhoades, K. (1989). The relation between child-rearing beliefs and the home environment in a sample of adolescent mothers. *Family Relations, 38,* 317-322.

Massat, C. R. (1993). Is older better? Adolescent parenthood and maltreatment. *Child Welfare, 74*(2), 325-336.

McCullough, M., & Scherman, A. (1991). Adolescent pregnancy: Contributing factors and strategies for prevention. *Adolescence, 26,* 809-816.

Miller, S. H. (1984). The relationship between adolescent childbearing and child maltreatment. *Child Welfare, 63* (6), 553-557.

Moore, K. A., Miller, B. C., Glei, D., & Morrison, D. R. (1995). *Adolescent sex, contraception, and childbearing: A review of recent research.* Washington, DC: Child Trends.

Murphey, D. A., & Braner, M. (2000). Linking child maltreatment retrospectively to birth and home visit records: An initial examination. *Child Welfare, 79* (6), 711-729.

Murphy, S., Orkow, B., & Nicola, R. M. (1985). Prenatal prediction of child abuse and neglect: a prospective study. *Child Abuse & Neglect, 9,* 225-235.

National Center for Health Statistics (NCHS). (1993). Advance report on final natality statistics. *Supplement to the Monthly Vital Statistics Report, 41* (9).

Robinson, R. B., & Frank, D. I. (1994). The relation between self-esteem, sexual activity, and pregnancy. *Adolescence, 29,* 27-36.

Santrock, J. W. (1996). *Child Development* (second ed.). Dubuque, IA: Brown & Brenchmark Publishers.

Schloesser, P., Pierpont, J., & Poertner, J. (1992). Active surveillance of child abuse fatalities. *Child Abuse & Neglect, 16,* 3-10.

Sherman, J. K., Evans, E., Boyle, M. H., Cuddy, L. J., & Norman, G. R. (1983). Maternal and infant characteristics in abuse: A case control study. *The Journal of Family Practice, 16* (2), 289-293.

Simmons, R. G. (1987). Self-esteem in adolescence. In T. Honess & K. Yardley (Eds.), *Self and identity: Perspectives across the lifespan* (pp. 172-192). New York, NY: Routledge & Kegan Paul.

Statistics Canada. (1996) *Census families in private households by number of persons, 1971-1996 censuses, Canada.* Retrieved August 27, 2002, from Statistics Canada web site: http://www.statcan.ca/english/pgdb/people/families/famil50a.html.

Steele, B. F. (1987). Psychodynamic factors in child abuse. In R. E. Helfer & C. H. Kempe (Eds.), *The battered child* (fourth ed., pp. 81-117). Chicago, IL: University of Chicago Press.

Steele, B. F. (1997). Psychodynamic and biological factors in child maltreatment. In M. E. Helfer & R. S. Kempe, & R. D. Krugman (Eds.), *The battered child* (pp. 73-103). Chicago, IL: The University of Chicago Press.

Stevens-Simon, C., & Nelligan, D. (1998). Strategies for identifying and treating adolescents at risk for maltreating their children. *Aggression and Violent Behavior, 3* (2), 197-217.

Straus, M. A., Gelles, R. J., & Steinmetz, S. K. (1980). *Behind closed doors: Violence in the American family* (1st -- ed.). Garden City, NY: Anchor Press/Doubleday.

Tarter, R. E., Hegedus, A. M., Winsten, N. E., & Alterman, A. I. (1984). Neuropsychological, personality, and familial characteristics of physically abused delinquents. *American Academy of Child Psychiatry,* 668-674.

Zongher, C. E. (1977). The self concept of pregnant adolescent girls. *Adolescence, 12,* 477-488.

In: Trends in Psychotherapy Research
Editor: M. E. Abelian, pp. 121-140

ISBN 1-59454-373-9
© 2006 Nova Science Publishers, Inc.

Chapter 6

PULL YOURSELF UP: FOSTERING POSITIVE YOUTH DEVELOPMENT ON AN ADOLESCENT SUBSTANCE ABUSE TREATMENT UNIT

Ralph J. Wood[1], Judy C. Drolet[2], Angela Robbins-Wood[1, 3] and Keri Diez[1,4]

[1] Department of Kinesiology and Health Studies;
SLU 10845 Hammond, LA 70402; e-mail: rwood@selu.edu
Ph: 985-549-2131; Fax: 985- 549-5119
[2] Mailcode 4632; Department of Health Education and Recreation
Southern Illinois University-Carbondale
Carbondale, IL 62901; e-mail: jdrolet@selu.edu; Ph: 618-453-2777
[3] Department of Human Development
SLU 10845; Hammond, LA 70402
Ph: 985-549-2131; Fax: 985- 549-5119
[4] e-mail: kdiez@selu.edu; Ph: 985-549-3800; Fax: 985- 549-5119

ABSTRACT

Every year thousands of youth participate in residential substance abuse treatment. The purpose of this study was to analyze the process of substance abuse treatment at the Generations Program and determine if the process of treatment was consistent with the constructs of the Positive Youth Development Model. A qualitative case study design was used for this study. A multi-method data collection approach was used for this case study including, field observations, interviews, and document analysis. Data analysis was an on-going process. Analysis began with construction of computer files of each interview and observation. Each file was reviewed and memos were written ranging from marginal notes to several paragraphs. These memos were used to generate additional interview questions. Data were compiled and reviewed; a case study record was constructed. A constant-comparative process was used to analyze all data. Analysis of the treatment process revealed the primary goal of treatment was to assist youth develop a belief in their ability to remain alcohol and drug free. This goal was achieved through the use peer support network, the development of self-control, and acquisition of treatment knowledge. Consistency was found between the process of substance abuse treatment and the Positive Youth Development Model. The content and process of substance abuse treatment at Generations Youth Program includes a number of components and strategies that provide the clients an opportunity to meet their basic human needs. Clients have the opportunity to develop a variety of competencies that are essential to healthy development. The Youth Development Model provides a unique framework for the delivery of primary, secondary, and tertiary prevention services to substance abusing adolescents. Specifically, this framework focuses on developing fully functioning adolescents prepared not only for sobriety, but also for complete living.

INTRODUCTION

Substance use and abuse is a major problem confronting adolescents (Denton & Kampfe, 1994). Adolescents who develop problems due to use and abuse of substances frequently need substance abuse treatment (USDHHS, 1995). The Substance Abuse and Mental Health Services Administration's Treatment Episode Data Set reveals over 650,000 youth participated in drug and alcohol treatment services between 1992 and 1999. (SAMHSA, 1999). The 1997 Uniform Facilities Data Set Survey reported the number of adolescents (individuals under the age of 18) in treatment for substance abuse problems had doubled.

THE PROCESS OF SUBSTANCE ABUSE TREATMENT

Historically, adult substance abuse treatment programming has served as the model for adolescent drug and alcohol treatment programs, however the needs of the substance abusing adolescents differ, from those of their adult counterparts (Kaminer, 1991; Newcomb & Bentler, 1989; Ralph & McMenamy, 1996; SAMHSA, 1993; NIH, 1999). Successful adolescent treatment must address not only substance use, but also developmental factors (Kaminer, 1991; SAMHSA, 1993; NIH, 1999). Due to the multiple problems facing adolescent substance abusers, a full range of comprehensive, integrated services must be available (SAMHSA, 1993; NIH, 1999).

Adolescent substance abuse treatment is a continuum of care. The components and methods of adolescent substance abuse treatment vary in name from program to program (DHHS,1999). Due to the early onset of substance use and abuse, frequently the focus of adolescent treatment is not rehabilitation (to return the individual to successful, independent functioning) but habilitation (assisting the individual attain a level of functioning previously unattained). One of the primary focuses of adolescent substance abuse treatment is the development of independent living skills (SAMHSA, 1993). The primary goal of habilitation can only be accomplished through developing skills and behaviors that foster resiliency, the process of successfully coping with chaotic, difficult, or challenging life events (Bernard, 1993, Richardson, Neiger, Jensen, & Kumpher, 1990, Werner, 1989). Through successful coping, a resilient individual builds additional coping and protective skills leading to successful youth development.

A short list of skills and competencies contributing to successful youth development include the ability to set goals, clearly communicate ideas, thoughts, and feelings, manage and cope with stressful life events, make informed decisions, develop bonds to family, school, and community, and understanding factors that contribute to life long health and vision for the future (Bernard, 1993; Fetro & Drolet, 2000;Werner, 1989). To enhance the adoption of these skills a framework is needed to serve as a road map for practitioners and recipients. The Youth Development Model provides such a framework - one that identifies basic human needs as well as skills and competencies to meet these needs.

Youth Development Model

The Youth Development Model provides a framework for developing basic personal competencies for youth. This model proposes that all youth are engaged in an on-going process of growth. This process includes attempts to meet basic personal and social needs, including a sense of security and safety, a sense of belonging and group membership, a sense of self-worth and contributing, a sense of closeness and relationships, a sense of independence, a sense of competence and mastery, and a sense of self-awareness (Pittman & Cahill, 1992). How young people meet their basic needs is dependent upon people, places, and possibilities (Pittman, O'Brien, & Kimball, 1993). Youth who lack basic competencies and skills will attempt to meet these needs in the form of behaviors that put them at-risk (Pittman et al, 1993; Pittman, 1991).

To successfully meet the demands of adolescence, youth must possess a wide array of skills and competencies that allow them to function and contribute in their daily lives (Pittman et al, 1993). The Youth Development Model provides a philosophy and framework that facilitates development of competencies in 5 specific areas: Health and Physical competence, Personal and Social competence, Cognitive and Creative competence, Vocational competence and Citizenship (Pittman et al, 1993; Pittman & Cahill, 1992).

This model is founded on a conceptual shift in prevention planning, a shift from thinking that youth risk behaviors are barriers to positive youth development, to thinking instead that youth development is the best approach to preventing at-risk behaviors (Pittman & Cahill,1992). The end product of this approach is fully-prepared adolescents, rather than the unrealistic goal of problem - free adolescents (Pittman & Cahill, 1992).

Purpose of the Study

While alcohol and drug treatment programs have existed for years, little qualitative research has examined the practices and procedures they involve. The purpose of this study was to describe the goal and process of substance abuse treatment at one adolescent treatment center, the Generations Youth Program, and determine if the process was consistent with the Youth Development Model. To the authors' knowledge this is the first study to explore adolescent substance abuse treatment through the use of the Youth Development Model.

METHODS

Research Design

A naturalistic case study design was used for this study. The target case for this study was a residential adolescent male substance abuse treatment unit at Generations (pseudonym) Youth Program in a medium-sized town in Illinois. The program consists of one female treatment unit and two male treatment units. Each male treatment unit houses 24 young men. Males on these units range from 12 to 18 years old and are referred to services due to problems arising from drug and alcohol use. The professional staff for each unit included a clinical coordinator, 4 counselors, 8 technicians, and one nurse who provided basic medical care to clients.

Data Collection

A multi-method data collection approach was used for this case study. Specifically, field observations, interviews, and document analysis were conducted to develop a comprehensive view of the case. A variety of facets of the treatment process were observed including static group, recreation groups, school, meal time, and day to day activities occurring at a residential treatment facility. All observation data initially were recorded in the form of hand-written field notes. Each field note contained specific identifying information including the location and setting of the observation, participants, activity being observed, and duration of the observation. In addition, the field notes contained a narrative that described the event in detail, accompanied by a personal reflection of the phenomena observed. Observations continued until saturation occurred, that is when observations yielded no new data. Saturation occurred after approximately 6 weeks (120 hours of observation) in the field.

In addition to participant observations, data for this study were collected via 10 semi-structured individual interviews with a variety of staff to gain their perspectives on the process and content of treatment. The staff interviewed included the Site Director, Upper Male Unit Coordinator, Upper Male Unit Counselors, Upper Male Unit Technicians, Family Therapist, Facility Nurse, Intake Coordinator, and Head Teacher. Interviews occurred on a voluntary basis. No interviews were conducted with adolescents participating in treatment. Interviews were audio-taped and transcribed verbatim.

The third data source was a review of programmatic documents. Documents were identified through interviews with respondents and observations of the treatment process. No documents were reviewed prior to conducting interviews. A total of 134 documents were reviewed, including unit operations directives, in-take forms, unit rules, and client treatment plans.

Data Analysis and Interpretation

Data analysis was an on-going process. A case study record was constructed from interview transcriptions, observation field notes, and reviews of documents. The case study record was constructed to reflect what new admissions might experience as they progressed through the treatment process. This description included both the content and process of treatment at Generations Youth Program.

As the case study record was being constructed, categorical aggregation was initiated. Each interview transcription, observation field note, and document was analyzed in conjunction with the case study record and indigenous codes were identified reflecting the language of the participants. As each successive observation, interview, or document review was completed, data were coded. Emergent themes were compared with existing indigenous codes. This constant-comparative process continued until all interview transcriptions, observation field notes, and documents were reviewed and coded.

After observations, field notes, interview transcriptions, and documents were indigenously coded, sensitizing codes were developed. In most cases, sensitizing codes were constructed by combining existing indigenous codes under a single code that was still consistent with the participant's language. Once all interview transcriptions, observation field notes, and documents were reviewed and coded, the case study record was completed, and emergent themes were finalized. The case study record and emergent themes were then compared to components of the Youth Development Model to determine the consistency between the content and process of substance abuse treatment and the model. Trustworthiness for this study was established through utilization of member checks triangulation of multiple data sources, and through use of an outside auditor.

RESULTS

The Site: Generations Treatment Program-Upper Male Unit

The Generations Youth Program is a residential substance abuse treatment facility for adolescent males and females. The facility has 60 beds, which when full serves 48 males and 12 females between the ages of 13 and 18. A large plaque in the administration building describes the program as follows,

> "Generations Youth Program views chemical abuse as a progressive disease which, without treatment, becomes more severe. The management and recovery from substance abuse encompasses all life areas including the physical, emotional, cognitive, and social individual. Generations' integrated approach to treatment consists of a number of components designed to provide quality services in a controlled environment. In addition to a holistic, therapeutic and educational approach to chemical dependency; Generations addresses such issues as thought disorders, emotional problems, behavior disorders, family dysfunction, vocational/educational preparedness, and psychiatric concerns."

The residential male treatment unit is a gray, stone building. The color at the base of the building is close to black and represents the early stages of recovery. The color becomes lighter as it approaches the roof, signifying the progression of the recovery process. The unit has two floors. The lower floor houses the Lower Male Unit. The upper floor houses the Upper Male Unit (UMU). Both the upper and lower male units have a capacity of 24 youths. Clients are assigned to the units based on the unit census.

When fully staffed, the Upper Male Unit has one Treatment Unit Coordinator, four counselors, four full-time technicians, two part-time technicians, one full-time over-night monitor, and one part-time over-night monitor. In addition to the unit staff, the Intake Counselor, Family Therapist, Registered Nurse, and Community Teachers play a significant role in the clients' treatment during their stay at Generations.

Staff Reflections on the Treatment Process

Amanda, Treatment Unit Coordinator, is responsible for the day-to-day functioning of the unit. Her duties include conducting weekly staff meetings, direct supervision of all other staff on the unit, constructing the staffing schedule, and developing the daily treatment schedule.

When fully staffed, four treatment counselors are responsible for delivery of treatment services. Each counselor is responsible for six clients when the unit is filled to capacity. The counselor is the primary person responsible for helping the client identify treatment issues to be addressed, monitoring progress on those issues, and ultimately making decisions about a client's discharge or termination from the program. The bond between client and counselor is one built on trust, dedication, and perseverance. The counselor is the client's motivator. Sarah, a counselor, explains her view of this role:

> "I think the kids put a lot into us like 'you have my life in your hands.' We try and help them. We are somebody who is concerned about them. We are directing them in the right direction with material and stuff they can use for themselves, that they do for themselves. It is not us doing the work for them."

Technicians make the unit function. They are constantly on their feet between 7:00 AM and 9:00 PM working with and directing the clients. They spend the greatest amount of time with the clients on a daily basis. Technicians ensure that clients stay focused and on task. In staffings they play an important role in identifying how clients function day-to-day. They see clients at their best and their worst. They are frequently the first unit staff member with whom the client comes into contact.

The Treatment Process

Data analysis resulted with the identification of one major theme of the treatment process, (belief in self) and three sub-themes, (peer support, self-control, and treatment knowledge). The primary goal of the treatment process is to help the client develop a sense of hope and belief in self. Through peer support, development of self-control, and acquisition of treatment knowledge, the client can begin to develop a new outlook on life, a belief that he can remain clean and sober (see Figure 1).

Figure 1. The process of Adolescent Substance Abuse Treatment at the Generations Program.

The Goal of Treatment: Belief in Self

The development of a sense of hope and a belief in self are the primary goals of the treatment process. As goals are accomplished, clients develop a belief that they can be successful and that they can complete treatment. Sarah notes,

> "A lot of them come in without goals and we like to see them realize that there are other things in life than drugs and other things to do…they gain self respect…become independent. They start to believe in themselves when they accomplish things. Like with their treatment goals, if they accomplish something and you say, 'See, you did this,' that gives them self worth."

Over the four to six months that a client spends in treatment, numerous small victories occur. Many, for the first time in their lives, have someone who believes in them and helps them to achieve their goals. The treatment planning process allows clients to identify the issues they wish to work on and allows them to identify a support network to accomplish these goals.

Leadership is one way in which a client can develop a belief in self. Leadership positions are given based on strength and accomplishment. Tim, a 16-year-old Caucasian male, had been in treatment for three months by the time I entered the unit. Tim was very friendly, but from the report of the counselors and his peers, he was doing very little in treatment. Over the next six weeks Tim became an active participant in the treatment process. He began to complete his treatment work and "pull himself up." As Tim "worked the program", he was rewarded with his first leadership role, the Maintenance Organizer position. The look on his face the day he was awarded this position was a combination of surprise and pride. As Tim continued to be active in the treatment process, he was given roles of leadership requiring more responsibility. One such role was Expediter. This position required Tim, who was typically, quiet and withdrawn, to take charge of his team side, ensuring that everyone was accounted for and lined up for meals. As I prepared to exit the field, he was finally moved up to House Coordinator, the highest leadership position. When he earned this position, he received a large round of applause from his peers and the staff. His counselor remarked, "See what you can do if believe in yourself." Tim still somewhat shocked, smiled from ear to ear, and replied, "If I can do this, I can stay clean."

In addition to leadership positions, success in school can help foster a belief in self. Marie, the head school teacher explains,

"It is about goal setting and accomplishment and positive results. Sometimes success in that [school] will encourage a kid to work a little harder in his treatment or start looking at himself as a kid who can do something positive and that will rub off on his treatment. A lot of these guys, they debilitated themselves with their using and have actually inflicted damage on their brains with the things that they have done."

The completion of treatment provides the staff and clients an opportunity to acknowledge the growth and success, and reinforce the primary goal. At the successful completion of treatment, the client is presented with a "Certificate of Growth" The client has his peers and staff sign as support for their discharge. The certificate reads:

"You have shared your joy, pain, and your humor with us. You have become part of us. You've torn down walls of fear and mistrust to allow us into your life. For all of this, we are grateful. You've given us the honor and privilege of knowing you and watching you grow, and by doing so have given us hope for ourselves. By allowing us to know who you are, you've helped us to begin understanding ourselves."

"We've learned together that with Honesty, Open Mindedness and Willingness our lives can change, the promises can come true and dreams can be fulfilled. We no longer have to be prisoners of our disease. There is Hope for all of us. You've learned tools for continuing to grow, take them with you, use them and Grow! With our Respect, Love, and Prayers."

Strategies for Success

The process of treatment includes a number of therapeutic strategies to assist clients in developing the belief that they can remain substance free and succeed in treatment. These strategies include the development of a peer support network, completion of treatment knowledge, and development of self-control. Specifically, these strategies provide the opportunity for the development of health enhancing behaviors, thus contributing to the goal of sobriety and positive youth development.

Peer Support

Generations Youth Program uses a Therapeutic Community paradigm. An integral component of this approach is use of peer support to enable recovery (DeLeon, 1994). Language used by both the treatment staff and clients reflect this peer support approach. The unit is divided up into team sides. The word "team" is the key for the proper functioning of the unit. Peer support provides the foundation for all therapeutic services. From the first day a client is admitted to treatment to their eventual discharge, their peers play a crucial role in treatment. During the first orientation group a technician explains, "Each member of the unit is important to the overall functioning of the unit. The behavior of one can effect the whole unit; much like life, each decision and resulting behavior can often impact someone other than themselves." Peer support is provided on the unit through a variety of strategies. Among these strategies are: use of leadership positions, pull ups, strokes, goodbye groups, and evening meditation.

Daily peer support is provided in the form of "pull ups" and "strokes." Pull ups and strokes are given by both peers and staff. Sarah describes how clients use pull ups as peer support. "They give each other encouragement to change negative behaviors. A pull up is like encouragement for them to be aware of their behavior." Clients may pull a peer up on a variety of behaviors such as rule infractions and relapse behaviors. Pull ups are used to draw the individual's attention to an inappropriate behavior. It is not unusual to hear one client tell another client, "Pull yourself up on your negative attitude," or "Pull yourself up on your lack of respect for staff."

While pull ups are given to address negative behaviors, strokes are given to encourage and reward positive behavior. Smoking is not permitted, however, clients smoke with regularity. When one client announced that he had not had a cigarette in 30 days, his peers responded with a loud and boisterous, "stroooookes".

Goodbye Groups are a time when the power of peer support can be felt. When a client is being discharged successfully, a Goodbye Group is held. The Goodbye Group starts with each member of the unit providing the departing person strokes and encouraging them to stay clean. The clients may say "you helped me out a lot" or "I know you're going to make it work." When each client has had a chance to provide words of encouragement, the person leaving addresses each member of the group, providing them pulls ups and strokes. Typically, Goodbye Groups can be, and often are, very emotional. Each day at Generations Youth Program ends with an evening meditation. The entire unit gathers in the group room. Standing shoulder to shoulder, arms around one another, they recite the Generations philosophy and serenity prayer.

A client then says, "Can we have a moment of silence for those suffering in and outside of Generations walls." The serenity prayer is followed by a moment of silence. Then someone asks, "Why are we here?" The clients respond by reciting the Generations philosophy, staying in unison and saying it with enthusiasm. The technician or counselor may encourage the clients by saying, "Louder." If the group gets out of unison they must stop and start again. Once finished, the group yells, "Another drug free day at Generations, hey," and proceed into reciting the Serenity Prayer.

Ideally, all clients would support one another, yet peer support varies on the unit. A number of factors effect peer support levels. For example, Laura a counselor explains:

"Sometimes we have a big shift in clients where a lot of people leave and new ones come in. That is when we have trouble with teamwork because they are all getting to know each other and they are not a team until they get to know each other and they have been here long enough."

In addition, it is not unusual for clients to have a negative attitude about treatment. This attitude affects other clients on the unit. For example, a client who was terminated from treatment and removed in hand cuffs and leg shackles disrupted the treatment process for his team side members.

Occasionally, a team side or the entire unit will stray away from the peer support approach. Typically, the first signs of this are covert behaviors and deterioration of client morale. When this situation occurs, the team side may be placed on "team side grounding". When a team side is placed on grounding the clients lose all free time privileges. If the entire unit is functioning poorly, the entire unit may be placed on house closing. When the house closes, both units lose free time and visitation privileges. To get off grounding or closing, the clients must pull together, work as a team, and support one another. Team work occurs when clients assume responsibility for each other's behavior. When a client receives a consequence for a negative behavior, the entire team side or unit receives the same consequence. The goal of this approach is to encourage clients to provide support and pull ups to one another.

Development of Self –Control

The primary goal of substance abuse treatment is "sobriety." To accomplish this goal, the treatment process focuses on providing the clients the necessary "tools" and "skills" to keep them on the road to sobriety when they leave the facility. Marie notes with regard to teaching skills for sobriety, "That is my number one priority."

There are a variety of skills that clients develop during their participation in treatment including refusal skills, hygiene skills, communication skills, and leadership skills. The two primary skills that clients need to be successful during treatment and after discharge are anger management skills and impulse control. These skills are vital to the client's recovery and success because they lead to a sense of self control. Amanda describes impulse control as the ability to "delay immediate gratification" and "identify appropriate ways to deal with conflict." The majority of clients admitted to treatment exhibit what Amanda calls the "King Baby Syndrome: I want what I want, when I want it." This behavior and pattern of thinking relates back to the clients' substance using behavior. Generally, clients do not realize that they lack impulse control. Laura notes, "They need to learn impulse control, which is also a skill that most don't have and don't even realize….Out on the streets if things didn't go their way, they would get high or they would get into a fight."

When a young person enters treatment they are faced with learning a large number of rules and the task of modifying their behavior in a short period of time. The greatest barrier to following the rules and adopting these new behaviors is an inability to control impulsive behaviors. Marie describes the importance of the development of impulse control, "…instead of being run by those patterns…if they can identify their own patterns then they have a leg up on gaining control….and then learn to manage their emotions and learn to manage the relapse cycle…" The treatment process helps the client develop impulse control in a number of ways, including use of house jobs, therapeutic groups, and unit rules. Therapeutic groups are used to assist clients learn impulse control through participation in an organized activity.

Closely related to impulse control is anger management. Laura notes, "I can name like two clients on the whole unit that don't have anger management problems, but they probably did when they were using." The goal of anger management is not for the client to not become angry. Rather, the goal is for the client to be able express anger in an appropriate manner.

A variety of strategies are used to enable a client to gain control of his anger. For some clients, use of quiet time is important, other clients might punch on the punching bag in the staff bathroom, others choose to write in an anger management journal. Over the course of treatment many clients become very proficient at learning to manage their anger and impulses. The result of learning these skills is an increase in flexibility and adaptability. Laura describes the importance of being able to adapt. "You have to be able to accept change here because it changes everyday; there is always something different going on…so you have to be real flexible." When clients are successful, this adds to feelings of self-esteem and self-worth. Sarah describes this process,

> "A lot of them set themselves up for failure. They will be like, 'I can't do that,' and then they change it and end up doing that and you're like, 'I thought you said you couldn't do that,'… they develop a sense of self-control and self- respect that they can take with them."

Treatment Knowledge

Development of treatment knowledge is the third major goal of the treatment process. Laura explains, "Treatment knowledge is really important…it is important for them to know what they are doing to their bodies….and know what the long term consequences are." Sarah adds, "….most of them don't understand the addiction process and the effects of their drug use."

Clients develop treatment knowledge in a variety of ways. The most common strategy used to develop treatment knowledge is "treatment work." Treatment work primarily consists of worksheets, workbooks, and other written assignments that increase the client's knowledge of treatment-related issues. These issues include information about different drugs and their effects of the body, Alcoholics Anonymous and/or Narcotics Anonymous, relapse triggers, anger, and family issues. Clients are provided approximately two to three hours a day to complete their treatment work. As treatment work is completed, it is reviewed with their counselor and new treatment work is assigned. Typically, this work is completed by the client without any assistance from their peers. Treatment work is to treatment as homework is to school.

In addition to treatment work, groups play a large role in communication of treatment knowledge. Therapy groups frequently focus on providing clients information in a lecture or experiential format. During this study, clients learned about STDs, condom use, and the Transtheoretical Model in therapy group. Didactic groups are primarily lecture based and focus on providing clients with basic information about drugs and alcohol. Amanda describes this group, "This group is more of a lecture group….if we want to teach them about marijuana or different types of drugs this is the type group we'll do." School complements acquisition of treatment knowledge. The majority of clients participate in daily school sessions. Marie, the head teacher explains the goal of school "is to provide the students a positive educational experience….complement what they are learning in treatment." Acquisition of treatment knowledge plays a role in a client's discharge. Laura explains, "Their discharge really depends on their behavior while they are here and whether or not they are doing the treatment assignments and they are really getting treatment knowledge…I sit down with them when they are getting ready to leave and ask them, 'What do you feel like you learned?' and then I'll have them write it out….I have them explain to me what they learned and how they will handle things differently."

Basic Human Needs in the Youth Development Model	Treatment Components at Generations
A sense of safety and structure	Client Rules Daily Schedule Organized Treatment Structure (sequential approach to recovery issues) Team-Side Closing House Closing
A sense of belonging / group membership -	Therapy Group Goodbye Group Confrontation Group Team-side Living Environment Peer Pull Ups
A sense of self-worth / contributing -	Treatment Work Peer Pull Ups and Strokes Confrontation Group
A sense of independence / control over one's life	Develop of an Individualized Master Treatment Plan One on One Counseling Sessions Treatment Work (Goal Setting, Anger Management) Participation in School (acquisition of reading skills, grade level attainment)
A sense of closeness / relationships -	One on One Counseling Goodbye Group Peer Pull Ups Confrontation Group
A sense of mastery -	Treatment Work (Anger Management, Relapse Prevention) School Leadership Positions House Jobs
A sense of self awareness -	One on One Counseling Goodbye Group Family Therapy School Treatment Work (Family Issues)

Figure 2.

The Development of Fully-Prepared Adolescents

The Youth Development Model provides a framework that encourages development of fully-prepared adolescents. To ensure that young people can meet these needs in positive, healthful ways, they must be presented opportunities to develop skills and competencies. The Youth Development Model identifies five basic competency areas which enable young people to meet their needs and become fully prepared for life. These competencies are: basic health and physical competence, personal and social competence, cognitive and creative competence, vocational competence, and citizenship and ethics.

Youth Development Competency in the Youth Development Model	Treatment Components at Generations
Health and Physical Competence	Hygiene Class Health Education on Sexually Transmitted Infections Physical Education and Recreation Treatment Work (Physical and Psychological affects of Substance Use)
Personal and Social Competence -	Intrapersonal Skills: Treatment Work (Anger Management, Emotional Health) Therapeutic Groups One on One Counseling Interpersonal Skills: Treatment Work (Communications Skills) House Jobs School Therapeutic Groups Coping Skills Interaction with legal system Treatment Work (Anger Management, Impulse Control) Stress Management Relapse Prevention Skills Judgement Skills Development of Master Treatment Plan Leadership Positions Peer Pull Ups
Cognitive and Creative Competence	Treatment Work (Process of completing the assigned work) School One on One Tutors for Special Needs Clients Art Therapy Group
Vocational Competence	Vocational Skills Group (Job Application Skills, Interviewing Skills) House jobs
Citizenship and Ethics	Team-Side Membership Activities Unit Membership Activities Recreational Activities Group Meditation

Figure 3

The purpose of this study was to document the content and process of adolescent substance abuse treatment occurring at the Generations Youth Program and then determine if the process and content was consistent with the Youth Development Model.

A comparison of content and process of substance abuse treatment on the Generations Upper Male Unit (UMU) with the major constructs of the Youth Development Model revealed consistency between the process and constructs (See Figures 2 and 3).

BASIC HUMAN NEEDS

A Sense of Safety and Structure

There are numerous strategies that the UMU uses to provide its clients a sense of safety and structure. The process and content of treatment on the UMU follows a highly structured schedule. There a number of client rules and guidelines. These rules and guidelines are used to provide clients a sense of safety and structure.

A Sense of Belonging / Group Membership

The UMU functions as a micro-community. The unit itself is divided into "team" sides, the implication being that treatment is a team effort. The Generations philosophy is that no client will be successful in treatment by himself. The process and content of treatment is based on the concepts of community and peer support. In addition, therapeutic groups foster a sense of belonging.

A Sense of Self-Worth / Contributing

As clients are successful in treatment, they develop a sense of self-worth and pride. This perception results from success. The content and process of treatment offers clients numerous activities to be successful, feel good about themselves, and contribute to their peers.

A Sense of Independence / Control Over One's Life

Clients participate in a number of activities that encourage independence and development of self-control. When the client arrives on the unit, he develops a master treatment plan in collaboration with his counselor. The client is encouraged throughout the treatment process to take responsibility for his treatment and to actively identify treatment issues and goals. Through this activity, clients begin to feel some level of control over their treatment.

A Sense of Closeness / Relationships

The development of sense of closeness / relationships is cultivated in a number of ways through the treatment process. Many clients develop a close relationship with their primary counselor. Therapeutic groups can, and frequently do, develop a sense of closeness between clients.

A Sense of Competence / Mastery

The content and process of treatment is designed to assist clients in the recovery process. As a client becomes responsible for his recovery, he experiences success in the treatment process. There a number of different components that provide clients an opportunity to gain competence and mastery. These components include treatment work, leadership positions, levels, and house jobs.

A Sense of Self-Awareness

A major goal of the treatment process on the UMU is that a client will become self-aware. Only through self-awareness can a client actively pursue his recovery. Individual sessions and therapeutic groups nurture a sense of self-awareness. Groups provide the client an opportunity to receive support and provide support.

YOUTH DEVELOPMENT COMPETENCIES

Health and Physical Competence

The majority of clients admitted to the UMU have little or no health and physical competence. All clients have been admitted due to behaviors that have compromised their overall health including drug and alcohol use and behaviors that increase their risk of STDs, HIV, and pregnancy. In addition, many have limited hygiene skills resulting in dental problems. A significant time is spent throughout the treatment process, providing clients treatment knowledge. The focus of treatment knowledge is to provide substance-specific information and information about the addiction process. In addition, groups focusing on sexually transmitted diseases and condom use are frequently offered.

Personal and Social Competence

Personal and social competence includes a wide variety of skills including: intrapersonal skills, interpersonal skills, coping skills, and judgment skills (Pittman & Cahill, 1992). Clients enter treatment with varying levels of personal and social competence. Some clients are quite articulate and are very adaptable while others have extreme difficulties getting along with peers and following the relate system. The majority of clients have problems with impulse control and anger management.

Intrapersonal Skills

A number of the components of the treatment process assist the client to develop intrapersonal skills. These elements include treatment work, therapeutic groups, one-on-one counseling, daily schedule, and unit rules.

Interpersonal Skills

Interpersonal skills are evidenced by the ability to work with others, develop friendships through communication, cooperation, empathizing, and negotiating (Pittman & Cahill, 1992). All components of the content and process of treatment build interpersonal skills. Clients must constantly interact in a socially appropriate manner. A variety of strategies are in place to assist clients in development of interpersonal skills. All of the groups require that clients develop interpersonal skills. Strokes, pull-ups, and announcements and confrontation groups require the clients practice their speaking and listening skills. In addition, these groups give clients time to empathize and provide peer support.

Coping Skills

The majority of clients enter treatment lacking coping skills, which frequently lead to problems with impulse control and anger management. Clients learn coping skills through interacting with the legal system, their families, and the treatment staff.

Judgment Skills

Clients, in general, have poor judgment skills at admission. These clients are impulsive, frequently going through few evaluative thought processes when making a decision. As a result, many have legal charges due to their actions. Development of judgment skills begins during the first week of treatment when the client assists his primary counselor to complete his treatment plan.

Clients who assume leadership positions also develop judgment skills through assigning jobs, working with staff, and evaluating their decisions.

Cognitive / Creative Competence

The majority of clients participating in treatment enter treatment with varying cognitive skills. Many have undiagnosed learning disabilities, are developmentally delayed due to their substance use, and/or have been truant from school. There are many facets of the treatment process that begin to build cognitive and creative competence in the client including school, treatment work, and therapeutic groups.

Vocational Competence

An integral component of the treatment process is the house job. House jobs are not designed to be vocational training, however these jobs do provide an opportunity to learn the value and importance of a job. If a house job is not completed, it affects the entire unit. Somebody else must complete the work, much like a real job. House jobs also provide clients a chance to be successful.

Citizenship and Ethics

The treatment unit operates as a micro-community. The unit has a history, rules, and consequences for not following the rules. Clients participate in running the unit, work with one another to support the treatment process, and take pride in their unit.

Clients learn about citizenship and ethics by actively participating in the treatment process. As clients support one another, they create an environment that is supportive of their recovery. The completion of the Generations Philosophy at the end of the day is designed to build a sense of community. They celebrate another day in treatment, another day sober. They are a group of individuals struggling to grow, to maintain their sobriety, and to support one another. For the time they are in treatment, they are part of a community, they share a history, and have an opportunity to help themselves by helping others.

The content and process of substance abuse treatment at Generations Youth Program includes a number of components and strategies that provide the clients an opportunity to meet their basic human needs. In addition, clients have the opportunity to develop a variety of competencies that are essential to healthy development. If the goal of treatment is an adolescent who has the skills and competencies that lead to resilience from a past of drug and alcohol abuse, the Youth Development Model is the framework for achieving this goal.

DISCUSSION

The process and content of substance abuse treatment at the Generations Youth Program attempts to address these threats as well as numerous others and assist adolescents develop basic skill and competencies that will enable them to live a better life. The majority of the young men who enter the Generation's Program lack basic skills to maintain an adequate level of holistic health. Most began using substances at a young age, have been abused, are involved with the legal system, and have had problems academically. The process and content of treatment is specifically designed to guide adolescents through the early steps of recovery from drugs and alcohol. In a much broader sense the content and process of treatment assists young people acquire skills and competencies that facilitate healthy development.

When a young man enters into treatment at Generation's, he is exposed to a multifaceted process; one that includes structured therapy groups, individual counseling, school, and recreation activities. In addition, if he participates in the program he develops a sense of community with other young people participating in treatment. He is provided the opportunity to be part of a team, to contribute to the unit, to learn skills to address their self-defeating behaviors, assist their peers, and develop sobriety. Belief in self is a result of participating in the treatment process. The counselors all indicated that as a client participates in the treatment process and experiences success he began to develop a belief in himself or hope.

Observations of the treatment process collaborate this assertion. As clients received leadership positions, received strokes, higher levels, and/or successfully completed treatment work, there was an improvement in their functioning. Many of the staff have described the results of this success as self esteem, self efficacy, and self worth. A belief in self, self-esteem and self-efficacy develop over the course of treatment through the development of skills and the opportunity to participate in treatment. Through giving and receiving peer support, gaining self-control, and acquiring treatment knowledge, the client obtains the necessary skills for sobriety. In addition, as a young man participates in treatment at Generations Youth Program he will receive and give a great deal of peer support. Through use of leadership positions, therapeutic groups, and pull-ups and strokes he will have the opportunity to provide peer support. DeLeon (1994) describes peer support as a key element in a therapeutic community. Peer support includes the use of participant roles, membership feedback, and use of unit membership as role models (Alterman, O'Brien, & McLellan, 1991;DeLeon, 1994; SAMHSA, 1993).

A major focus of treatment on the Generations' UMU is self-control. Self control is a key skill clients must develop to be successful in treatment, and ultimately in their sobriety. Development of self control enables the client to fully participate in treatment, thus becoming a contributing member of the community. A young man will develop self control by learning how to handle anger, problem solve, and remediate impulsive behaviors. These strategies include treatment work, house jobs, and leadership. The acquisition of treatment knowledge is essential for the successful completion of the treatment program. The majority of clients at admission have limited knowledge about the addiction process and the effects of substances on their body, emotions, and family. A variety of strategies are used to develop treatment knowledge. These include treatment work, didactic and therapy groups, and membership feedback. Development of treatment knowledge through the used Didactic and education groups are described as an essential component of a residential treatment program (SAMHSA, 1993).

IMPLICATIONS FOR PRACTICE

The Youth Development Model provides a unique framework for the delivery of primary, secondary, and tertiary prevention services to substance abusing adolescents. Specifically, this framework focuses on developing fully functioning adolescents prepared not only for sobriety, but also for complete living.

The utilization of this model by adolescent substance abuse treatment professionals will require few changes in the treatment content and process. In fact, many of the key components of adolescent substance abuse treatment are key elements of the Youth Development Model. The National Institute on Drug Abuse recommends that drug and alcohol treatment address the multiple needs of the client through development of interpersonal relationships, community bonding, cognitive and developmental therapies, development of coping strategies, and stimulus and urge control (NIDA, 1999). These recommendations certainly are in line with the goal of the Youth Development Model. The chief benefit of utilizing this model as a framework for the treatment of adolescent substance abusers is that it ensures professionals would consider the client's basic human needs, as well as ensure the development of competencies that encourage healthy development. If the goal of adolescent substance abuse treatment is habilitation, then the Youth Development Model is a powerful tool that can be used to reach that goal.

This study demonstrated that while these adolescents were receiving treatment for their alcohol and drug use they were also receiving primary and secondary prevention services. Education about contraception and sexually transmitted infections, basic hygiene skills, the development of stress management skills, and education about communicable diseases such as colds, flu as well as self-care illustrate primary and secondary prevention services. Consistent with personal and social skill development, the treatment process develops primary prevention skills-goal setting, stress management, communication skills, and decision making (Fetro & Drolet, 2000). Substance abuse treatment requires a full continuum of prevention strategies.

The Youth Development Model provides a framework to deliver this full continuum of prevention services that cuts across all content areas. The primary goal of substance abuse treatment will continue to be development of sober and substance free adolescents. A Youth Development approach helps achieve this goal by assisting substance - abusing adolescents become fully prepared for the challenges of sobriety, enhance protective factors, and foster resilience.

REFERENCES

Benard, B. (1993). *Fostering resiliency in kids: Protective factors in the family school and community.* Western Regional Center for Drug-Free Schools and Communities. Portland, Oregon: Northwest Regional Educational Laboratory.

Carnegie Council on Adolescent Development (1989). *Turning points: Preparing American youth for the 21st century.* Carnegie Council on Adolescent Development: Washington D. C.

Creswell, J. W. (1998). *Qualitative inquiry and research design: Choosing among five traditions.* Thousand Oaks: CA: Sage Publications.

DeLeon, G. (1994). The therapeutic community: Toward a general theory and model. In F. Tims, G. De Leon, & N. Jainchill (Ed.), *Therapeutic communities: Advances in research and application* (NIDA Publication NO. 94-3633, pp. 16-53). Washington DC Government Printing Office.

Denton, R. E., & Kampfe, C. M. (1994). The relationship between family variables and adolescent substance abuse: A literature review. *Adolescence, 29*(6), 475-495.

Fetro, J. V. & Drolet, J. C. (2000). Personal and social competence: Strategies for communication, decision making, goal setting, stress management. Santa Cruz, CA: ETR Associates

Jackson, A. W. & Davis, G. A. (2000). Turning points 2000: Educating adolescents in the 21st century. New York: Teachers College Press.

Kaminer, Y. (1991). Adolescent Substance Abuse. In R. J. Frances, & S. I. Miller,

(Eds.), *Clinical textbook of addictive disorders* (pp.320- 346). New York, NY: Guilford

Press.

Lincoln, Y. S., & Guba, E. G. (1985). *Naturalistic inquiry.* Beverly Hills: Sage Publications.

Marcus, M. T. (1998). Changing carreers: Becoming clean and sober in a therapeutic community. *Qualitative Health Research, 8*(4), 466-480.

National Institutes of Health (1999). *Principles of drug addiction: A research-based guide.* NIH Publication No. 99-4180. Washington D. C. Government Printing Office.

Newcomb, M. D., & Bentler, P.M. (1989). Substance use and abuse among children and teenagers. *American Psychologist, 44*(2), 242-245.

Pittman, K.J. (1991). *Promoting youth development.* Testimony before the House Select Committee on Children, Youth and Families. The Center for Youth Development and Policy Research of The Academy for Educational Development

Pittman, K. J., & Cahill, M. (1992). *Pushing the boundaries of education: The implications of a youth development approach to education, policies, structures and collaboration.* Washington DC: The Center for Youth Development and Policy Research of The Academy for Educational Development.

Pittman, K. J., O'Brien, R., & Kimball, M. (1993). *Youth development and resiliency research: Making connections to substance abuse prevention.* Commissioned for The Center for Substance Abuse Prevention, Washington DC: The Center for Youth Development and Policy Research of The Academy for Educational Development.

Ralph, N., & Mc Menany, C. (1996). Treatment outcomes in an adolescent chemical dependency program. *Adolescence, 31*(121), 91-108.

Richardson, G. E., Neiger, B. L., Jensen, S., & Kumpfer, K. L. (1990). The resiliency model. *Health Education, 21*(6), 33-39.

Substance Abuse and Mental Health Services (1993a). *Guidelines for the treatment of alcohol-and other drug-abusing adolescents.* (DHHS Publication No. (SMA) 93-2010). Washington D. C. Government Printing Office.

Substance Abuse and Mental Health Services (1999). *Treatment Episode Data Set: 1992-1997.* DHHS Publication (Drug and Alcohol Services Information System Series: S-7) Washington D. C. Government Printing Office.

United States Department of Health and Human Services (1995). *Effectiveness of substance abuse treatment.* (DHHS Publication No. (SMA) 95-3067). Washington D. C. Government Printing Office.

Werner, E. E. (1989). High-risk children in young adulthood: A longitudinal study from birth to 32 years. *American Journal of Orthopsychiatry, 59*(1), 72-81.

In: Trends in Psychotherapy Research
Editor: M. E. Abelian, pp. 141-159

ISBN 1-59454-373-9
© 2006 Nova Science Publishers, Inc.

Chapter 7

A GROUP INTERVENTION WHICH ASSISTS PATIENTS WITH DUAL DIAGNOSIS REDUCE THEIR TOBACCO USE

Stephen R. Kisely

Departments of Psychiatry and Community Health & Epidemiology, Dalhousie University, Queen Elizabeth II Centre, Halifax, Canada

Neil J. Preston

Mental Health Directorate, Fremantle Hospital and Health Service, WA 6160, Australia

ABSTRACT

There is a well-recognised association between substance use and psychotic disorders, sometimes described as 'dual diagnosis'. Approximately one half of individuals in the community with a psychotic disorder have a substance use disorder, and the same proportion of those who abuse substances have a psychiatric disorder. Most interventions have concentrated on opiates, psychostimulants, hallucinogens and marijuana and there has been much less emphasis on the treatment of co-morbid nicotine use. Tobacco use is especially high in chronic schizophrenia and people with this diagnosis are more likely to be nicotine dependent than smokers in the general population or those with other psychiatric disorders. Smoking may contribute to the 60 percent increase in deaths from respiratory disorders, and a 30 percent increased chance of heart disease. Patients with psychotic disorder may also spend up to 40% of their income on tobacco. This chapter looks at possible psychological and pharmacological treatments such as nicotine replacement and bupropion. It particularly focuses on the effectiveness of a manualised group intervention based on motivational interviewing and cognitive behavioural therapy, which also includes advice on nicotine replacement. Using a waitlist-treatment crossover design, we recruited 38 subjects of whom nineteen completed the waitlist and intervention phases. There were no significant differences between subjects and dropouts. During the waitlist period there were no significant changes in tobacco use. At the end of the intervention, almost a quarter had stopped smoking, (z=-2.24, p=0.02). Other outcome measures included smoking cessation, motivation to stop, the Fagerstrom Test for Nicotine Dependence (FTND), urinary cotinine and psychiatric symptoms on the

General Health Questionnaire. Subjects showed significant improvements on state of change, FTND score and urinary cotinine levels. These improvements were maintained at three-month follow-up (n=10), with no adverse effect on psychiatric morbidity. Although this intervention shows promise, larger randomised controlled trials are indicated to determine the relative contributions of nicotine replacement, bupropion and group interventions to smoking cessation in this population. We also need to consider intervention early on in the course of schizophrenia and other psychotic disorders. In our subsequent survey of patients attending an early psychosis service (n=60), half were smokers, of whom 60% wished to stop. These smoking rates were roughly mid-way between the general population and a long-term psychiatric population and they may be more susceptible to intervention than patients with chronic psychotic illness. This should include primary prevention aimed at ensuring that non-smokers do not start smoking, and a secondary prevention programme aimed at existing smokers

BACKGROUND

There is a well-recognised association between substance use and psychotic disorders, sometimes described as 'dual diagnosis'. Approximately one half of individuals in the community with a psychotic disorder have a substance use disorder, and the same proportion of those who abuse substances have a psychiatric disorder (Fowler *et al*, 1998; Schneier *et al*, 1987; Siegfried, 1998; Regier *et al*, 1990). The special needs of this group of patients have been increasingly recognised in Great Britain, the United States and Australia (Dawe & Mattick, 1997; Department of Health, 2002). These include increased symptoms of depression, suicidal ideation and psychosis (Strakowski *et al*, 1994, Krausz *et al*, 1996; Dixon, 1999), reflected in higher admission rates to psychiatric units (Martinez-Aravelo *et al*, 1994).

Most interventions have concentrated on opiates, psychostimulants, hallucinogens and marijuana and there has been much less emphasis on the treatment of co-morbid nicotine use. This chapter looks at the prevalence of co-morbid nicotine use in this population and possible pharmacological and psychological treatments. It particular, focuses on the effectiveness of a group intervention based on motivational interviewing and cognitive-behavioural therapy

PREVALENCE

While smoking rates in the general population have declined, up to 80% of individuals with psychiatric disorder continue to smoke (Lasser *et al*, 2000; SANE, 1997; Hall *et al*, 1995; Ziedonis *et al* 1994; Kisely *et al* 2000; de Leon *et al*, 1995; Wilhelm 1998). In North America, 50 to 80% of individuals with psychiatric disorders smoke (Lasser *et al*, 2000), similar levels being reported in Victoria, Australia (SANE, 1997). Furthermore, smokers with a past history of depressive illness stop smoking at half the rate of patients with no such history (Glassman, 1993) In addition, Hall *et al* (1995) found higher than average rates of major depressive disorder amongst smokers especially those who were nicotine dependent. This has been confirmed in a community survey of Australian smokers (Jorm *et al*, 1999).

Tobacco use is especially high in psychotic disorder such as schizophrenia and people with this diagnosis are more likely to be nicotine dependent than smokers in the general population or those with other psychiatric disorders (Lasser *et al,* 2000; SANE, 1997; Hall *et al*, 1995; Ziedonis *et al* 1994; Kisely *et al* 2000; de Leon *et al*, 1995; Wilhelm 1998). In some studies, up to 80% of patients with chronic schizophrenia smoke (Hughes 1993; SANE, 1998). Individuals with schizophrenia are three times as likely to be smokers and 13 times more likely to smoke high tar cigarettes than patients with other psychiatric disorders such as depressive, anxiety, personality and adjustment disorders (Kisely *et al,* 2000). Smoking may contribute to the 60 percent increase in deaths from respiratory disorders, and 30 percent increase chance of heart disease in individuals with mental illness (SANE, 1997). They may also spend up to 40% of their income on tobacco (Lasser et al, 2000; SANE, 1997). Although lower than rates for people with schizophrenia, smoking is still higher in patients with alcohol dependence, agoraphobia, panic disorder and major depression than in the general population (Hall *et al*, 1995; Jorm *et al*, 1999).

REASONS FOR THIS ASSOCIATION

One reason for this association is nicotine's augmentation of dopamine release. Dopamine release in the nucleus accumbens and the prefrontal area is associated with pleasurable activities such as eating and sex, as well as exposure to substances such as cocaine, amphetamines and nicotine. This is particularly relevant in the case of schizophrenia where negative symptoms such as social withdrawal and poor motivation may be due to hypofrontality inherent in the disease process. (Lyon 1999). Nicotine also releases noradrenaline and acetylcholine that may result in improved cognitive performance (Wilhelm, 1998). It may also affect an auditory gating mechanism leading to an improvement in auditory hallucinations, while the reverse is true in controls (Wilhelm, 1998).

There may also be psychosocial factors. Patients with schizophrenia report feeling less anxious after smoking (Lyon 1999), which may be especially marked in this population because other sources of recreation are so limited (Lyon 1999). Negative and affective symptoms, particularly in schizophrenia, may hinder attempts to stop (George *et al,* 2000). Co-morbid depression is associated with increased smoking, more difficulty in stopping smoking and a greater subsequent relapse rate (Lyon 1999)

IMPORTANCE OF INTERVENTION

There are a number of benefits to smoking cessation aside from the reduced mortality from carcinoma, respiratory disease and other smoking related conditions in stopping smoking. Nicotine also lowers the level of serum psychotropic medications, so smokers require larger doses of medication, with consequent increased side effects and the risk of chronic neurological problems such as tardive dyskinesia. (Wilhelm, 1998)

TYPES OF INTERVENTION

There have been relatively few studies of the effectiveness of intervention in 'dual diganosis' patients and these favour integrated treatments addressing both issues using cognitive-behavioural and motivational interviewing frameworks (Drake *et al*, 1998; Drake & Mueser, 2000; Department of Health, 2002). These studies have not specifically addressed nicotine dependence.

However, a variety of treatments for nicotine dependence have been investigated in the general population of which advice by a doctor, bupropion and nicotine replacement therapy (NRT) in standard doses have all been evaluated in the general population and been the most successful (Law *et al* 1995; Jorenby *et al*, 1999). Nortriptyline, cognitive behavioural therapy (CBT) and high dose nicotine replacement therapy (NRT) have also shown promise (Hall *et al* 1998; Dale *et al*, 1994)

It is unclear how applicable or acceptable interventions such as brief physician advice, health education packages, CBT or nicotine patches would be to patients with severe mental illness.

In uncontrolled studies, smoking cessation groups and nicotine replacement therapy (NRT) resulted in reduced tobacco use in about 40% of subjects and cessation in 16% at three months (Ziedonis *et al*, 1997; Addington *et al*, 1998). The use of clozapine (an atypical antipsychotic) has been associated with reduced smoking but widespread use is precluded by the risk of agranulocytosis (George *et al*, 1995). For instance, we have previoulsly reported that four out of nine subjects on clozapine (44%) were non-smokers as opposed to one out of 15 (6%) of those who were not on clozapine, this result reaching statistical significance in spite of the small numbers. (OR=12.0 (95%CI=1.1-134) (Fisher's Exact test=0.04) (Kisely et al, 2000). In a controlled trial of group therapy in patients with schizophrenia, two other atypicals (olanzapine and risperidone), in conjunction with NRT, were associated with the highest cessation rates and reduced carbon monoxide levels (George *et al*, 2000). Nortriptyline (an antidepressant) and cognitive-behavioural therapy showed promise in a controlled trial of individuals with a history of major depression (Hall et al, 1998). None of these studies confirmed the results of self-report measures with cotinine levels. Although the benefits of bupropion are well documented in the general population (Jorenby *et al*, 1999), only one study has evaluated its effect on smoking in individuals with severe mental illness (George *et al*, 2002). Smoke –free in-patient units have also been suggested as an intervention (Hughes 1993),

Any study of the treatments for nicotine dependence in patients with severe mental illness therefore needs to take into account other predictors of smoking outcome such as severity and type of psychiatric diagnosis, or concurrent prescription of psychotropic medication such as nortriptyline or clozapine.

The American Psychiatric Association (APA) guidelines for managing nicotine withdrawal have highlighted how staff attitudes towards smoking are one of the barriers to helping inpatients stop smoking (1996). For instance, it is difficult for individuals to stop smoking unless the unit or facility they are attending is smoke-free. Letting staff smoke while in contact with patients also makes it more difficult for people with psychiatric disorder to stop smoking. In addition, describing time away from the ward or unit as a 'smoking break' can implicitly condone smoking.

APA Guidelines also stress that psychiatric history taking should detail the smoking history of the patient and others in their household, the relationship to psychiatric illness, previous attempts to stop and an assessment of motivation (1996). Staff should also distinguish between smoking and nicotine dependence, and the presence of the latter should be documented in the notes (American Psychiatric Association, 1996; Wilhelm, 1998).

Standardised instruments for nicotine dependence are available, but have not been validated in this group of patients against serum or urine cotinine levels. A group programme for psychiatric patients in Victoria has been developed but had not been formally evaluated before our study (SANE, 1997). The virtues of a group-based approach include the positive impact of group belonging, the sharing of information about harm-reduction strategies by members of the group, and cost effectiveness.

In this chapter, we initially describe the effectiveness compared to standard treatment of a manualised group intervention use in helping psychiatric patients, including those with dual diagnosis, reduce their tobacco use. We also need to consider intervention early on in the course of schizophrenia and other psychotic disorders. In the second half of the chapter we describe the results of a subsequent survey of patients attending an early psychosis service to see if their rates are nearer to those of the general population or a long-term psychiatric population, and establish their desire to stop smoking. This would be a first step to introducing a primary or secondary prevention programme for this population.

Why a Special Anti-Smoking Programme for Patients with Dual Diagnosis?

In the late 1990s, SANE in Victoria, Australia developed a smoking cessation programme for people with a mental illness (1997). SANE is a national charity in Australia that helps people seriously affected by mental illness through applied research, dissemination of resource materials and advocacy (1997). Reasons behind the development of a special programme included the increased difficulty faced by people with mental illness in coping with withdrawal symptoms, and their reluctance in discussing the effect of withdrawal on their psychiatric symptoms in group programmes for the general poulation. There was also a risk of facilitators without any professional experience of mental illness becoming overwhelmed in helping someone with a psychiatric disorder cope with both withdrawal and any consequent increase in psychopathology. Community based programmes for the general poulation often charge attendance fees that can stretch the finances of patients on a limited income, who may already be spending a large proportion of their resources on tobacco.

The group intervention designed by SANE includes health education, motivational interviewing, cognitive-behavioural therapy and advice about nicotine replacement (1997). The programme was designed prior to the introduction of bupropion to Australia.

It consists of around 10 sessions. Early group sessions focus on developing knowledge and motivation through discussion about the positive and negative effects of smoking, reasons for smoking, and the short- and long-term benefits of stopping. Participants set initial and long-term goals for reduction and cessation. Subsequent sessions cover different methods of stopping, cognitive-behavioural strategies to deal with difficult situations, relapse prevention and a smoke-free lifestyle. This includes exercise, alternative social activities and a healthy diet.

Table 1. Stages of change (Prochaska *et al*, 1986; SANE 1997)

Stage	Smoking example
Pre-contemplative:	Not thinking about stopping in the next 6 months
Contemplative:	Thinking about stopping in the next 6 months
Preparation stage:	Planning to stop smoking in the next 30 days
Action stage:	The first six months after stopping
Maintenance stage:	More than six months after stopping

In our study, these were collapsed into 8 weekly 1½-hour sessions (Kisely *et al*, 2003). A psychologist conducted the intervention, with an additional facilitator as needed.

EVALUATING THE ANTI-SMOKING PROGRAMME

Subjects

We recruited participants (inpatients or outpatients) by referral from Fremantle Hospital Mental Health Services in Western Australia. Inclusion criteria were

1. Being regular smokers (at least 10 cigarettes or equivalent daily),
2. Aged between 18 and 65 years and clinically stable.
3. A willingness to discuss their nicotine use in a group setting;
4. Able to converse in English without an interpreter
5. Absence of developmental disability sufficient to impair participation in the group process

Measures

The following domains were assessed at baseline, the start of the intervention, the end of the intervention, and at three month follow-up: demographic details; clinical diagnosis; medication; number and strength of cigarettes; details of past and concurrent attempts to stop smoking including use of nicotine replacement therapy (NRT) and bupropion; motivation as assessed by the five stages of change (pre-contemplation, contemplation, preparation, action and maintenance scored from 1-5 respectively) (Table 1) (Prochaska & DiClemente, 1986); nicotine dependence as determined by the Fagerstrom Test for Nicotine Dependence (FTND) a 6-item questionnaire with a maximum score of 10 (Heatherton *et al*, 1991), and urinary cotinine.

We also assessed any change in psychiatric symptom using the 12-item General Health Questionnaire (GHQ-12) (Goldberg & Williams, 1988). We reviewed the case notes of participants to assess the number of times tobacco use was recorded in the notes, as well as any record of counselling on reduction of use.

Study Design and Procedure

We used a waitlist-treatment crossover design. Each subject underwent an initial assessment and was then placed on an eight-week waitlist. After the eight weeks, they were re-assessed and invited to join the treatment group. Further assessments were carried out after treatment 8 weeks later and at 3-month follow-up. Other smoking cessation treatments were recorded but not restricted.

All participants received standard community mental health services, including case management, routine inpatient or outpatient services, and a daytime rehabilitation programme.

Analysis

Differences between subjects completing the intervention and dropouts were assessed using the chi-square test and independent samples t-test as appropriate. Changes in measures of tobacco use and psychiatric symptoms between baseline and the start of the intervention; the start and end of the intervention, and the end of the intervention and three-month follow-up respectively were assessed using the paired samples t-test. The results were confirmed with the equivalent non-parametric test (Wilcoxon signed ranks test). We also calculated the number needed to treat (NNT) with 95% confidence intervals (CI). Other influences on cessation or measures of tobacco use were assessed using logistic or multiple regression respectively.

RESULTS

Patient Characteristics

52 subjects were referred by treating clinicians of whom 38 consented to participate. Sixty percent were female (n=23) and 40% male (n=15), with a mean age of 41.1. A third had completed post-secondary education (n=14). All were outpatients. Just over 40% had schizophrenia (n=17), and another 40% mood disorder (n=16). The remainder had an organic mental (n=4) or personality disorder (n=1). Subjects had smoked an average of 20 years. Twenty patients were on antidepressants, three on clozapine, fourteen on other atypical antipsychotics and eleven on conventional antipsychotics. Only two were on bupropion and one on NRT who later dropped-out.

The records of 34 subjects were included in the audit of case-notes as the remaining four were of patients with less than 2 years contact. Tobacco use was recorded at least once in the two years prior to the study in 52% of case notes (n=18), and counselling documented in 38% (n=13).

Of the 38 subjects, eight dropped out during the waitlist period and a further eleven during the intervention. This left 19 subjects who completed the waitlist and intervention phases in four cohorts. There were no significant differences between subjects who completed the study and those who dropped out in terms of demographics, diagnosis, medication, psychological symptoms or measures of tobacco use (Figures 1 and 2). Ten subjects were followed up three months later.

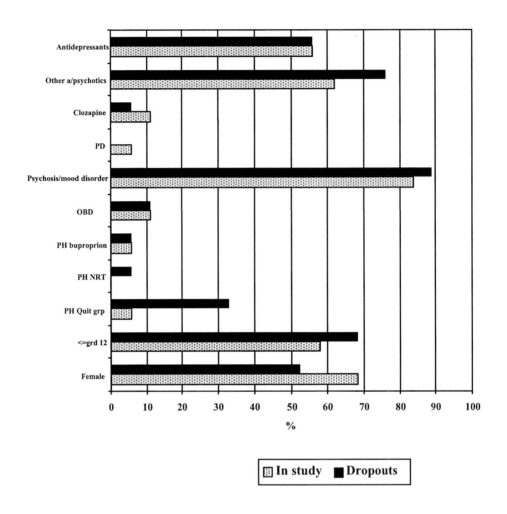

Figure 1. Differences between particpants and drop-outs

Changes During the Wait-List Period

During the waitlist period, all 19 subjects continued to smoke. There were no significant changes in the two self-reported measures of tobacco use. These were state of change (t-test=-0.97, df=18, p=0.35), or FTND score (t-test= 1.51, df=18, p=0.15) (Figure 3). This was confirmed by urinary cotinine levels (t-test= 0.16, df=18, p=0.87)(Figure 4). Psychiatric morbidity as measured by the GHQ-12 also showed no change (t-test= 0.42, df=18, p=0.68)(Figure 4).

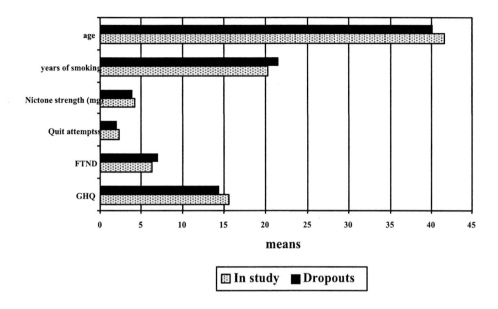

Figure 2. Differences between participants and drop-outs (continuous varaibles)

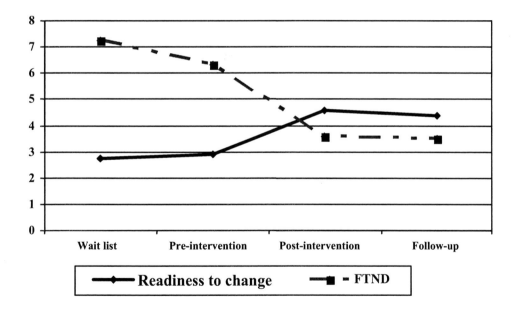

Figure 3. Changes in self-report measures of tobacco use

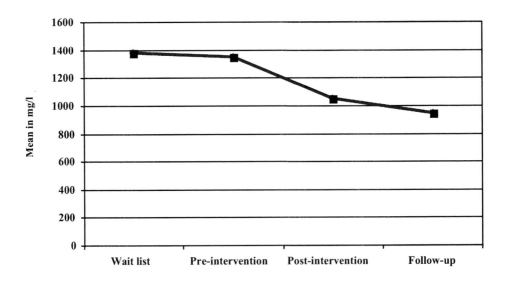

Figure 4. Changes in cotinine level

Psychiatric morbidity as measured by the GHQ-12 also showed no change (t-test= 0.42, df=18, p=0.68) (Figure 5).

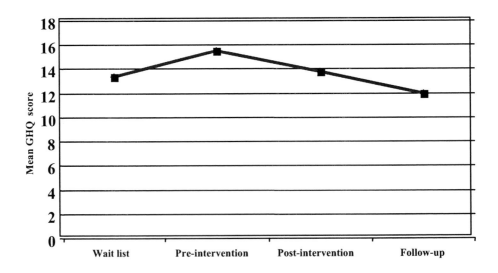

Figure 5. Changes in psychiatric morbidity

Treatment Outcome at the End of the Intervention

By the end of the 8-week intervention, almost a quarter (n=5) had stopped smoking (NNT=3.8 (95%CI=3.6-4.0)). This was statistically significant (z=-2.24, p=0.02). Subjects also showed significant improvements in the two self-reported measures of tobacco use

(Figures 3 and 4), in terms of state of change (t-test=-4.14, df=18, p=0.001), or FTND score (t-test= 3.81, df=18, p=0.002). This was mirrored by similar significant falls in urinary cotinine levels (t-test= 2.25, df=18, p=0.046).

Psychiatric morbidity on the GHQ-12 showed no significant change (t-test= 1.22, df=18, p=0.24) (Figure 5). Two subjects remained on bupropion.

Treatment Outcome at Three Month Follow-Up

We followed up 10 subjects three months after the end of the intervention. Of these, three continued not to smoke (NNT=3.3 (95%CI=3.0-3.6)). Subjects maintained their improvement on self –report measures of tobacco use with significant improvements in stages of change (t-test=-2.28, df=9 p=0.046), and FTND score (t-test= 3.14, df=9, p=0.004) from the beginning of the intervention (Figures 3 and 4). There was no adverse effect on psychiatric morbidity as measured by the GHQ-12 (t-test=0.61, df=9, p=0.56) (Figure 5).

Other Results

We found the same results using non-parametric equivalents of the paired samples t-test. On multivariate analysis, we found no association between socio-demographic characteristics, diagnosis, atypical antipsychotic or antidepressant prescription and tobacco use. Table 2 shows the results for cotinine levels at the end of the intervention.

Table 2. Potential confounders associated with cotinine levels post-intervention

	Unstandardized Coefficients		Standardized Coefficients	t	Sig.
	B	Std. Error	Beta		
length smoking in years	24.29	25.29	0.32	0.96	0.36
gender	-939.08	616.96	-0.49	-1.52	0.16
age	-13.17	47.68	-0.13	-0.28	0.79
diagnosis	17.24	179.93	0.04	0.10	0.93
SNRI antidepressants	282.61	745.73	0.13	0.38	0.71
SSRI antidepressants	-12.13	965.81	-0.01	-0.01	0.99
atypical antipsychotics	699.42	641.26	0.38	1.09	0.30

WHAT ABOUT PATIENTS WITH EARLY PSYCHOSIS?

We also wanted to find out whether patients at the time of first presentation with psychosis show the same levels of smoking as those with long-term illness, or whether their levels are nearer to those in the general poulation. We therefore surveyed patients of the Nova Scotia Early Psychosis Programme (NSEPP) in Canada.

The Nova Scotia Early Psychosis Programme (NSEPP) is a multidisciplinary programme that provides care for individuals who suffer with Early Psychosis. NSEPP was formed in 1995 as a partnership between Dalhousie University Department of Psychiatry and the Nova

Scotia Hospital. It is currently part of the Capital District Mental Health Program and operates at both the QEII Health Sciences Centre (Abbie J. Lane site) and the Nova Scotia Hospital. It has a Province-wide mandate and accepts referrals form the whole of Nova Scotia.

All patients who presented to the Nova Scotia Hospital (NSH) site for a two-month period were asked to complete a standard questionnaire regarding smoking history. This included demographic details, medication; number and strength of cigarettes; details of past and concurrent attempts to stop smoking including use of nicotine replacement therapy (NRT) and bupropion. We also assessed motivation using the five stages of change (Table 1) (Prochaska & DiClemente, 1986).

Sixty questionnaires were completed. Nineteen of the subjects were female (31.7%) and 41 male (68.3%). The mean age at first contact with NSEPP was 25.20 (SD=6.86). Thirty (50%) of the sample were smokers and there were no statistically significant difference in age between these two groups on the t-test between smokers (mean age=24.34 (SD=5.11)) and non-smokers (mean age=26.06 (SD=8.25)).

Table 3 illustrates the characteristics of the smokers. There was no statistically significant gender difference in terms of age of starting to smoke, amount of cigarettes smoked, and duration of smoking. Neither were there statistically significant gender difference in terms of antidepressant therapy (Males=8 / 15, Females=2 / 5) or level of interest in stopping smoking (Males=13 / 10, Females=5 / 2). Interestingly, although 18 out 30 subjects (60%) were at the contemplative stage of change or above, this is significantly lower than that reported in a study of patients attending general psychiatric services where 77 out of 87 patients (88%) were at the contemplative stage or above (Chi square=12.7, df=1, =0.0004) (Kisely et al 2000).

Table 3. Characteristics of smokers attending NSEPP

	Smokers (N=30)
Demographics	
Mean Age (sd)	24.3 (5.1)
Male (%)	23 (76.7%)
Tobacco use Mean Length Smoking In Years (sd)	9.03 (5.57)
Cigarettes per day (sd)	20.0 (10.5)
Smoking cessation Stage of change >= contemplative (%)	18 (60.0%)
Psychotropic medication Antidepressants (%)	10 (33.3%)

Table 4 compares the characteristics of smokers attending NSEPP with those attending general psychiatric services in Fremantle who were approached to participate in our evaluation of the group intervention. Patients attending the early episode psychosis service were significantly more likely to be male. As expected they were significantly younger and had been smoking less long. There were no significant differences between the two groups in the level of antidepressant prescription.

Table 4. A comparison of smokers attending NSEPP with those attending general psychiatric services in Fremantle

	NSEPP (N=30)	Fremantle (N=38)	Significance
Demographics			
Mean Age (sd)	24.3 (5.1)	40.0 (10.2)	t-test=2.0, df=66, p=0.049
Male (%)	23 (76.7%)	15 (39.4%)	Chi square=9.27, df=1, =0.002
Tobacco use Mean Length Smoking In Years (sd)	9.03 (5.57)	20.9 (10.4)	t-test=2.0, df=66, p=0.049
Psychotropic medication Antidepressants (%)	10 (33.3%)	21 (55.6%)	NS

DISCUSSION

Comparison with Previous Work

We need more research to define the most effective content, shape and form of interventions that will help people with dual diagnosis reduce their tobacco use. Although not specifically about tobacco use, Drake et al (1998) reviewed published studies in the area of dual diagnosis, and identified a number of methodological flaws, including non-randomised non-controlled experimental designs, low numbers of participants, and the lack of standardised assessment instruments.

This is the first attempt to evaluate a group intervention targeted for individuals with psychiatric disorder using a controlled design and confirming self-report measures with cotinine levels. By using a wait-list design, each case acted as their own control. To our knowledge, the second part of the study is also the first time that anyone has measured the prevalence of smoking in an early episode psychosis service.

Our findings support the view that integrated treatment is effective for people with psychotic disorders, whose illness is complicated by substance use, including tobacco (Drake *et al.*, 1998; Siegfreid, 1998; Drake & Mueser, 2000; Department of Health, 2002). Integrated interventions incorporate aspects from both mental health and substance use treatments and are delivered simultaneously by the same personnel (Ley *et al* 2001). We have shown that this approach can be employed in a group-based intervention within routine clinical service settings. It is also promising that patients of an early episode psychosis service show rates of smoking that although higher than those of the general population, are lower than those in longer-term patients (Hughes 1993; SANE, 1998). However, although 60% were at the very least thinking of smoking cessation, it is of concern that motivation to change was significantly lower than patients in other psychiatric settings (Kisely et al, 2000). This group should be a particular focus for primary and secondary prevention of smoking.

Limitations of the Study

Limitations of the study include small numbers, and the impossibility of blinding participants and group facilitators to intervention status. The wait-list design meant we could not control for the therapeutic effects of social contact through recruitment to the study. We were reliant on self-report measures for some of our outcomes, and there has been little research on the psychometrics of the Fagerstrom Test for Nicotine Dependence in patients with psychotic or other psychiatric disorders.

Our project did not consider reasons for substance use in the group intervention. Work in patienst with dual diagnosis who are using substances other than nicotine has suggested that group treatments that incorporate this approach may be of benefit (James *et al*, 2004).

Other limitations include the 50% dropout rate from referral to receiving the intervention, and non-blinded assessment of outcome. We only assessed 10 subjects at three-month follow-up. The small number meant we could not assess the contributions of demographic, clinical or treatment variables like NRT, bupropion and the group intervention to smoking cessation.

Strengths of the Study

Strengths of the study included the absence of significant differences between participants and dropouts, and the use of urinary cotinine levels to confirm the results of self-report instruments.

This project showed that it was possible to reduce levels of smoking in individuals with mental illness, up to three months afterwards, and without deterioration in their mental state. Assessment of numbers needed to treat indicated moderate efficacy (Bandolier, 2002). In spite of the high rate of cigarette smoking among people with psychiatric disorder, our audit of case-notes and survey of drugs prescribed on entry to the study indicated that few had received interventions such as bupropion or NRT. However, rates of counselling were still higher than those reported in primary care (Goldstein *et al*, 1998).

Unlike other work, atypical antipsychotic prescription did not result in lower tobacco use, but our numbers were small and we didn't prescribe NRT (George *et al*, 2000). Larger randomised controlled trials are indicated to assess the contribution of NRT, bupropion and group interventions using multivariate analyses to control for confounders such as psychotropic medication. This is because atypical antipsychotics have been shown to augment the effects of both nicotine replacement and bupropion in studies of smoking cessation in patients with schizophrenia (George *et al*, 2000 & 2002).

Another area for further research is a direct comparison between group programmes designed for this population and those intended for the general poulation. Although there are good reasons why specifically designed programmes should be superior (SANE 1998), they have not been shown to be conclusively better than generic interventions (George 2000).

Other areas for research would be to investigate whether looking at individual's reason for tobacco use might be of therapeutic benefit. Research into other substance use suggests that this approach may help. A number of studies have investigated motivations for substance use in psychosis (Spencer *et al*, 2002; Test *et al*, 1989; Dixon *et al.*, 1991; Warner, 1994; Baigent *et al.*, 1995; Addington & Duchak, 1997; Fowler *et al.*, 1998; Mueser *et al.*, 1995). This work was applied to the evaluation of a manualised group intervention tailored to participants' stage of change and motivations for drug use (James *et al*, 2004). The active intervention consisted of weekly 90-minute sessions over 6 weeks, and at three-month follow-up there were improvements in psychiatric morbidity, alcohol and illicit substance use, severity of dependence and need for inpatient treatment. Substances covered were primarily alcohol, cannabis and amphetamines (Wynne *et al*, 2002).

Our survey of Nova Scotia Early Psychosis Programme (NSEPP) patients suggests that primary and secondary intervention may be indicated early in the presentation of psychotic and other psychiatric illness. Based on these results we plan to offer both

- A primary prevention programme aimed at ensuring that non-smokers do not start smoking, and
- A secondary prevention programme aimed at existing smokers based on a group programme tailored for people with psychiatric disorder, supplemented by medication.

Given the high rate of antidepressant prescription in this population and the need for caution in the use of bupropion when patients are being prescribed antidepressants (British Medical Association, 2003), it may be that nicotine replacement therapy would be more appropriate as the first line of therapy.

ACKNOWLEDGMENTS

The evaluation of the group intervention was funded by Healthway (Western Australia).

REFERENCES

Addington J, el-Guebaly N, Campbell W, Hodgins D, Addington D (1998). Smoking cessation treatment for patients with schizophrenia. *Amercian Journal of Psychiatry*,155,974-6.

Addington, J., and Duchak, V. (1997) Reasons for substance use in schizophrenia. *Acta Psychiatrica Scandinavica*, 96, 329-333.

American Psychiatric Association (1996). Practice guideline for the treatment of patients with nicotine dependence *Amercian Journal of Psychiatry*, 153s, 1-16

Baigent, M.; Holme, G.; and Hafner, R. J. (1995) Self reports of the interaction between substance abuse and schizophrenia. *Australian and New Zealand Journal of Psychiatry*, 29, 69-74.

Bandolier Library (2002) *Number needed to treat (NNT)* [Cited 28 September 2002] available from URL: http://www.jr2.ox.ac.uk/bandolier/band59/NNT1.html#box3

Barrowclough C, Haddock G, Tarrier N et al. (2001) Randomized controlled trial of motivational interviewing, cognitive behavior therapy, and family intervention for patients with comorbid schizophrenia and substance use disorders. *American Journal of Psychiatry*, 158, 1706-1713

Bond, G.R.; McDonel, E.C.; Miller, L.D.; & Pensec, M (1991). Assertive community treatment and reference groups: an evaluation of their effectiveness for young adults with serious mental illness and substance abuse problems. *Psychosocial Rehabilitation Journal,* 15, 31-43.

British Medical Association and the Royal Pharmaceutical Society of Great Britain (2003). *British National Formulary.* London: British Medical Association.

Dale LC, Hurt RD, Offord KP, Lawson GM, Croghan IT, Schroeder DR. (1995). High-dose nicotine patch therapy. Percentage of replacement and smoking cessation. *JAMA.,*274,1353-8.

Darke S. Hall W. Wodak A. Heather N. Ward J. (1992) Development and validation of a multi-dimensional instrument for assessing outcome of treatment among opiate users: the Opiate Treatment Index. *British Journal of Addiction.* 87:733-42.

de Leon J, Dadvand M, Canuso C, White AO (1995) Schizophrenia and smoking: an epidemiological survey in a state hospital. *American Journal of Psychiatry,* 1995,152,453-5.

Department of Health (2002) Mental Health Policy Implementation Guide: Dual Diagnosis Good Practice Guide. Department of Health Publications. London

Dixon L (1999) Dual diagnosis of substance abuse in schizophrenia: prevalence and impact on outcomes. *Schizophrenia Research.* 35, 93-100.

Dixon, L.; Haas, G.; Weiden, P. J.; Sweeney, J.; and Frances, A. J. (1991) Drug Abuse in schizophrenic patients: clinical correlates and reasons for use. *American Journal of Psychiatry,* 148: 224.

Drake, R.E., and Mueser, K.T. (2000) Psychosocial approaches to dual diagnosis. *Schizophrenia Bulletin,* 26, 105-118.

Drake, R.E., Mercer-McFadden, C., Mueser, K.T., McHugo, G.J. & Bond, G.R. (1998). Review of integrated mental health and substance abuse treatment for patients with dual disorders. *Schizophrenia Bulletin,* 24, 589-608.

Dual Diagnosis Steering Group (2002). Mental Health Policy Implementation Guide. Dual diagnosis Good Practice Guide. London: Department of Health

Fowler, I. L., Carr, V. J., Carter, N. T., & Lewin, T. J. (1998). Patterns of current and lifetime substance abuse in schizophrenia. *Schizophrenia Bulletin,* 24, 443-445.

George T, Sernyak M, Woods S. Effects of clozapine on smoking in chronic schizophrenic patients. *J Clin Psychiatry* 1995, 56, 344-6.

George TP, Vessicchio JC, Termine A, Bregartner TA, Feingold A, Rounsaville, BJ, Kosten TR. (2002). A placebo controlled trial of bupropion for smoking cessation in schizophrenia. *Biological Psychiatry,* 52, 53-61

George TP, Ziedonis DM, Feingold A, Pepper WT, Satterburg CA, Winkel J, Rounsaville BJ, Kosten TR (2000). Nicotine transdermal patch and atypical antipsychotic medications for smoking cessation in schizophrenia. *American Journal of Psychiatry,*157,1835-42.

Glassman AH (1993). Cigarette smoking: implications for psychiatric illness. *American Journal of Psychiatry,* 150, 546-53

Goldberg DP, Williams P.(1988) *A Users Guide to the General Health Questionnaire: GHQ.* Windsor: NFER-NELSON

Goldstein MG, DePue JD, Monroe AD, Lessne CW, Rakowski W, Prokhorov A, Niaura R, Dube CE (1998). A population-based survey of physician smoking cessation counseling practices. *Preventive Medicine,*27,720-9.

Hall RG, Duhamel M, McClanahan R, Miles G *et al.* (1995) Level of functioning, severity of illness, and smoking status among chronic psychiatric patients. *Journal of Nervous Mental Disease* 183, 468-71.

Hall S, Munoz R, Reus V (1991). Smoking cessation, depression & dysphoria. *NIDA Research Monograph*, 105,312-3

Hall S, Reus VI, Munoz RF, Sees KL, Humfleet G, Hartz DT, Frederick S, Triffleman E (1998). Nortriptyline & CBT in the treatment of cigarette smoking. *Archives of General Psychiatry*, 55,683-9

Heatherton TF, Kozlowski LT, Frecker RC, Fagerstrom KO (1991). The Fagerstrom Test for Nicotine Dependence: a revision of the Fagerstrom Tolerance Questionnaire. *British Journal of Addiction*,86,1119-27

Hellerstein, D.J.; and Meehan, B. (1987). Outpatient group therapy for schizophrenic substance abusers. *American Journal of Psychiatry,* 144, 1337-1339.

Hughes JR (1993). Possible effects of smoke-free inpatient units on psychiatric diagnosis and treatment. *Journal of Clinical Psychiatry*; 54: 109-114

Hughes JR. (1993) Possible effects of smoke-free inpatient units on psychiatric diagnosis and treatment. *Journal of Clinical Psychiatry*, 54, 109-114

Huxley N, Rendall M, Sederer L (2000) Psychosocial treatments in schizophrenia: a review of the past 20 years. *Journal of Nervous and Mental Diseases* 188, 187-201

James W , Koh G, Spencer C, Preston N, Kisely S, Castle D (2002). *Managing Mental Health & Drug Use*. Perth, Western Australia: Uniprint.

James W, Preston N, Koh G, Spencer C, Kisely S, Castle D (2004) A group intervention which assists patients with dual diagnosis reduce their drug use. *Psychological Medicine* (In press)

James, W, Castle D. (2003). Substance abuse comorbidity in schizophrenia. In: Castle DJ, Copolov D, Wykes T (eds.) *Pharmacological and Psychosocial treatments for Schizophrenia*. London: Martin Dunitz. Pp.75-87

Jorenby DE, Leischow SJ, Nides MA, Rennard SI, Johnston JA, Hughes AR, Smith SS, Muramoto ML, Daughton DM, Doan K, Fiore MC, Baker TB (1999). A controlled trial of sustained-release bupropion, a nicotine patch, or both for smoking cessation. *New England Journal of Medicine*, 340,685-91

Jorm AF, Rodgers B, Jacomb PA, Christensen H, Henderson S, Korten AE (1999). Smoking and mental health: results from a community survey. *MJA*; 170: 74-7

Kavanagh, D. J (1995) An intervention for substance abuse in schizophrenia. *Behaviour Change*, 12: 20-30.

Kavanagh, D.; Saunders, J.; Young, R.; Jenner, L.; and Clair, A (1998). *Start Over and Survive Treatment Manual. Evaluation of a brief intervention for substance abuse in early psychosis*. Brisbane, Australia: University of Queensland

Kisely S, Preston N, Shannon P (2000). Smoking in Mental Health Settings: A pilot study. *Health Promotion Journal of Australia*, 10, 60-62.

Kisely S, Wise M, Preston N, (so good you named me twice!!!) Shannon P (2003). A group intervention to reduce smoking in individuals with psychiatric disorder. *Australian and New Zealand Journal of Public Health*; 27: 61-63

Krausz, M., Haasen, C. Mass, R., Wagner ,H.B. Peter, H. and Freyberger, H.S. (1996) Harmful use of psychotropic substances by schizophrenics: coincidence, patterns of use and motivation. *European Addiction Research* 2, 11-16.

Lasser K, Boyd JW, Woolhandler S, Himmelstein DU *et al.* (2000) Smoking and mental illness: A population-based prevalence study. *JAMA*, 284,2606-10

Law, M, Tang JL (1995). An analysis of effectiveness of interventions intended to help people stop smoking. *Archives of Internal Medicine*,155, 1933-41

Ley A, McLaren S, Siegfried N (2001) Treatment programmes for people with both severe mental illness and substance misuse (Cochrane Review). Cochrane Library, Issue 1

Lyon ER. (1999) A review of the effects of nicotine on schizophrenia and antipsychotic medications. *Psychiatric Services*; 50:1346-50.

Martinez-Aravelo, M.J., Calcedo-Ordonez, A. & Varo-Prieto, J.R. (1994). Cannabis consumption as a prognostic factor in schizophrenia. *British Journal of Psychiatry,* 164:679-681.

Minkoff, K. (1989). An integrated treatment model for dual diagnosis of psychosis and addiction. *Hospital and Community Psychiatry*, 40, 1031-1036.

Mueser, KT. Nishith, P. Tracy JL. DeGirolamo, L. Molinaro, M. (1995) Expectations and motives for substance use in schizophrenia. *Schizophrenia Bulletin*. 21 (3): 367-378.

Noordsy, D., & Fox, L. (1992). Group intervention techniques for people with dual disorders. *Psychosocial Rehabilitation Journal,* 15, 67-78.

Osher, C.F., & Kofoed, L.L. (1989). Treatment of patients with psychiatric and psychoactive substance abuse disorders. *Hospital and Community Psychiatry,* 40, 1025-1030.

Prochasca, J. & DiClemente C (1986) Toward a comprehensive model of change. In Miller & Heather (eds), Treating addictive behaviours: process of change. Plenum: New York.

Regier, D. A., Farmer, M. E., Rae, D. S., Locke, B. Z., Keith, S. J., Judd, L. L., & Goodwin, F. K. (1990). Comorbidity of mental disorders with alcohol and other drug abuse. *Journal of the American Medical Association,* 264, 2511-2518.

SANE (1997). *Cessation of smoking in long term psychiatric patients.* Victoria: SANE

Schneier, F. R., and Siris, S. G. (1987). A review of psychoactive substance abuse and schizophrenia: Patterns of drug choice. *Journal of Nervous and Mental Disease*, 175, 641-652.

Siegfried, N. (1998). A review of comorbidity: Major mental illness and problematic substance use. *Australian and New Zealand Journal of Psychiatry*, 32, 707-717.

Spencer C, Castle D, Michie P (2002) An examination of the validity of a motivational model for understanding substance use among individuals with psychotic disorders. Schizophrenia Research, 28, 233-247

Strakowski, SM. McElroy, SL. Keck,PW. and Wesy, SA. (1994) The co-occurrence of mania with medical and other psychiatric disorders. *International Journal of Psychiatry Medicine* 22, 305-328.

Test, M. A.; Wallisch, L. S.; Allness, D. J.; and Ripp, K. (1989) Substance abuse in young adults with schizophrenic disorders. *Schizophrenia Bulletin*, 15, 465-476.

Warner, M. B.; Taylor, D.; Wright, J.; Sloat, A.; Springet, G.; Arnold, S.; and Weinberg, H. (1994) Substance use among the mentally ill: Prevalence, reasons for use and effects on illness. *American Journal of Orthopsychiatry*, 64, 30-39.

Wilhelm K (1998). The relevance of smoking & nicotine to clinical psychiatry. *Australasian Psychiatr,* 6, 130-1

Zeidonis, D.M; and Fisher, W. (1994). Assessment and treatment of comorbid substance abuse in individuals with schizophrenia. *Psychiatric Annals,* 24, 477-483.

Ziedonis DM, George TP (1997). Schizophrenia and nicotine use: report of a pilot smoking cessation program and review of neurobiological and clinical issues. *Schizophrenia Bulletin*, 23, 247-54.

Ziedonis DM, Kosten TR, Glazer WM, Frances RJ (1994). Nicotine dependence and schizophrenia. *Hospital & Community Psychiatry*, 45, 204-6.

In: Trends in Psychotherapy Research
Editor: M. E. Abelian, pp. 161-181

ISBN 1-59454-373-9
© 2006 Nova Science Publishers, Inc.

Chapter 8

WRITING YOUR WAY TO HEALTH?
THE EFFECTS OF DISCLOSURE OF
PAST STRESSFUL EVENTS IN GERMAN STUDENTS

Lisette Morris, Annedore Linkemann and Birgit Kröner-Herwig[*]
Clinical Psychology and Psychotherapy
University of Göttingen, Germany

ABSTRACT

In 1986 Pennebaker and Beall published their renowned study on the long-term beneficial health effects of disclosing traumatic events in 4 brief sequential writing sessions. Their results have been confirmed in various studies, but conflicting results have also been reported. The intent of our study was to replicate the experiments from Pennebaker and Beall (1986), Pennebaker et al. (1988), and Greenberg and Stone (1992) using a German student sample. Additionally, essay variables that point to the emotional processing of events (e.g., depth of self-exploration, number of negative/positive emotions, intensity of emotional expression) were examined as potential mechanisms of action. Trait measures of personality which could moderate the personal consequences of disclosure (alexithymia, self-concealment, worrying, social support) were also assessed. In a second study the experimental condition (disclosure) was varied by implementing "coping" vs. "helping" instructions as variations of the original condition. Under the coping condition participants were asked to elaborate on what they used to do, continue to do, or could do in the future to better cope with the event. Under the helping condition participants were asked to imagine themselves in the role of a adviser and elaborate on what they would recommend to persons also dealing with the trauma in order to better cope with the event. The expected beneficial effects of disclosure on long-term health (e.g., physician visits, physical symptoms, affectivity) could not be corroborated in either the first or the second study. None of the examined essay variables of emotional processing and only a single personality variable was able to explain significant variance in the health-related outcome variables influence. Nevertheless, substantial reductions in posttraumatic stress symptoms

[*] Prof. Dr. B. Kroener-Herwig; Georg-Elias-Mueller-Institut für Psychologie; Dep. Clinical Psychology and Psychotherapy; Gosslerstr. 14; D - 37073 Goettingen; Email: bkroene@uni-goettingen.de

(e.g., intrusions, avoidance, arousal), were found in both experiments. These improvements were significantly related to essay variables of emotional expression and self-exploration and were particularly pronounced under the activation of a prosocial motivation (helping condition).

Repeated, albeit brief, expressive writing about personally upsetting or traumatic events resulted in an immediate increase in negative mood but did not lead to long-term positive health consequences in a German student sample. It did, however, promote better processing of stressful or traumatic events, as evidenced by reductions in posttraumatic stress symptoms. The instruction to formulate recommendations for persons dealing with the same trauma seems more helpful than standard disclosure or focusing on one's own past, present, and future coping endeavours. Overall, expressive writing seems to be a successful method of improving trauma processing. Determining the appropriate setting (e.g., self-help vs. therapeutic context) for disclore can be seen as an objective of future research.

INTRODUCTION

Pennebaker & Beall's (1986) study published under the title "Confronting a traumatic event: Towards an understanding of inhibition and disease" caused quite a sensation among clinical psychologists and incited numerous replication studies, primarily in the USA. In their original study, the authors asked students to write about personally upsetting or traumatic experiences from one of the following three perspectives: emphasising feelings without describing the actual experience (trauma-emotion condition), emphasising factual aspects of the experience without mentioning feelings (trauma-fact condition), or describing both the experience and the associated feelings (trauma-combination condition). In a control condition, students were instructed to write in an factual manner about different trivial topics (e.g., their living room, the shoes they were wearing). In all four conditions, writing took place on 4 consecutive days for a period of 15 minutes per day.

The physical symptoms and mood of the students were assessed directly prior to and following writing and a number of health-related variables were assessed at follow-up 4 to 6 months later. Short-term effects of writing were not found for physical symptoms, but significant effects were found, as expected, for mood. Ss in all three trauma conditions reported a deterioration of mood subsequent to writing, whereas controls reported improved mood.

The most important effect, however, was the significantly better health status found in the trauma-combination condition at follow-up. Ss in both the trauma-emotion and trauma-combination conditions reported significant reductions of health problems (4-month) relative to the other conditions, while significantly fewer days with illness-related restriction of activity (4-month) and fewer visits to the university health care centre (6-month follow-up) were found only in the trauma-combination condition.

The authors concluded that written disclosure of traumatic or stressful experiences in a manner that combines emotional expression and factual description is beneficial to health, at least in a sample of young students. Thus, it seemed that with the disclosure paradigm a simple intervention capable of enhancing physical, and perhaps even psychological, health had been found.

Numerous replication studies conducted by Pennebaker and associates as well as by independent researchers followed and various modifications were made to the original paradigm. In some studies Ss were asked to write about specific events like job loss (Spera et al, 1994), entering college (Pennebaker et al., 1990; Pennebaker & Francis, 1996) or suffering from rheumatic disease (Kelly et al, 1997). In some of the studies disclosure took place not through writing but by oral report (e.g., Pennebaker et al. 1987; Donnelly & Murray, 1991; Esterling et al, 1994) or bodily expression (Krantz & Pennebaker, 1996). Additionally, the length of writing sessions was varied (e.g., up to 45 minutes by Schoutrop et al, 1996), as was the number of sessions (1 session by Greenberg et al, 1996; 5 sessions by Spera et al, 1994).

Nearly all early studies corroborated the negative short-term effect of expressive writing on mood (e.g., Petrie et al, 1995; Francis & Pennebaker, 1992, Greenberg et al, 1996) and many further studies found the postulated short-term increase in physical symptoms (e.g., Pennebaker et al, 1988; Greenberg & Stone, 1992; Booth et al, 1997). The long-term beneficial effects on physical health were supported by numerous studies which documented improvements ranging from reductions in health care utilization (e.g., Pennebaker et al, 1990, Pennebaker & Francis, 1996, Pennebaker et al, 1988) to improved immunological parameters (e.g., Esterling et al, 1994; Pennebaker et al, 1988; Lutgendorf et al, 1994; Petrie et al, 1995). In other studies, however, expressive writing did not positively affect subjective health measures (e.g., Petrie et al, 1995; Spera et al, 1994; Murray & Segal, 1994). Results concerning the long-term effect of disclosure on psychological well-being were also contradictory. Pennebaker et al's (1988) results as well as the findings from Schoutrop et al (1996) pointed to long-term improvements of mood following writing. No effect, however, was seen by Greenberg and Stone (1992) and an unexpected long-term increase in negative affect was reported by Greenberg et al (1996).

Overall, however, the studies seemed to support the theoretical model formulated by Pennebaker (1988, 1989) on inhibition and confrontation. Based on the tenet that people have an innate desire to express their feelings and to communicate significant experiences, Pennebaker postulated that hindered interpersonal expression, due to feelings of guilt or shame or feared negative response of others, leads to negative physical and psychological consequences.

Inhibition was defined by Pennebaker (1989) as the process of consciously holding back or otherwise suppressing thoughts, feelings and behaviours. It entails physiological work and leads to an activation of the autonomic nervous system. In the long run, it places cumulative stress on the body, increasing the likelihood of stress-related physical and psychological symptoms or illness. Confrontation is seen as the opposite of inhibition. It is the process of actively facing significant personal experiences, while acknowledging and dealing with the associated feelings and thoughts. Confronting significant experiences makes the physiological work of suppressing associated thoughts and feelings obsolete and can, via reductions in overall stress level, negate the long-term effects of inhibition on physical health and psychological well-being.

Later the focus of attention was shifted more to the cognitive level (Francis & Pennebaker, 1992; Pennebaker et al., 1997). From this perspective, inhibition is seen as an impediment to the emotional processing of traumatic experiences, a hindrance to their assimilation and resolution. The inadequately processed experiences maintain their distressfulness as they resurface in the form of rumination or associated cognitive symptoms. Written or verbal confrontation, which entails the translation of traumatic memory into language, negates inhibition and works to promote the understanding and assimilation of the experiences, thereby facilitating their closure. The relevance of the reorganisation of traumatic memory and its integration into the autobiographical memory and self-concept echoes back to Horowitz (1976) and coincides with current models of the processes underlying confrontation therapy in posttraumatic stress disorder (Ehlers, 2000).

As the vast majority of the early studies were conducted in the USA and Canada, Petrie et al (1995), Paez et al. (1999), and Schoutrop et al (1996) are several exceptions, we were interested in the effect of disclosure on a German sample. The intent of our experiment was to replicate the studies from Pennebaker and Beall (1986), Pennebaker et al (1988) and Greenberg and Stone (1992) in order to find out whether we would achieve effects of disclosure comparable to those in the USA. Furthermore, we intended to study the disclosure process more closely by assessing relevant essay characteristics (e.g., frequency of positive and negative emotional expressions) and examining their influence on the short- and long-term effects of disclosure. A number of personality variables were also examined as potential moderators of the effects of disclosure.

Two studies were conducted, each on a different sample of students. In the first study, standard disclosure and control conditions were implemented. In the second study, two new variations of expressive writing were examined, one instructing the Ss to focus on coping endeavours and a second emphasising a "helping" perspective (see Methods: Study II).

STUDY I: METHODS

The design was based on the studies from Pennebaker and Beall (1986), Pennebaker et al (1988), and Greenberg and Stone (1992) and employed analogous assessment instruments. A two factorial control group design with repeated measures was implemented in accordance with Pennebaker et al (1988). In the disclosure condition, Ss were instructed to write about a very upsetting or traumatic personal experience in their past and to emphasise revealing their deepest thoughts and feelings in their essays, while control Ss were asked to write about their daily routine and time management in an detailed and factual manner. A total of 3 writing sessions were held, each lasting 20 minutes. Long-term effects of disclosure were assessed 6 weeks after writing in accordance with Pennebaker et al, (1988).

The sample consisted of 61 students, who were randomly assigned to one of the two conditions. Because of our focus on variables which could potentially moderate disclosure effects, a greater number of Ss were assigned to the experimental condition (40 vs. 21 in the control condition).

The following instruments, commonly employed in disclosure research, were used (in German translation) to assess the *short-term* effects of expressive writing (pre - post comparison):

- Pennebaker Physical Symptom Scale (PPSS)
- Pennebaker Negative Mood Scale (PNMS)

Long-term effects (pre - 6-week follow-up comparison) were assessed using the following common instruments / measures:

- Pennebaker Inventory of Limbic Languidness (PILL)
- self-reported number of illness days
- self-reported number of days with illness-related activity restriction
- self-reported number of illness-related physician visits
- Positive and Negative Affect Schedule (PANAS, Watson, Clark & Telegen, 1988)
- subjective rating of the long-term effect of writing.

As an additional measure of long-term outcome, the self-report version of the PTSD Symptom Scale (PSS-SR, Foa et al, 1993) was administered to the Ss of the disclosure group.

The following essays characteristics, posited as potential mechanisms of action, were assessed in the disclosure condition:

- relative frequency of negative emotional expressions (Negative Affect Scale, Westbrook, 1976)
- relative frequency of positive emotional expressions (Positive Affect Scale)
- relative frequency of emotional expressions on the whole.

Additionally, the intensity of both positive and negative emotional expression in the essays was rated by independent judges on a 6-point scale (scale anchors taken from Schmidt-Atzert, 1981). The judges also rated the depth of self-exploration exhibited in the essays, yielding the variables average depth of self-exploration and change in self-exploration from day 1 to day 3. Self-exploration, which has proven its relevance for the course and efficacy of client-centred therapy (German Scale: Tausch, 1970), seemed a fitting construct for disclosure research. Finally, Ss in both conditions were asked to rate how emotionally revealing and personal their essays were.

Four personality variables were selected for examination as potential moderators of the short- and long-term effects of disclosure on the basis of their theoretical fit with Pennebaker's theory of inhibition and confrontation. The following instruments were employed for their assessment in the German version:

- Self-Concealment Scale (SCS, Larson & Chastain, 1990)
- Toronto Alexithymia Scale (TAS, Taylor et al, 1985)
- Penn State Worry Questionnaire (PSWQ, Meyer et al, 1990)
- Social Support Questionnaire (F-SozU, Fydrich et al, 1987)

Finally, Ss in the disclosure group were requested to rate the extent to which the experience was personally upsetting at the time of its occurrence and on the first day of writing.

The participants were recruited via placards and handouts distributed in university facilities that provided information about the research project and its aim of tapping *"physiological responses to writing about personal experiences"* (Blood pressure and other physiological parameters were assessed during the experiment, but will not be reported here). Ss received a postpaid monetary incentive or partial course credit for participation in the study. Anonymity of personal data and essays was assured and enforced through strict adherence to data protection procedures. An offer of free counseling was made for any participants who felt emotionally shaken or upset after writing.

STUDY I: RESULTS

A total of 39 female and 22 male Ss with a mean age of 23 years participated in the study (see tab. 1). Half of the Ss were psychology majors. Under the predetermined quota of 2:1 in favour of the experimental group, Ss were randomly assigned to the conditions. The Ss in the two conditions did not differ significantly with regard to sex or age.

Table 1. Characteristics of study I sample

Variable	Condition	
	Disclosure (n=40*)	Control (n=21)
Age (m,sd)	23.9 (4.1)	23.3 (4.0)
Sex (n, % female)	23 (57.5%)	16 (76%)
Major		
Psychology	47,5%	52%
Business/ Economics	32.5%	23.8%
Social sciences	5%	14.3%
Other	15.5%	9.9%

* 1 drop-out at follow-up

As a manipulation check subjects were asked to rate how personal and how emotionally revealing their essays were. Ss in the disclosure group gave significantly higher ratings with regard to both aspects (personal: $m_{disclosure}$ = 5.71 (1.12), $m_{control}$ = 2.79 (1.03), $p < .001$; emotionally revealing: $m_{disclosure}$ = 5.25 (0.95), $m_{control}$ = 1.86 (.85), $p < .001$). Analysis of the essay contents in the disclosure group corroborated the personal nature of the essays and revealed that Ss wrote about a broad spectrum of life events (tab. 2). The Ss rated the experiences described in their essays as quite upsetting at the time they occurred (m=5.8, sd=1.5, scale 1-7), though somewhat less so at the time of writing (m=4.0, sd=1.4). Nevertheless, the latter rating indicates that Ss wrote about experiences that continued to have a negative impact in their lives. Inspection of the essays of the control group revealed compliance with the writing instructions.

The first hypothesis tested relates to *short-term* effects of writing. The disclosure group was expected to show an increase in negative mood and physical symptoms following writing (see tab. 3, mean of all sessions). The hypothesis was statistically supported for negative mood, but not for physical symptoms.

Table 2. Contents of essays in study I disclosure group

Problems with boyfriend / girlfriend	15%
Severe illness or death of family member or close friend	15%
Own severe illness or deformity	12%
Problems with friends or peers	12%
Problems with family members	10%
Separation or divorce of parents	7%
Sexual or physical abuse	7%
Stressful events (not interpersonal)	7%
Major personal failure	5%
Other	10%

Table 3. Short-term effects of writing (study I): Item means (m), standard deviation (sd), and results from analysis of variance (interaction terms*)

Short-term effects			
Variables	Period	Condition	
		Disclosure	Control
1. PPSS	pre	1.63 (.40)	1.58 (.39)
(m,sd) $\alpha = 0.59^{+}$	post	1.65 (.43)	1.54 (.56)
2. PNMS	pre	1.87 (.64)	1.93 (.88)
(m,sd) $\alpha = 0.81$	post	2.05 (.74)	1.73 (.79)
VA(1)*: F (1,59) = 0.62, p > .10			
VA(2)*: F (1,59) = 12.70, p= .001			

$^{+}$ Cronbach's alpha
* period x condition

The second hypothesis related to *long-term* effects and postulated an improvement in physical health in the disclosure group. Results did not confirm the hypothesis. Ss in disclosure group failed to show a significant improvement relative to the control group in any of the health-related variables (see tab. 4). On the contrary, inspection of means revealed deteriorations in 2 of the 4 health-related variables, albeit in both the disclosure and control condition. The third set of hypotheses relates to the expected long-term improvement of psychological well-being in the disclosure group, predicting more positive and less negative affectivity relative to the controls, and also predicting a reduction of posttraumatic stress symptoms within the disclosure group. The hypothesis cannot be confirmed regarding affectivity. However, significant reductions in PSS-SR scales indicate a decreased presence of maladaptive processing 6 weeks after writing. Both re-experiencing and autonomic arousal are reduced (effect sizes d = .72 and .54, respectively), as are posttraumatic stress symptoms on the whole (d = .56).

Asked about long-term positive and negative effects of writing at follow-up, Ss in the disclosure group rate both effects to be stronger than the controls (positive: $m_{disclosure} = 2.43$ (1.32), $m_{control} = 1.57$ (.98), t-test: p = 0.006; negative $m_{disclosure} = 1.55$ (1.09), $m_{control} = 1.0$ (1.0); t-test: p = 0.003).

Table 4. Long-term effects of writing (study I): Item means (m), standard deviation (sd), and results from analysis of variance (interaction terms*) and t-tests

Health	Period	Condition	
		Disclosure	Control
1. PILL (m,sd) α = 0.91	pre	1.03 (0.46)	1.11 (0.37)
	follow-up	0.99 (0.51)	1.07 (0.44)
2. Illness-related visits to physician[+] (m,sd)	pre	0.43 (0.90)	0.48 (1.25)
	follow-up	0.40 (1.08)	0.52 (0.98)
3. Days with illness-related restriction of activity[+] (m,sd)	pre	2.63 (3.83)	2.55 (3.67)
	follow-up	5.75 (17.27)	3.00 (6.60)
4. Illness days[+] (m,sd)	pre	2.30 (3.31)	1.93 (2.67)
	follow-up	4.03 (9.42)	3.86 (7.02)
Affectivity			
5. PANAS: negative (m,sd) α = 0.89	pre	2.05 (0.73)	1.78 (0.65)
	follow-up	1.90 (0.66)	1.75 (0.67)
6. PANAS: positive (m,sd) α = 0.82	pre	3.37 (0.56)	3.17 (0.61)
	follow-up	3.15 (0.56)	3.14 (0.71)
VA(1) *: $F_{(1,59)}$ = .00, p > .10 VA(2) *: $F_{(1,59)}$ = .04, p > .10 VA(3) *: $F_{(1,59)}$ = .48, p > .10 VA(4) *: $F_{(1,59)}$ = .01, p > .10 VA(5) *: $F_{(1,59)}$ = .47, p > .10 VA(6) *: $F_{(1,59)}$ = 1.87, p > .10			
PSS-SR [§]			Statistics
7. Re-experiencing (m, sd)	pre	0.92(0.64)	df=38 t=4.52
	follow-up	0.54 (0.45)	p=.000**
8. Avoidance (m, sd)	pre	0.81 (0.69)	t=1.16
	follow-up	0.70 (0.65)	p=.127
9. Arousal (m, sd)	pre	0.78 (0.58)	t=3.38
	follow-up	0.54 (0.56)	p=.001**
10. Total severity score	pre	0.83 (0.55)	t=3.50
	follow-up	0.61 (0.53)	p=.001**

* Period x condition
[+] Mean frequency
[§] Only assessed in disclosure group

All essay variables were examined for their influence on short- or long-term outcome. Only 4 of the 108 correlations examined reached significance (p < .001, see tab. 5). The results indicate that autonomic arousal is reduced to a larger extent when essays include more positive emotions and when the positive emotions are of greater intensity. Reductions in avoidance and total posttraumatic stress symptoms are greater, when self-exploration increases from day 1 to day 3.

The moderating effect of personality variables on short- and long-term outcome was also examined. Of the 48 correlation coefficients, only one reached significance (tab. 5): The long-term reduction of physical symptoms was more attenuated, the greater the extent of self-concealment.

In a last step of analysis, the influence of personality variables on the manner of writing, as assessed with the essay variables, was examined. The only personality variable that correlated significantly with the examined essay characteristics was "worrying". Essays written by habitual worriers contained relatively more emotional expressions on the whole ($r = .435$, $p = .005$) and more negative emotional expressions in particular ($r = .511$, $p = .001$) than non-worriers' essays. Also, the stronger the tendency to worry, the deeper the self-exploration exhibited in the essays ($r = .378$, $p = .016$)

Table 5. Significant correlations ($p \leq 0.01$) between moderator variables (essay or personality variables) and outcome variables (short- and long-term) in the disclosure group (study I)

Moderator variable	Outcome	Correlation: r
Frequency of positive emotions in essay	Reduced arousal (PSS-SR)	.452 ($p = .002$)
Intensity of positive emotions in essay	Reduced arousal (PSS-SR)	.421 ($p = .004$)
Increasing self-exploration day 1 to day 3	Reduced posttraumatic stress symptoms (PSS-SR)	.424 ($p = .004$)
Increasing self-exploration day 1 to day 3	Reduced avoidance (PSS-SR)	.376 ($p = .009$)
Self-Concealment	Physical symptoms (PILL)	-.366 ($p = .01$)

STUDY II: METHOD

Because of the unexpected negative outcome regarding the postulated long-term beneficial effect of expressive writing on physical health, a second study was conducted to examine whether disclosure instructions modified to promote self-efficacy and coping would produce more positive effects. Therefore, in addition to the standard disclosure condition, two further experimental conditions, "coping" and "helping", were implemented, in which modifications were made to the writing instructions given on day 3. In the "coping" condition, Ss were instructed on to reflect upon what they have done in the past, continue to do, or could do in future to better cope with the traumatic experience they wrote about during the first 2 sessions. This instruction aimed at increasing Ss' awareness of their past, present, and future coping behaviour and thereby at increasing their sense of self-efficacy in dealing with the traumatic experience. It was postulated that the instruction could elicit a constructive reappraisal of the experience which would, in turn, facilitate emotional resolution (see Murray et al, 1989). In the "helping" condition, Ss were asked to imagine themselves in the role of an adviser and to elaborate on what they would recommend to persons dealing with the same trauma they experienced in order to better cope with the event. Midlarsky & Kahana (1994) as well as Berking (1998) have presented data indicating that adopting a prosocial role can have positive cognitive and emotional consequences. A control condition analogous to study I was also implemented, in which Ss were asked to write about their daily routine and time management in a detailed and factual manner.

22 Ss were randomly assigned to each of the four conditions. This time a different set of instruments, selected based on the psychometric quality of the validated German versions, was used for the assessment of long-term effects. The circumstance that the study I instruments were, for the most part, translations of questionnaires originally developed for Anglo-American samples and not yet psychometrically evaluated for German samples was seen as a limitation worthy of amelioration in study II.

Physical symptoms (prior PILL) were assessed via the Complaints Schedule (Beschwerden-Liste, von Zerssen, 1976), affectivity (prior PANAS) through a validated German version of the Profile of Mood States (McNair et al, 1971), and PTSD symptoms via the tested German version of the Impact of Event Scale (Horowitz et al, 1979). The individual health-related items from study I (e.g., illness days) were implemented, as was a questionnaire scale tapping satisfaction with one's health (Fahrenberg et al, 1986). To assess the effect of writing on mood regulation, which is posited as one of the mechanisms underlying health improvement, the questionnaire "Generalized Expectancy for Negative Mood Regulation" (Catanzaro & Mearns, 1990, Catanzaro & Greenwod, 1994) was administered. Furthermore, an item assessing self-efficacy regarding coping with the critical event was added. The conductance of study II was similar to study I in all other aspects.

STUDY II: RESULTS

The sample comprised a total of 84 Ss, the majority of which were female and whose average age varied in the four conditions between 21 and 24 years (see tab. 6). Four Ss dropped out of the study (i.e., did not return follow-up data). Like in study I, most of the participants were students majoring in psychology. No significant differences between groups were found with regard to sociodemographic variables. Analysis of the essay contents in the three experimental conditions (disclosure, coping, helping) indicates that Ss wrote about experiences similar to those in study I. Problems with boyfriend / girlfriend were, however, more frequently written about in study II, while problems with friends and peers, and own severe illness or deformity were less frequent than in study I.

Two two-factorial analyses of variance (condition x period) on the *short-term* effects of writing showed significant differences between groups regarding physical symptoms (PPSS) and negative mood (PNMS, see tab. 7). A post-hoc Scheffé test revealed that this effect can be attributed to differences between the disclosure and control conditions: The disclosure group reported more physical symptoms and greater negative mood directly after writing.

The postulated *long-term* effect of improvements in physical health could not be corroborated in this study. None of the analyses of variance on the health-related variables yielded significant interaction effects, reflecting the absence of health differences between the controls and the three experimental groups, in which the Ss had written in an emotionally expressive manner about traumatic experiences (see tab. 8).

Table 6. Characteristics of study II sample

Variable	Condition			
	Disclosure n = 20*	Coping n = 21	Helping n = 22	Control n = 21
Age (m,sd)	24.1 (5.7)	21.8 (2.4)	22.2 (3.2)	21.2 (2.6)
Sex (n, % female)	13 (65%)	14 (67%)	15 (64%)	14 (67%)
Major				
Psychology	50%	76.2%	45.5%	57.1%
Law	5%	4.8%	13.6%	19%
Other	35%	19.0%	40.9%	19.0%
Non-students	10%			4.8%

*deviation from n = 22: drop-outs at follow-up

Table 7. Short-term effects of writing in study II: Item means (m), standard deviations (sd), and results from analysis of variance (interaction terms) and post-hoc Scheffé-tests

Variables	Period	Condition			
		Disclosure	Coping	Helping	Control
1. PPSS (m,sd)	pre	1.41 (.40)	1.36 (.32)	1.49 (.39)	1.60 (.57)
	post	1.64 (.40)	1.35 (.37)	1.54 (.39)	1.42 (.33)
2. PNMS (m,sd)	pre	1.56 (.64)	1.67 (.97)	1.65 (.70)	1.51 (.58)
	post	1.98 (1.05)	1.79 (1.16)	1.72 (.78)	1.41 (.48)
VA (1)* F (3,80)= 3.75, p = .014					
VA (2)* F (3,80) = 4.16, p = .009					
Post-hoc Scheffé (1): control / disclosure, p = .016					
Post-hoc Scheffé (2): control / disclosure, p = .010					

Analyses of variance conducted on the long-term effects of writing on affectivity and yielded significant differences between groups regarding depression, fatigue and vigour. A post-hoc Scheffé test revealed that this interaction reflects differences between the helping and coping conditions: Ss in the coping condition reported feeling less vigorous and more fatigued than Ss in the helping group.

Analysis of variance of PTSD symptoms (IES) revealed a significant interaction effect for intrusion and a marginally significant interaction effect for avoidance. These effects can be attributed to the expected lack of change in the control group and reductions in intrusions and avoidance found in the disclosure and helping conditions, respectively. The post-hoc Scheffé test supported this interpretation (see tab. 8). Overall, the highest average effect on symptoms of posttraumatic stress was found in the helping group (d = .71), while the other experimental conditions yielded somewhat attenuated effects (disclosure: d = .52, coping: d = .43) and no change occurred in controls (d = .07).

Table 8. Long-term effects of writing in study II: Means (m), standard deviations (sd), and results from analysis of variance (interaction terms) and post-hoc Scheffé-tests

Variable	Period	Condition			
		Disclosure	Coping	Helping	Control
Health					
1. Symptoms	pre	0.77 (.43)	0.78 (.33)	0.78 (.33)	0.84 (.42)
	follow-up	0.80 (.36)	0.77 (.49)	0.65 (.39)	0.76 (.35)
2. Satisfaction with health	pre	2.91 (1.12)	2.92 (1.23)	3.13 (.97)	3.02 (.96)
	follow-up	2.89 (1.01)	3.29 (1.29)	3.24 (1.02)	2.82 (.70)
3. Visits to physician[+]	pre	0.05 (.22)	0.05 (.22)	0.14 (.35)	0.33 (.73)
	follow-up	0.40 (1.57)	0.10 (.44)	0.05 (.21)	0.00 (.00)
4. Activity restriction[+]	pre	1.75 (3.16)	1.11 (1.70)	0.77 (2.19)	1.19 (2.32)
	follow-up	3.16 (6.83)	1.53 (2.32)	0.86 (1.49)	0.91 (1.76)
5. Illness days[+]	pre	2.05 (4.57)	1.43 (2.01)	1.45 (2.46)	2.19 (6.49)
	follow-up	2.65 (6.47)	1.95 (4.77)	0.77 (1.60)	0.71 (1.68)
Affectivity: POMS					
6. Depression α = 0.92*	pre	0.89 (.85)	(.69)	0.86 (.69)	1.10 (.65)
	follow-up	0.81 (.63)	1.23 (1.21)	0.55 (.45)	0.90 (.68)
7. Fatigue	pre	1.22 (.88)	1.07 (.67)	1.22 (.72)	1.25 (.79)
α = 0.89	follow-up	1.36 (.80)	1.68 (.65)	1.10 (.70)	1.37 (.58)
8. Anger	pre	(1.09)	0.94 (.71)	0.77 (.51)	0.94 (.72)
α = 0.90	follow-up	1.10 (.96)	1.05 (.87)	0.72 (.57)	1.20 (.85)
9. Vigor	prä	1.86 (.83)	1.85 (.70)	1.49 (.79)	1.61 (.76)
α = 0.90	follow-up	1.47 (.79)	1.24 (.71)	1.70 (.81)	1.63 (.90)
IES (scale 0 - 3)					
10. Intrusion	pre	1.36 (.76)	1.24 (.82)	1.22 (.73)	0.99 (.60)
α = 0.82	follow-up	.79 (.63)	1.00 (.91)	0.69 (.68)	0.92 (.75)
11. Avoidance	pre	1.06 (.70)	0.84 (.59)	1.08 (.66)	0.92 (.60)
α = 0.75	follow-up	0.89 (.61)	0.63 (.50)	0.65 (.61)	0.93 (.63)

VA (1)* F (3, 80) = 1.22 p > .10
VA (2)* F (3, 80) = 2.56 p = .061
VA (3)* F (3, 80) = .58 p > .10
VA (4)* F (3, 80) = .65 p > .10
VA (5)* F (3, 80) = 2.02 p > .10
VA (6)* F (3, 80) = 2.91 p = .04
VA (7)* F (3, 80) = 5.40 p = .002
VA (8)* F (3, 80) = .51 p > .10
VA (9)* F (3, 80) = 5.56 p = .002
VA (10)* F (3, 80) = 3.23 p = .027
VA (11)* F (3, 80) = 2.29 p = .084

Post-hoc Scheffé: (2) control / helping, p = .071
Post-hoc Scheffé: (6) helping / coping, p = .055
Post-hoc Scheffé: (7) control / coping, p=.083; helping / coping, p = .003
Post-hoc Scheffé: (9) control / coping, p=.060; disclosure / helping p=.082; helping / coping, p = .005
Post-hoc Scheffé: (10) control / disclosure, p = .076
Post-hoc Scheffé: (11) control / helping, p = .086

* Cronbach's Alpha
[+] Mean frequencies

While analysis of variance yielded no significant long-term effects of expressive writing on mood regulation (assessed with the NMR), a significant interaction effect (period x condition) was found for Ss' perceived coping self-efficacy. On the descriptive level, the increase in self-efficacy was most pronounced in the helping condition followed by the coping condition. Inquired as to the positive and negative long-term effects of writing, Ss in the helping group reported significantly more positive consequences than controls. No other differences were found.

Table 9. Mood regulation and coping competency in study II:
Item means (m), standard deviation (sd), and results of analysis variance (interaction terms*)

Variables		Period	Condition			
			Disclosure	Coping	Helping	Control
1.	Mood regulation (m,sd) α = 0.85[+]	pre	3.40 (.40)	3.31 (.43)	3.41 (.42)	3.35 (.39)
		follow-up	3.52 (.40)	3.31 (.50)	3.59 (.48)	3.43 (.47)
2.	Coping competency (m,sd) α = 0.82[+]	pre	1.70 (.73)	1.74 (.87)	1.55 (1.06)	1.81 (1.08)
		post[§]	1.85 (.99)	2.16 (.96)	2.09 (.68)	1.76 (.83)
		follow-up	1.75 (1.07)	2.10 (1.02)	2.10 (1.07)	1.81 (.93)
VA (1)* F (3,80) = 1.14, p > .10						
VA ($2_{pre\text{-}post}$)* F (3,80) = 1.79, p > .10						
VA ($2_{pre\text{-}follow\text{-}up}$)* F (3,80) = 2.71, p = .05						

[+] Cronbachs Alpha
[§] After 3rd writing session
*period x condition

STUDY I: DISCUSSION

In many studies a relative increase in negative mood directly after writing about upsetting events has been observed, an effect which Pennebaker (1993) has postulated as being a prerequisite for the long-term positive effects of disclosure. This negative effect on mood was corroborated in our study, though inspection of means revealed the effect to be attributable to an improvement of mood in the control group and a comparable deterioration of mood in the disclosure group. It is important to emphasise that the disclosure Ss wrote about truly upsetting and traumatic events, as shown by the analysis of essay contents and the self-rating of the extent to which the experience was troubling at occurrence and now.

The expected short-term increase in physical symptoms due to the emotional impact of expressive writing, which has been observed at least in some prior studies, was not shown in our data. This may be due to inadequacies of the German version of the PPSS, an interpretation supported by the relatively low internal consistency of the scale (α = .59 vs. α = .75 reported by Pennebaker, 1982). Data of the second study should decide on this interpretation.

The positive long-term effect of expressive writing on physical health could not be found at 6-week follow-up for any of the health-related variables assessed in the study. Thus, the beneficial effects of disclosure on physical health reported by Pennebaker and colleagues

(1986, 1988) could not be replicated in our German sample. In fact, increases in both illness days and days with illness-related restriction of activity were found in the disclosure condition at follow-up. Such increases, however, were also observed in the control group and seem quite likely due to the seasonal influence of follow-up taking place during winter. The very high variance within Ss (see e.g. "illness-related restriction of activities") indicates the presence of heterogeneous health trajectories, especially in the disclosure group.

It should be pointed out that all health-related variables in our study were of a subjective nature. Unlike American universities, Germany universities do not operate student health care centres, a source from which objective health data was obtained in prior studies. Though possible that health improvement not apparent in subjective measures might be found in objective health data, the likelihood of such a divergence of health measures is small. Furthermore, it bears attention that our study was not unique in being unable to corroborate health improvement: Significant health-related differences between conditions were also absent in other studies (Greenberg & Stone, 1992; Murray et al, 1989; Murray & Segal, 1994; Gidron et al, 1996).

The results concerning long-term effects of expressive writing on psychological well-being are contradictory. Though no improvement relative to controls was found for positive or negative affectivity, significant reductions were found in maladaptive processing 6 weeks after writing: Re-experiencing, autonomic arousal and posttraumatic stress symptoms on the whole occurred less frequently.

The study also focussed on potential mechanisms of written disclosure by examining the relationship between a number of essay variables and the postulated short- and long-term effects of disclosure. The essay characteristics were assessed by self-report (e.g., rating of extent to which the essay was emotionally revealing) as well as by independent judges' rating (e.g., depth of self-exploration). Despite the overall lack of significant long-term effects of disclosure on health status and affectivity, meaningful correlations between essay characteristics and outcome variables could have been found that would lend support to Pennebaker's theory of inhibition and confrontation. However, only 4 out of 108 calculated correlations reached significant and the few significant correlations were all related to the domain of posttraumatic stress symptoms, the only outcome variables for which significant effects were found. Interestingly, the significant correlations were not exclusive to the scales for which long-term effects were found: Re-experiencing, though significantly reduced at follow-up, was not associated with any of the examined essay characteristics, while avoidance, though not significantly changed following disclosure, was. Associations were found between the more frequent and intense expression of positive emotions in essays and a higher the reduction in arousal. This effect, though not predicted by inhibition theory, seems quite plausible in light of Lazarus' stress coping model, in which positive reappraisal reduces the stress response. Associations were also found between increasing self-exploration (day 1 to day 3) and reductions in avoidance as well as posttraumatic stress symptoms on the whole.

Surprisingly, the assessed personality variables were of little to no relevance for short- and long-term consequences of disclosure. The constructs of personality variables like alexithymia (lack of ability to perceive and express emotions) and self-concealment (conscious inhibition of expressing emotions to others) made the hypothesis of their influence on the disclosure process and its outcome highly probable. Nevertheless, only one significant correlation was found regarding self-concealment and *long-term* change of physical symptoms. The unexpected absence of these theoretically highly plausible associations may be indicative of a weakness in the theory of inhibition and confrontation.

STUDY II: DISCUSSION

The second study was conducted to determine whether the negative results of study I might be due, in part, to inadequacies in the German versions of the selected assessment instruments. More importantly, however, was the study's aim of examining whether modified disclosure instructions promoting self-efficacy and coping would be more successful in producing the postulated positive effects on physical health and psychological well-being.

Negative short-term effects of expressive writing were found in study II for both mood and physical symptoms. Interestingly, the increases in both were most pronounced in the disclosure condition, which differed significantly from the control condition. The coping and helping conditions, on the other hand, evidenced only slight, if any, increases in physical symptoms and negative mood.

As in study I, positive long-term effects of writing on physical health were conspicuously absent. Not only were there no effects with regard to the Complaints Schedule, an instrument specifically validated for German samples, none of the subjective health measures indicated a beneficial effect of expressive writing on physical health.

The observed long-term effects on mood were unexpectedly attributable to differences between the helping and coping conditions, controls were not involved. Nevertheless, the deterioration of mood in the coping Ss, relative to the helping Ss, merits comment. The only predicted long-term improvements of psychological well-being were found with the Impact of Event Scale. A marginally significant interaction effect was revealed for "avoidance" and a significant interaction effect for "intrusion". Altogether the helping group showed the largest reduction in posttraumatic stress symptoms,

The newly explored variable "expectancy of negative mood regulation" did not respond to expressive writing, either in its standard or modified form. Self-rated coping competency did, however, as evidenced by the significant interaction effect in the analysis of variance on follow-up data. Though the post-hoc Scheffé-test did not reveal any significant pairwise differences, inspection of means showed that the largest increase in perceived coping competency was found in the helping condition, marginal increases were found in the other experimental groups, while the controls evidenced no change.

Regarding global estimate of positive effects of writing by the Ss, the helping group gives the highest rating and the control the lowest.

SUMMARY

In both of our studies, the main assumption made by Pennebaker that confronting personally upsetting experiences via a brief writing intervention, can lead to positive long-term health consequences could not be corroborated. The vision of being able to achieve improvements in physical health and psychological well-being by writing in an emotionally expressive way about negative experiences does not seem to be warranted by the results of the present study. Thus, our findings contradict not only the early disclosure studies but also the results of a metaanalysis from Smyth (1998), in which medium effect sizes were reported for both physical health (d = .42) and psychological well-being (d = .66).

We want to point, however, that the effects reported in some studies did not reflect improvement in the disclosure condition, but rather a deterioration of health in the control group (Pennebaker & Beall, 1986; Pennebaker & Francis, 1996; Greenberg et al, 1996). Taken together with our negative results on health improvement and the lack of substantial correlations between theoretically fitting personality constructs and outcome variables, a more sceptical view of disclosure seems warranted.

On the other hand, however, we found substantial changes in symptoms of post traumatic stress. In the first experiment re-experiencing and autonomic arousal were reduced after disclosure and a decrease in posttraumatic stress symptoms on the whole was found. In the second experiment, the positive effect of disclosure on these symptoms could be replicated using an instrument that was psychometrically validated for German samples. A significant reduction in intrusions was found as well as a marginally significant reduction of avoidance. These effects (reduction of symptoms) were most pronounced in the helping group. It seems that taking on the role of an adviser and recommending coping strategies to others dealing with the same experience can increase perceived coping competency and thereby facilitate improved emotional processing. Contrary to our expectations, the coping instruction was not as effective. It is plausible that the coping instruction may have reactivated the memory of unsuccessful coping endeavours in some of the Ss. On the other hand Cameron & Nicholls (1998) found positive effects in their somewhat different coping intervention.

Thus, disclosure had a positive long-term effect on the processing of traumatic experiences but not on physical health or mood. Perhaps the effects on trauma processing, which are of medium size in the helping and disclosure group were not strong enough to have consequences for general health.

Conclusions from our studies are that writing about upsetting or traumatic events can be useful as a self-help strategy to improve coping with the trauma but it can not replace more comprehensive professional interventions when the negative impact of the stressful event on the individual is strong.

Is there any explanation for the discrepancy between our results and the beneficial health effects reported in the early studies from Pennebaker and Beall (1986) and others? Our samples do not differ from the others with regard to Ss' status and age. The marginal gender difference between conditions in study I cannot explain the discrepancies, as gender had no moderating effect on outcome. The experiences the Ss wrote about are similar to the essay contents reported by Pennebaker and Beall (1986) or Pennebaker et al (1988). The health-related assessment measures and instruments were analogous, with the exception of a lack of objective health data. It seems highly unlikely, however, that self-report measures of health should be less sensitive to change than objective parameters. It could be argued that our follow-up assessment was premature, the time span of 6 weeks being too short for the beneficial effects on health to occur. This argument, however, loses its strength in view of the health improvements reported by Pennebaker et al (1988), who implemented a follow-up of the same length, and found reductions in health centre visits and increased immunocompetence 6 weeks after writing. Improvements in health have even been reported for as short a time span as 4 weeks after writing (Greenberg et al, 1996). It cannot be ruled out that sociocultural factors may play a role in the discrepant results as nearly all supporting findings originate from the USA and Canada. What factors these might be, however, is far from clear.

Interest in the theory of inhibition and confrontation has not waned over the years: Since the first wave of research in the late eighties and the nineties, numerous new studies using the disclosure paradigm have been conducted. The study samples have grown more diverse ranging from prisoners (Tromp, 1998; Richards et al, 2000), individuals in mourning (Eddins, 1999, Ströbe et al, 2002), persons afflicted with cervical dysplasia (Cook, 2001) and prostate cancer (Rosenberg et al, 2002[prostate cancer]), to patients presenting with somatisation (Schilte et al, 2001), fibromyalgia (Gillis, 2002) and major depression (Hitt, 2001). College students were examined by Marlo & Wagner (1999) and Kloss & Lisman (2002), school children (8-13 years) by Reynolds et al (2000), and Klapow et al (2001) tested the disclosure hypothesis on a sample of primary care patients of an older age (66 years or older).

Beneficial effects of disclosure are reported in some of the studies, e.g. by Gillis et al (2002), who found functional improvement in patients with fibromyalgia as well as better sleep quality. Rosenberg et al (2002) reported reductions of physical symptoms and health care utilisation in prostate cancer patients, though no effect was found on psychological variables or disease-related parameters of immunocompetence. Richards et al's (2000) psychiatric prisoners showed a reduction in postwriting infirmary visits. Reduced health care utilisation was also found in older primary health care patients, though somatic symptoms and distress remained unchanged (Klapow et al, 2001). Whether Tromp's report (1998) of increased mental health care utilization in prisoners points to a positive effect (more sensitivity to psychological symptoms) or a negative effect (more symptoms) remains unclear.

In other studies, however, disclosure was less successful in promoting psychological or physical health (Wilson, 2000; Marlo & Wagner, 1999; Schilte et al, 2001; Ströbe et al, 2002; Reynolds et al, 2000; Kloss & Lisman, 2002). Thus, evidence seems to be accumulating that the effects of disclosure are less positive and less dramatic than assumed after the first studies. Unfortunately, outcome variables indicative of the dysfunctional processing of traumatic events were rarely assessed, so that further support for the results of our studies is lacking.

Furthermore, the variables mediating and moderating the effect of disclosure are far from clear. Additional research is needed to systematically analyse relevant variables and elucidate the mechanisms of action. The current focus of disclosure research on health-related variables and the neglect of psychological processing seems adversarial to the clarification of the potential utility of written disclosure as a means of self-help or in conjunction with psychotherapy.

REFERENCES

Berking, M. (1998). Vom hilflosen Patienten zum hilfreichen Experten? Empirische Studie über Möglichkeiten therapeutischen Arbeitens mit altruistischen Wirkfaktoren bei chronischen Schmerzpatienten. (From the helpless patient to a helpful expert? Empirical study of the chance to work with altruistic motivation in the treatment of chronic pain). Unpublished master thesis, Georg-August-University of Göttingen.

Booth, R.J., Petrie, K.J. & Pennebaker, J.W. (1997). Changes in circulation lymphocyte numbers following emotional disclosure: Evidence of buffering? *Stress Medicine*, 13, 23-29.

Cameron, L.D. & Nicholls, G. (1998). Expression of stressful experiences through writing: Effects of a self-regulation manipulation for pessimists and optimists. *Health Psychology*, 17, 84-92.

Catanzaro, S.J. & Greenwood, G. (1994). Expectancies for negative mood regulation, coping, and dysphoria among college students. *Journal of Counseling Psychology*, 41, 34-44.

Catanzaro, S.J. & Mearns, J. (1990). Measuring generalized expectancies for negative mood regulation: initial scale development and implications. *Journal of Personality Assessment*, 54, 546-563.

Cook, B.L. (2001). Relationships between cognitive-affective processing of past trauma and psychophysiological and immune parameters in women at risk for cervical cancer. Dissertation Abstracts International: Section B: *The Sciences & Engineering*, 61, 5556.

Donnelly, D.A. & Murray, E.L. (1991). Cognitive and emotional changes in written essaya and therapy interviews. *Journal of Social and Clinical Psychology*, 10, 334-350.

Eddins, C. (1999). Self-disclosure and the course of midlife conjugal bereavement. (coping strategies, mourning). Dissertation Abstracts International: Section B: *The Sciences & Engineering*, 60, 1849.

Ehlers, A. (2000). Posttraumatische Belastungsstörungen. (Posttraumatic anxiety disorders). *Göttingen*, Hogrefe.

Esterling, B.A., Antoni, M.H., Fletcher, M.A., Margulies, S. & Schneidermann, N. (1994). Emotional disclosure through writing or speaking modulates latent Eppstein-Barr-virus antibody titers. *Journal of Consulting and Clinical Psychology*, 62, 130-140.

Fahrenberg, J., Myrtek, D., Wilk, D. & Kreutel, K. (1986). Multimodale Erfassung der Lebenszufriedenheit: eine Untersuchung an Herz-Kreislauf-Patienten. (Multimodal assessment of life satisfaction: a study on CHD patients). *Psychotherapie, Psychosomatik, Medizinische Psychologie*, 36, 347-354.

Foa, D.B., Riggs, D.S., Dancu, C.V. & Rothbaum, B.O. (1993). Reliability and validity of a brieg instrument for assessing post-traumatic stress disorder. *Journal of Traumatic Stress*, 6, 459-473.

Francis, M.E. & Pennebaker, J.W. (1992). Putting stress into words: The impact of writing on physiological, absentee, and self-reported emotional well-being measures. American *Journal of Health Promotion*, 6, 280-287.

Fydrich, T., Sommer, G., Menzel, G. & Höll, B. (1987). Fragebogen zur sozialen Unterstützung (Kurzform, Sozu-K-22). (Questionnaire of social support). *Zeitschrift für Klinische Psychologie*, 16, 434-436.

Gidron, Y., Peri, T., Connolly, J.F. & Shalev, A.Y. (1996). Written disclosure in posttraumatic stress disorder: Is it benificial for the patient? *Journal of Nervous and Mental Disease*, 184, 505-507.

Gillis, M.E. (2002). The effects of written emotional disclosure on adjustment in fibromyalgia syndrome. Dissertation Abstracts International: Section B: *The Sciences & Engineering*, 63, 1562.

Greenberg, M.A., & Stone, A. (1992). Emotional disclosure about traumas and its relation to health: Effects of previous disclosure and trauma severity. *Journal of Personality and Social Psychology*, 63, 75-84.

Greenberg, M.A., Wortman, C.B. & Stone, A.A. (1996). Emotional expression and physical health: Revising traumatic memories or fostering self-regulation? *Journal of Personality and Social Psychology,* 71, 588-602.

Henderson, B.N., Davison, K.P., Pennebaker, J.W. & James, W. (2002). Disease disclosure patterns among breast cancer patients. *Psychology & Health,* 17 (1), 51-62.

Hitt, S. K. (2001). Disclosure, psychophysiology, and major depression. Dissertation Abstracts International: Section B: *The Sciences & Engineering,* 61, 5566.

Horowitz, M.J. (1976). Stress response syndromes. (2nd ed.) Northvale, NJ: Jakob Aronson.

Horowitz, M.J., Wilner, N. & Alvarez, W. (1979). Impact of event scale: a measure of subjective stress. *Psychosomatic Medicine,* 41, 209-218.

Klapow, J.C., Schmidt, S.M., Taylor, L.A., Roller, P. & Li, Q. (2001). Symptom management in older primary care patients: feasibility of an experimental, written self-disclosure protocol. *Annals of Internal Medicine,* 134, 905-11.

Kloss, J.D. & Lisman, S.A. (2002). An exposure-based examination of the effects of written emotional disclosure. *British Journal of Health Psychology,* 7 (1), 31.46.

Kelley, J.E., Lumley, M.A. & Leisen, J.C.C. (1997). Health effects of emotional disclosure in rhematoid arthritis patients. *Health Psychology,* 16, 331-340.

Klapow, J.C., Schmidt, S.M., Taylor, L.A., Roller, P., Li, Q., Calhoun, J.W., Wallander, J. & Pennebaker, J.W. (2001). Symptom management in older primary care patients: feasibility of an experiment, written self-disclosure protocol. *Annals of Internal Medicine,* 134, 905-911.

Kloss, J.D. & Lisman, S.A. (2002). An exposure-based examination of the effects of written emotional disclosure. *British Journal of Health Psychology,* 7(1), 31-46.

Krantz, A., & Pennebaker, J.W. (1996). Bodily versus written expression of traumatic experience. Manuscript submitted for publication [Zit. nach Pennebaker, 1997, S. 164].

Larson, D.G. & Chastain, R.L. (1990). Self-concealment: Conceptualization, measurement, and health implications. *Journal of Social and Clinical Psychology,* 9, 439-455.

Linkemann, A. (2001). Schreiben über belastende Lebensereignisse und dessen Einfluss auf körperliches und psychisches Wohlbefinden. (Writing about threatful life events and its influence on physical and psychological well-being). Unpublished PhD, University of Göttingen.

Lutgendorf, S.K., Antoni, M.H., Kumar, M. & Schneidermann, N. (1994). Changes in cognitive coping strategies predict EBV-antibody titer change following a stressor disclosure induction. *Journal of Psychosomatic Research,* 38, 63-78.

Marlo, H. & Wagner, M.K. (1999). Expression of negative and positive events through writing: Implications for psychotherapy and health. *Psychology & Health,* 14,193-215.

McNair, D.M., Lorr, M. & Droppleman, L.F. (1971). ETIS manual for the Profile of Mood States. San Diego, California: Educational and Industrial Testing Service.

Meyer, T.J., Miller, M.L., Metzger, R.L. & Borkovec, T.D. (1990). Development and validation of the Penn State Worry Questionnaire. *Behavior Research and Therapy,* 28, 487-495.

Midlarsky, E. & Kahana, E. (1994). Altruism in later life. Thousand Oaks, California: Sage.

Murray, E.J., Lamnin, A.D. & Carver, C.S. (1989). Emotional expression in written essays and psychotherapy. *Journal of Social and Clinical Psychology,* 8, 414-429.

Murray, E.J. & Segal, D.L. (1994). Emotional processing in vocal and written expression of feelings about traumatic experiences. *Journal of Traumatic Stress,* 7, 391-405.

Paez, D., Velasco, C. & Gonzalez, J.L. (1999). Expressive writing and the role of alexithymia as a dispositional deficit in self-disclosure and psychological health. *Journal of Personality & Social Psychology,* 77, 630-641.

Pennebaker, J.W. & Beall, S.K. (1986). Confronting a traumatic event: Toward an understanding of inhibition and disease. *Journal of Abnormal Psychology,* 95, 274-281.

Pennebaker, J.W., Hughes, C.F. & O'Heeron, R.C. (1987). The psychophysiology of confession: Linking inhibitory and psychosomatic processes. *Journal of Personality and Social Psychology,* 52. 781-793.

Pennebaker, J.W., Kiecolt-Glaser, J.K. & Glaser, R. (1988). Disclosure of traumas and immune function: Health implications for psychotherapy. *Journal of Consulting and Clinical Psychology,* 56, 239-244.

Pennebaker, J.W. (1988). Confiding traumatic experiences and health. In S. Fisher & J. Reason (Eds.), Handbook of life stress, cognition and health. *Chichester: John Wiley & Sons.*

Pennebaker, J.W. (1989). Confession, inhibition, and disease. In L. Berkowitz (Ed.), Advances in Experimental and Social Psychology, 22, 211-244. New York: *Academic Press.*

Pennebaker, J.W., Colder, M. & Sharp, L.K. (1990). Accelerating the coping process. *Journal of Personality and Social Psychology,* 58, 528-537.

Pennebaker, J.W. & Francis, M.E. (1996). Cognitive, emotional, and language processes in disclosure. *Cognition and Emotion,* 10, 601-626.

Pennebaker, J.W., Mayne, T. & Francis, M. (1997). Linguistic predictors of adaptive bereavement. *Journal of Personality and Social Psychology,* 52, 863-871.

Petrie, K.J., Booth, R.J., Pennebaker, J.W., Davison, K.P. & Thomas, M.G. (1995). Disclosure of trauma and immune response to a hepatitis B vaccination program. *Journal of Consulting and Clinical Psychology,* 63, 787-792.

Reynolds, M., Brewin, C. R. & Saxton, M. (2000). Emotional disclosure in school children. *Journal of Child Psychology and Psychiatry and Allied Disciplines,* 41, 151-9.

Richards, J.M., Beal, W.E. & Seagal, J.D. (2000). Effects of disclosure of traumatic events on illness behavior among psychiatric prison inmates. *Journal of Abnormal Psychology,* 109, 156-160.

Rosenberg, H.J., Rosenberg, S.D. & Ernstoff, M.S. (2002). Expressive disclosure and health outcomes in a prostate cancer population. International *Journal of Psychiatry in Medicine,* 32, 37-53.

Schilte, A. F., Portegijs, P., Blankenstein, A.H., van der Horst, H.E. & Latour, M. B. (2001). Randomised controlled trial of disclosure of emotionally important events in somatisation in primary care. *British Medical Journal,* 323, 86-89.

Schmidt-Atzert, L. (1981). Die verbale Kommunikation von Emotionen: Eine Bedingungsanalyse unter besonderer Berücksichtigung physiologischer Prozesse. (Verbal communication of emotions: an analysis with regard to physiological processing). Unpublished PhD thesis. Justus-Liebig-University, Giessen.

Schoutrop, M.J.A., Lange, A., Davidovich, U. & Salomon, H.B. (1996). The effects of writing assignments in traumatised individuals: An experimental study. *Psychosomatic Medicine,* 58, 64.

Smyth, J.M. (1998). Written emotional expression: Effect sizes, outcome types, and moderating variables. *Journal of Consulting and Clinical Psychology,* 66, 174-184.

Spera , S.P., Burhfeind, E.D. & Pennebaker, J.W. (1994). Expressive writing and coping with job loss. *Academy of Management Journal,* 37, 722-733.

Ströbe, M.; Ströbe, W., Schut, H., Zech, E. & van-den Bout, J. (2002). Does disclosure of emotions facilitate recovery from bereavement? Evidence from two prospective studies. *Journal of Consulting and Clinical Psychology,* 70, 169-78.

Tausch, R. (1970). Gesprächspsychotherapie (Client-centered therapy) (4. ergänzte Aufl.). Göttingen: Hogrefe.

Taylor, J.T., Ryan, D. & Bagby, R.M. (1985). Toward the development of a new self-report alexithymia scale. *Psychotherapy and Psychosomatics,* 44, 191-199.

Traue, H. C. (1998). Emotion und Gesundheit. (Emotion and health). Heidelberg: Spektrum Akademischer Verlag.

Tromp, S.N. (1998). Use of self-guided writing therapy as an intervention for trauma: A sample of incarcerated women. Dissertation Abstracts International: Section B: *The Sciences & Engineering,* 58, 3936.

Westbrook, M.T. (1976). Positive affect: A method of content analysis for verbal samples. *Journal of Consulting and Clinical Psychology,* 44, 715-719.

Wilson, L. (2000). The health and psychological effects of sequenced and unsequenced emotional expression regarding college adjustment experiences. Dissertation Abstracts International Section A: *Humanities & Social Sciences,* 60, 3274.

Zerssen, D. von, (1976). Die Beschwerden-Liste. (Symptom list). Weinheim: *Beltz.*

INDEX

B

C

D